Cancer

JUNE 22–July 23

Aquarius
Sagitarius
Gemini
} difficulty with commitment

QUANTITY SALES

Most Dell books are available at special quantity discounts when purchased in bulk by corporations, organizations, and special-interest groups. Custom imprinting or excerpting can also be done to fit special needs. For details write: Dell Publishing, 666 Fifth Avenue, New York, NY 10103. Attn.: Special Sales Department.

INDIVIDUAL SALES

Are there any Dell books you want but cannot find in your local stores? If so, you can order them directly from us. You can get any Dell book in print. Simply include the book's title, author, and ISBN number if you have it, along with a check or money order (no cash can be accepted) for the full retail price plus $2.00 to cover shipping and handling. Mail to: Dell Readers Service, P.O. Box 5057, Des Plaines, IL 60017.

Dell Horoscope

PRESENTS

1991

DAY-BY-DAY

Cancer

JUNE 22–July 23

A DELL BOOK

Published by
Dell Publishing
a division of
Bantam Doubleday Dell Publishing Group, Inc.
666 Fifth Avenue
New York, New York 10103

Copyright © 1990 by the Editors of DELL HOROSCOPE MAGAZINE

How to Find Your Moon's Sign and Degree—charts by Grant Lewi from *Astrology for the Millions*.

All rights reserved. No part of this book may be reproduced or transmitted in any form or by any means, electronic or mechanical, including photocopying, recording, or by any information storage and retrieval system, without the written permission of the Publisher, except where permitted by law.

The trademark Dell® is registered in the U.S. Patent and Trademark Office.

ISBN: 0-440-20693-6

Printed in the United States of America
Published simultaneously in Canada

August 1990

10 9 8 7 6 5 4 3 2 1
OPM

EDITOR'S NOTE

For the second year in a row, the editors of *Dell Horoscope Magazine* present a series of twelve astrological books—one for each sign in the zodiac. With the resources of the world's most popular astrology magazine at our disposal, we bring you a capsule of the history of astrology; your personal and professional astrological indicators; sign descriptions; financial, health, and career advice; hobbies and pastimes inherent in your personal sign; advice for parents; relationship guidance; unique stellar combinations; how to determine where each planet was at the time of your birth and its astrological meaning; and fifteen months of daily predictions from two of *Horoscope*'s most experienced and skilled forecasters—all of which can help you to achieve personal fulfillment and greater self-understanding, assist you in decision-making for your important life choices, and aid you in your quest to find greater peace of mind in your place on this planet and within the boundaries you share with your closest associations.

I'd like to extend a special thanks to Edward Kajkowski for his efforts in research and his astrological and editorial wisdom; to Jack Pettey for his wonderful introduction and his keen editorial and astrological advice; to Julia Lupton Skalka, Heidi Rain, and Evy Tishelman for the many valuable and insightful articles they wrote exclusively for this series; and to Lloyd Cope and Doris Kaye for their top-notch daily forecasts.

RONNIE GRISHMAN
Editor

CONTENTS

Introduction	*ix*
Astrology Through the Centuries	*1*
Personality Traits for Cancer	*12*
Sun Signs Around the Zodiac	*14*
How to Maintain Good Health	*24*
Your Guide to Friends and Lovers	*26*
Career-Wealth Potentials	*29*
Hobbies for Fun and Profit	*32*
Stellar Tips for Parents	*34*
Your Birthday's Planetary Ruler	*37*
Your Moon Sign	*41*
Your Unique Sun and Moon Portrait	*80*
Your Rising Sign and Sun-Sign Combination	*87*
Mercury: Mind Over Matter	*92*
Venus: Love and Attraction	*112*
Mars: The Spark of Life	*132*
Jupiter: Fortune and Bounty	*148*
Saturn: The Teacher	*159*
Uranus: The Unexpected Visitor	*167*
Neptune: The Dreamer	*170*

viii Contents

Pluto: The Power Planet	173
Successful Planning With the Moon Sign Guide	190
Daily Predictions	193

INTRODUCTION

Today, while the tenth and final decade of the twentieth century is still young, curious minds and seekers within the astrological field have vast resources at their fingertips. If we want to check a point to back up a statement we have made or a belief that we hold, if we want to gain a better understanding of the meaning of a particular aspect in a friend's birth chart, or if we want to grasp a more psychological approach to the underlying mythological background of the natal chart, we have but to go, in some cases, to our own home libraries. In most large cities we can travel to a top-notch New Age bookstore and ask to be directed to the subject of our inquiry. Or we can take a class and start with the basics of astrology, building up a storehouse of knowledge that we can trust, add to, and draw on as time-tested theories wedge their way into the accepted lexicon of astrology.

Many centuries ago, when time, as we know it, was nascent and humankind consisted of primitive beings who had no means of committing thoughts, environmental conditions, or progress to words, the only reference book in existence was the great expanse of sky overhead—a seemingly stable and stationary rooftop of bright, some not so bright, shining lights that appeared each night in a sea of dark. Early humankind's experience of the heavens was virtually the same from day to day, year to year. But against the starry backdrop of this upper world came the nocturnal visitations of one object in particular—noticeable to those below by its much more rapid movement across the sky. This was the Moon. And during the day a bright shining ball coursed across the sky from one side of the known world's existence to its opposite point 180 degrees away. This was the Sun, and living in a totally physical world, humans soon noticed five other relatively rapid moving lights across the sky. These were the five visible planets—Mercury, Venus, Mars, Jupiter, and Saturn—and the ancient world came to know them as wanderers because they did not stay in the same place like the other stars.

Speculation has it that as early as 8000 B.C. humans became fascinated with the movements occurring overhead and soon thereafter began to note physical earthly connections to the shifting patterns above. The earliest inhabitants soon learned what time was best to grow and harvest crops. The ancient Egyptians noticed that the rising of the Dog Star, Sirius, the brightest star in the Northern Hemisphere, coincided with the flooding of the Nile Valley. Some noticed that the ocean rose and fell with the tides and connected this to the pull of the Moon's rays. Was there a natural order to the universe, some accountability for the birth and death, the growth and decay that were such a noticeable part of the environment? Could it be possible that individual destinies were part of the plan, if indeed it was a plan at all? Life was filled with mysteries for those first observers of the sky to unravel.

Astrology was born of observation and mathematical calculation. An overview of the evolution of astrology is contained in the first chapter of this book. The Chaldeans of ancient Babylonia are credited as the first astrologers. They combined astronomy and astrology in a marriage of science and divination or spirituality until it came under attack by the outbreak of rationalism during the Age of Reason of the eighteenth century. They were first to use the twelve principal constellations as forerunners of the zodiac as we know it today. Every two hours the constellations shifted one-twelfth of a complete circle or thirty degrees. The constellations consist of seven bestial figures, four human, and one that is neither (Libra, the sign of

justice or the scales). The system of houses is sep&
from that of the constellations, although there were dele
gated twelve houses, equal to the number of zodiac signs.
Numbering from the east down below the horizon and
around to complete the circle, the Chaldeans designated
these twelve sections to encompass twelve areas or planes
of the life experience.

THE DEVELOPMENT OF THE CALENDAR

It is reasonable to assume that early inhabitants of the
planet Earth, having noted the difference between day (the
Sun) and night (the Moon), next perceived the changes in
climate and the recurring pattern of these changes. The
lunar month became the guidepost of the first calendars.
Time after time people saw the Moon increasing in light
(the waxing Moon), followed by a period when it became
smaller or decreased in light (the waning Moon). This cycle
became the lunar month, and its repetition in the skies was
easily discernible. The need for a reliable timetable grew
out of the requisites for the success of agriculture. The
planting of crops could not operate by human whim, for
the ripening of vegetables and grains had to occur before
winter. Humankind's intelligence soon learned that there
was a regular pattern to climate, and it was by observation
of celestial patterns and the two main bodies or wanderers
of the solar system (the Sun and Moon, called the Lights)
that mastery of agricultural practices might take place.
Julius Caesar, with the help of Egyptian astronomers,
established the Julian calendar in 46 B.C. Using the solar
rotation as a guide, he fixed the length of the year at 365¼
days. Since the Egyptians had discovered that every four
years Sirius, by which they set the start of their year, rose
one day late, Caesar decreed that every fourth year should
have 366 days to make up for the accumulation of quarter
days.

The modern calendar, as we know it, is the Gregorian
calendar, which corrects the length of the solar day. This
revision, initiated under Pope Gregory XIII in 1582, al-
lowed the spring equinox to remain at March 21 because

Introduction

the Julian calendar was eleven minutes and fourteen seconds out of step with the Sun each year. All this is just a very brief and sketchy synopsis of the progress of the calendar, presented here to stress the importance of the Sun and Moon in guiding humankind to an understanding of time to the present day and as important celestial markers of our day-to-day lives. If we live our every waking moment to the rhythm of the Sun and the Moon, as evidenced by the invention of the modern-day calendar, then might we not also be influenced by the other heavenly bodies?

THE BIRTH CHART AND THE TWELVE ZODIACAL SIGNS

Like the calendar and its constant need for revision to keep up with the unflagging pace and tempo of the Earth's Lights, the twelve signs of the zodiac, as we know them by the passage of our Sun through each constellation, are not fixed in precise time from year to year. For instance, the Sun enters Leo this year on July 22 (9:23 P.M. EST), but next year it will enter Leo on July 23 (3:12 A.M. EST). The Sun enters Aquarius in 1991 on January 20. Thus, the dates differ from year to year for each of the signs, and an ephemeris (a daily account of each planet's place in the heavens) is required to know one's correct sun placement.

The birth chart is a circular depiction of the ten known planets (Sun and Moon included here as planets) in relationship to the planet Earth. Some are above the horizon; some are below. Others may be east or west of the meridian (the imaginary line separating the north and south points of the horizon—the top and bottom of the visual chart). Therefore, when you view the pictograph of the individual birth chart which represents your entrance into this life, you must visualize yourself as at the exact center of the chart, with its twelve pielike slices constituting the circle. At the center is the planet Earth, and on it you are being born. The exact time of birth (the first intake of human breath) is required because what you are actually getting in the picture of your birth chart is a depiction of the exact placements of the Sun, the Moon, and the eight planets as they relate to the time and location of your birth. The birth chart, then, is a picture of the self within you, the individual essence that you are, the center of your being. It does not tell us your sex or your racial and collective background. What it does portray is the conscious level you are living on, the stage of development you have reached to be lived out in this lifetime. It has often been said that the construction of the chart is a science (astronomy) and the interpretation of the chart is an art (astrology).

The sign where a planet is placed is like the adjective that modifies a noun. The planets are energies, but the signs tell us how these energies are predisposed to action; they are the background that colors the affairs of the individual planet. We all know that there are twelve astrological signs and that these signs correspond to the twelve constellations that constitute the outer circle of our universe. Brief overviews of each sign appear later in this book (see "Sun Signs Around The Zodiac"), but here we present a different way of regarding the signs—a mythological overlay that can serve as a kind of archetypal guidepost.

ARIES is the point of all beginnings. It is the first sign in the natural zodiac and thus begins the system of the twelve houses. It begins with the spring equinox, when day and night are of equal length and winter's thaw gives rise to new birth. Symbolically life renews itself and begins again. This is why many astrologers refer to Aries as the new-start sign, for it encourages pioneerism and the conquering of new vistas. Early Christians chose to celebrate Easter at a time close to the spring equinox because it marked a time of rebirth and renewal. "I am," cries Aries, for here is born the concept of individuality. The myth behind Aries (whose bestial symbol is the battering ram) is that of the conquering hero (the self) who slays the dragon (the overthrowing of the old order) and asserts his independent and individual spirit. The old order is dead (the ruling structure into which the hero is born—i.e., the father), and a free spirit is born. This is the embodiment of Aries, and inherent in this concept is a sense of the rugged, outdoorsy physical self. Aries, Mars (its ruler), and the first house rule the physical body. Aries men and women often outwardly display a physical sensibility that is common to their sign. You see them in physical jobs, at the gym, at home in the military, and working with tools in their backyards. In summation, then, Aries is the solar hero, who has courage and confidence and faces challenges easily; he sets his own rules, wants to see results immediately, and then seeks out a new challenge in the ever-present spirit of moving onward. You may detect shades and gradations of this solar hero in friends who have a number of planets in Aries, many first-house planets, Aries rising, or just a strongly placed Aries Sun. Aries is the search for a separate identity.

TAURUS represents the earth of springtime, ripe with fertility and ready to receive the seed which will ultimately result in prosperity. This mental image conjures up visions of creativity and wealth. The earth gives rise to produce, and Taurus says, "I have; I own; I possess." Symbolized by the bull, the zodiac's second bestial figure, Taurus cannot be pushed into activity unwillfully. The attachment to comfort, security, and beauty which Taurus feels is the inherited structural foundation of this sign. Venus, its ruler, is renowned for her feeling nature, creative impulses, love of beauty, and sociable tendencies. The myth behind this sign is that of King Minos, who claimed the throne of Crete by divine right. Covetousness motivated him to keep for himself a bull sent by the god Poseidon and offer in sacrifice a substitute. Of this subterfuge was born the Minotaur, whose ogreish reputation was enhanced by the literal feeding of youths and maidens to appease him in his labyrinthine prison. As tyrant-monster the Minotaur represents the challenge for Taurus, that of single-minded covetousness and overwhelming senses, as opposed to the earthly power to accrue wealth as a natural unadulterated gift of true merit. Those who have many planets in Taurus, the second house, Taurus rising, or even just a very strong Taurus Sun placement are being asked to examine their resources, both inner and outer (material possessions), and find their own true value system. Taurus is involved in a lifelong search for meaning, an evolution leading to the inner realms through earthly dealings with the world of matter.

GEMINI, the sign of duality, says to the world, "I think." As opposed to the feeling type of person, Gemini lives his life in the head; he sifts experience through the analytical sieve of the mind, filtering out emotional baggage. This youthful sign represents the eternal adolescent, for unlike Taurus/earth (the seed which must ripen and mature) and Aries/fire (the young and virile hero), the mind grows in wisdom but has no intrinsic properties that connect with physical aging. Mercury, the Messenger, is the planetary ruler of this sign, whose symbol is that of the twins. This is the first human symbol found in the natural zodiac, implying that the process of thought is what distinguishes human from beast. Gemini's underlying myth, some say, is that of the twins Castor and Pollux, one mortal, the other divine. The theme implied here is that of two forces in opposition—one a force of dark, the other of light. Gemini must learn to face his own oppositeness, which he will ultimately experience through another. Here there is the need to focus, to reason out conflicts with rivals (often a sibling). Gemini stands at a crossroads and must learn to unite the two selves within. You'll notice the playfulness, anxiety, and duality in those who have many Gemini planets, planets in the third house, Gemini rising, or a strong Gemini Sun.

CANCER, the fourth sign and first of the water element, has as its nonhuman symbol that crustacean of the sea, the slow-moving crab. Insecure, the crab is never far from home because it carries its home on its back; the shell is its fortress against life's frequent invasions. "I feel," says Cancer, for like the tides of the ocean, Cancer swells with highs and lows of emotional pulse. Cancer's lifelong search is for security, emotional and otherwise. Just as the crab might clamp its pincers to your toe and not let go, the person of this sign clings to people in his or her life. Emotional, nondirect, protective, mother-loving (the home), Cancerian imagery evokes creative, earth mother symbolism. The Moon, symbol of women and the mother in particular, rules Cancer, and mythology offers us examples of mother-goddess figures that would opt for destruction of their offspring rather than lose their dominant and emotional hold on them to the forces of free will and individual selfhood. Confronting life via the search for emotional security is a predominant theme in those with fourth-house planets, several planets in Cancer, a strongly placed Cancer Sun, and Cancer rising.

LEO rules the Sun in the natural zodiac and is symbolized by the lion, the hot-blooded fiery beast of the jungle. In myth the story always involves the taming of the beast; the lion is not permitted to remain in its aggressive impassioned state but must come to its individuality through the creative process of self-discovery. As king of the jungle, the lion embodies the animal form (showmanship, self-involvement) before the sign evolves to compassion and maturity through life's experiences. Leo's quest to shine (like the sun) in the limelight grows out of a strength of will and the passion of the heart for self-recognition; Leo's search for the self must surpass erotic leanings and hedonism and strive for more spiritual and compassionate involvement in life to be successful. Individualism, Leo must learn, grows out of the journey away from insensitive self-involvement toward a sense of spiritual inner meaning. You will find that people with many fifth-house planets or planets in Leo, like Leo rising and the Leo Sun, have honesty, nobility, creativity, a sense of joy about them, and a spirit of generosity when they have evolved beyond the base ego of their bestial form.

VIRGO, the sign of humble service, looks at life and its workings with the motor blades of the mind turning, analyzing, and assimilating experience. A materialistic earth sign, Virgo leads a search for perfection—oftentimes through service to others. This sign has a fondness for order and precision. Virgo's symbol is that of the Virgin or Maiden holding a sheaf of barley or wheat, this itself a symbol of the earth's harvest. Virgo is the second human symbol in the zodiac, and its mission or search for a meaningful way to employ human energy and to be productive in this lifetime is integral to the experience of humanity, as opposed to beasthood, just as Gemini accents the human gift of intelligent selection. Virgo shares its ruler, Mercury, with Gemini. Mercury (or Hermes), in mythology is the clever and cunning messenger who has access to all worlds—that above, the mortal realm, and that below, or Hades. Mercury's flexibility via access to heavenly, earthly, and subterranean realms has important implications in its rulership of Virgo. Virgo must come to its sense of purity and perfection by traveling to the inner world of the subconscious and making choices according to inner laws rather than live life according to what is expected by the outer world. People with a strong Virgo Sun, Virgo rising, many planets in the sixth house, or a preponderance of Virgo planets are guided by a strong inner moral ethic when evolved. They can be overly critical, anxious, high-strung, and shy, at times, but through the lessons of humble service and patience, Virgos can reach the highest perfection.

LIBRA marks the beginning of the fall season and is the seventh sign in the natural zodiac. Thus, it is a turning point because one half of the circle of twelve signs has been completed. The journey now veers from that of the personal (or personality) to the universal (or soul). Strategic in this midway point, Libra says to the world, "I balance." The symbol for Libra, that of the scales of justice, is the only one in the zodiac that is neither human nor beast. It is an inanimate and tactile object. As opposite to the first house of the self (Aries), this turning point embodies the self in alliance with another or others; it is the house of you and me, the area of our partnerships and how we relate to others in this life. Venus is the planetary ruler of this sign of fairness and impartiality, and congenial Venus has a great desire to receive affection and appreciation from others. The mythological background of this friendly sign is constructed around the need to make fair and objective assessments, to judge according to personal and ethical codes, thereby upholding a moral balance of the universal principles of right and wrong. Libra's search for the perfect balance extends beyond the temporal quest for a complementary partner or soul mate for this life. The indecision associated with this sign stems from the thrusting of decision-making situations into Libra's life and a strong desire not to violate the principles of idealism inherent in this individual's deep inner value system. You will note that people with several seventh-house planets, a number of planets in Libra, strong Libra Sun Signs, and perhaps Libra rising can be very diplomatic, thoughtful, civilized, and sometimes quite vacillating as they deal with the relationships that enter their daily lives.

SCORPIO is often cited as the most complex of the twelve signs; it is called the mystery sign of the zodiac and is the one many astrologers find hardest to read for. The dark imagery of this sign's background is reflected in Scorpio's association with murky water—those waters with superficial oil spillings or clouded debris that do not allow one to see beneath the surface to what may lie below. In the natural zodiac Scorpio rules the eighth house of sex and death, indisputably two of life's most mystifying experiences. Mythic images pit the individual against the dark and destructive dragon, suggesting that Scorpio's battle lies in coping with evil and rage and emotional darkness in order to give birth to change and light. Scorpio is called upon to meet the darkness that lies within the soul on a personal level—through relationships and life's pursuits—and purge and transform it to a higher plane. The scorpion is the symbol for this sign. The fifth bestial figure we are to meet in the zodiac is the lowest form of this sign. The phoenix, the legendary bird that rose from its own ashes to live again, is the highest, implying that Scorpio must face darkness that lies within the personality and transcend to a soul level. Pluto, lord of the underworld, rules this sign and, through the myth of Persephone, conjures up a mythic tale of rape and pillage. There is the potential for great strength and power in Scorpio, once the individual rises, like the phoenix, above personality issues to the realm of the soul. In addition to strength, you will note a secretiveness, a stubbornness, and a strong reserve in people with strong Scorpio influences and eighth-house planets in their birth charts.

SAGITTARIUS in symbol form appears to us as the centaur, half man and half horse. The glyph for this fiery sign is represented by the archer aiming an arrow toward the heavens, his four-footed bestial frame supporting him. This is the sign of perception of the higher mind or the search for wisdom that comes from experience. Pictorially this sign suggests man's struggle to release himself from his lower (bestial) nature. Mythology portrays Sagittarius as part immortal and part beast. The race of the centaurs was bred from the coupling of a goddess (Hera) and a mortal. Chiron, the king of the centaurs, was famed as a scholar and healer. Poisoned by a wound to the thigh, he could not die because he was immortal, but he could not live either because the poison had no antidote. This implies that an element of depression underlies the bright optimistic surface of Sagittarius, popularly cited for a friendly, optimistic, and extroverted approach to life. The function of the physical wound is to turn Sagittarius' outgoing and fiery spirit inward to the realm of the superconscious, wherein lie wisdom and knowledge beyond the grasp of the mere mortal. From this one can sense in this sign the duality that exists between the flesh and the spirit. An aversion to rigid rules and the expectations of others create in Sagittarius an overwhelming desire for freedom and independence which in turn makes for difficulties in relationships at times. Jupiter, as planetary ruler of this ninth-house sign, brings the gifts of spirituality, understanding, and forward movement—or progress into the future. You will notice that those who have many planets in Sagittarius, the ninth house, a strongly placed Sagittarian Sun, or Sagittarius rising love to be on the move, have some spiritual or philosophical leanings, and face life head-on with a smile and a buoyancy that looks forward to tomorrow.

CAPRICORN, ruled by the persevering mountain goat, is the tenth-house mid-heaven sign in the natural zodiac. This sector is associated with how others see you, your reputation, the business world, and your parents. A practical sign, Capricorn uses available assets to get the most from them. Capricorn marks the time of the winter solstice, when the days start to grow colder and the natural out-of-doors fire of summer is replaced by home and the heated hearth. The tone is more serious, less airy. Saturn rules this sign and is known as a cold, unfeeling planet. Material affairs and steady concentration of effort are more important to Saturn than is the realm of the feelings. The myth behind this sign involves, as it does with Aries, the confrontation between father and son—or the sacrifice of the king to give birth to fertility on the earth. In *The Astrology of Fate* Liz Greene says: "Capricorn almost always seems to find the personal father a disappointment, just as Leo does, for the father he seeks is nothing less than divine." Saturn, frequently called the lesson giver of the zodiac, is closely associated with the father. Its symbol or glyph is shaped like the sickle (which Father Time holds, as does the Grim Reaper). Capricorn's lessons involve the loss of faith and the limitations imposed on life. An interest in worldly success, material strength, ambition, persistence, and hard work are part of the Capricorn ethic, and you will notice these traits or qualities among your friends who are strongly Capricornian—either through tenth-house planets, a strong Sun in Capricorn, several planets in the sign, or Capricorn rising.

AQUARIUS is known as the water bearer but is, in fact, an air sign. It is the fourth and last of the human representations in the zodiac. The symbol for this sign depicts a human figure pouring water from an urn onto the earth, symbolizing the dissemination (or communication) of ideas from one individual (the single container) to all humanity (the fertilization by water of the earth). Communication, then, is a keyword for Aquarius, as it is for all the air signs, but for this air sign there is more of a sense of altruism and an involvement of the collective in the dispersal of knowledge and information. The fast-moving and forward-thrusting planet Uranus rules this sign. Aquarius is interested in progress and the future. This inventive and socially minded sign has a great concern with the group, or humankind as a collective, rather than an individual, being. Mythology emphasizes this group orientation and the need to help others in the story of Prometheus, who saved humankind from darkness by stealing fire from the gods, thus bringing light (science/progress) to earth. But revenge, guilt, and suffering enter the myth, for this deed did not go unpunished. Accompanying a genuine wish to spread goodwill among humankind are a self-doubt and an impulse toward self-punishment in the background of Aquarius. Those with many planets in Aquarius or the eleventh house, a strong Aquarius Sun, or Aquarius rising are often experienced as forward thinkers, somewhat detached emotionally, rebellious, and highly individualistic. The struggle in this sign involves Uranus (liberation) and Aquarius' co-ruler Saturn (discipline). When these two primarily incompatible forces are integrated within the individual, there is great potential for spiritual evolvement.

PISCES rules the feet in the human body and, under an astrological parallel, bottoms out the natural cycle of the zodiac by virtue of its placement as the twelfth and final sign. Pisces' search is for inner spiritual peace. The bestial symbol for this sign is the fish, and the symbol for Pisces features two fishes swimming in opposite directions. One swims toward the realm of the soul, and the other toward the world of the personality. One frequently hears that if the spiritual inclinations of this sign do not overpower and conquer the personality dimensions of the Pisces individual, then there is much suffering in the life. Indeed, Pisces, holding domain over the twelfth sector in the natural zodiac, is identified with suffering, just as is the tie-in of the twelfth house in astrology, for only through suffering is the spirit released from bondage to the personality. Neptune, the planet representing fantasy or that which is not real, is the ruler of this sign. Pisces is sensitive, compassionate, and emotional and has a feeling connection to all life-forms, and its mythic role is either to save and redeem humankind through selfless service or to identify with the role of victim and dissolve into chaos. This duality is embodied in the figure of Dionysus, god of the vine and the grape (hence drunkenness), who was called upon to travel annually to visit the underworld (the unconscious) and be born again. This helps somewhat to explain the connection of Pisces and the twelfth house to the realm of solitude. Pisces needs to escape from the world, to retreat from time to time, and to overcome a sensual response to life. Shyness, sweetness, sensitivity, a sense of separateness, and sacrifice—these are all parts of the person who has planets in Pisces, the twelfth house, the Pisces Sun, and Pisces rising.

This very brief journey through the zodiac is meant to set the flavor and tone for the journey that lies ahead in the pages of this book. Learning about your own birth chart is a thrilling experience, for it holds the key to what your life is all about. It is not a rare occurrence to hear someone bemoan his or her personal birth chart. "Oh, I wish I had a chart like yours," your friend may say to you, or, "What I wouldn't give to have a chart like his!" But the true fact is the only chart that is right for you is the one you were born with.

Cancer

JUNE 22–July 23

ASTROLOGY THROUGH THE CENTURIES

No one knows exactly when the notion of divining by the stars caught hold of the human mind. In every part of the world, in every culture and clime, the Sun, Moon, planets, and stars have played some part in the mythological scheme of human society. It is inevitable that this should be so, for what is more breathtaking than the sunrise? What is more awesome than the countless beads of starlight? It is no wonder that primitive people revered them.

Although societies have generally delegated some significance to astrology, not all of them have ascribed an astrological meaning to the planets and the signs of the zodiac. The earliest records we have of a belief in astrology were unearthed in Mesopotamia. The stellar art began developing into its "modern" form around 4000 B.C., when the first temples were built along the banks of the Euphrates River in honor of the Sumerian star gods. These ingenious people were adept in many branches of divinatory practices, including a technique of interpreting the patterns of oil poured into a bowl of water, observing the flight of birds, and studying the entrails of sacrificed animals. They were the first to devise a primitive astroscopy that involved the observation of the Sun, Moon, and planets, without, however, taking note of their relative positions in the zodiac.

The Sumerians were later to develop the twelve-house system of horoscopy in combination with the twelve signs of the zodiac, which were then identified with the constellations of the ecliptic. Dating from about 2870 B.C., during the reign of Sargon of Agade, documents have been found involving predictions based upon the positions of the Sun, Moon, and the five known planets, also including such phenomena as comets and meteors. At this time astrology had already begun to acquire a distinctively modern flavor.

In 3000 B.C. the house system was already described in the same fashion as that used in contemporary astrology: first house—self-assertiveness; second—poverty/riches, finances; third—brothers, sisters, communications; fourth—parents, home life; fifth—children, creativity; sixth—illness/health, work; seventh—wife/husband, marriage; eighth—death, sex; ninth—religion, education; tenth—dignities, career; eleventh—friendship, hopes; and twelfth—enmity, restrictions, subconsciousness.

With the spread of Sumerian culture, astrology became of central importance to early civilized humankind. From the Mesopotamian mythogenetic zone, astrology, the religion and science of the priestly cult, spread into Egypt, Persia, and India. From there it eventually crossed into Europe and to the East, encountering the primitive civilizations of China and Japan, and finally into Central and South America. Astrology had so great an influence on the beginning of technological humankind that the finest, most beautiful, and long-lived architectural works of the ancient world were none other than temples to the planetary deities, to the wanderers, places of worship that were also used as observatories. The priests ruled their people with absolute authority and were felt to be in touch with the very source of nature itself (in their eyes) and able to predict exactly what would befall their people.

There was no direct communication between the Sumerians and the builders of Stonehenge in England, but that marvelous work of primitive architecture was, in fact, a megalithic computer, begun sometime around 2500 B.C. The gigantic stones of this pre-Druidic temple are situated so that the rising and setting of the solstitial Sun and Moon, plus solar and lunar eclipses throughout the year, could be seen between two of the strategically placed colossal standing stones.

Astrology entered India at least as early as 3000 B.C.,

and even now the stellar science plays an all-important role in the lives of most Hindus. The main difference between Oriental and Occidental horoscopy today is that, in the East, an actual sidereal zodiac is the rule, observing the positions of the planets in relation to the constellations. In the West, however, the position of the Sun on the first day of spring is taken to be the first degree of Aries; because of the precession of the equinoxes, the Western "Aries" is now almost into the constellation Aquarius, marking the beginning of a new eon or "great year."

Soon after astrology was introduced in India from Sumerian sources, it was carried by way of trade routes into China, where it was received, as usual, with reverence. The Chinese themselves elaborated to some extent on the Indian form of astrology, combining it with the indigenous Taoist religion and the philosophy of the *I Ching*. Correlating the five elements, the cardinal points and the zenith, the five known planets, colors of the spectrum, emotional dispositions, and so forth, the Chinese evolved a highly complex system of divination that resembles the Hebrew Kabbalah in many ways. In association with native religion, astrology was successful as an aid in the ruling of the Chinese Empire for thousands of years.

The Chinese signs of the zodiac were not placed on the ecliptic, as are the signs of Indian and Western astrology, but on the equator. Each of the twelve signs ruled a two-hour period of the day, one of the months of the year, and one entire year during a twelve-year cycle. Therefore, it can be said that one was born in the Year of the Rat or the Year of the Monkey, and these animals would convey a particular astrological significance. The Chinese names for the signs of the zodiac are as follows: Dog, Boar, Rat, Ox, Tiger, Hare, Dragon, Snake, Horse, Goat, Monkey, and Cock.

In the seventh century before the Christian Era, King Ashurbanipal of Assyria built a great library in the city of Nineveh and furnished it with thousands of astrological cuneiform tablets, some dating from around 4000 B.C. In the year 612 B.C. Nineveh was conquered by the Chaldeans and the library was destroyed. The assailants, however, were soon to become masters of stellar divination themselves, and the name Chaldean was later synonymous in the West with an adept of the occult arts.

Astrology entered the Hellenic world at least as early as the Alexandrian wars, when hosts of Greek warriors fought their way to the banks of the Indus River and came under the influence of Egypt, Persia, and Babylonia, on the one hand, and of the mystical, introspective philosophies of India and the Far East, on the other. Astrological works said to have been written by the pharaoh Nechepso and the priest Petosiris were translated into Greek around 150 B.C. and became the cornerstone of pre-Christian European astrology.

As the Roman Republic was gradually infiltrated by Asian religious and philosophical thought, its citizens turned to astrology as the central theme of this new consciousness. The star-minded prophets of Baal and Ishtar were evicted from Rome in 139 B.C. along with the Jews, but as the Eastern cults gained massive public support over the years, the Roman government could eventually do nothing but tolerate the existence of various astrological sects. During the time of the Roman general Pompey (106–48 B.C.), the senator Nigidius Figulus wrote a textbook on the science in Latin. More influential were the studies of Posidonius of Apamea, written at the end of the republic.

With the founding of the Roman Empire in 27 B.C. and the subsequent official adoption of Oriental cults, astrology was accepted by nearly everyone. The emperor Tiberius turned from the worship of the elder gods in favor of the new science, which everywhere manifested itself more as a religion than as the pure mathesis (science) it is. It was thought then, as it is sometimes believed today, that the planets and signs (being representatives of theological and exalted paganism that replaced the old, stale forms of Roman religion) controlled events on earth. Astrology gained such a hold on Rome that the nation's citizens did nothing without consulting its oracles. According to one report, the Romans would not even take a bath without the assurance that it would be astrologically profitable.

The Alexandrian scholar Claudius Ptolemaeus, or Ptolemy, wrote the famous treatise on astrology entitled *Tetrabiblos* during the second century A.D., probably drawing on Egyptian and Babylonian sources. With the aid of such eminent minds as this, astrology became ingrained in the people's thinking to such an extent that virtually all philosophy and scientific thought in this period were dependent on its precepts. *The Dream of Scipio* by Cicero, written some two hundred years before Ptolemy's treatise, speaks of the heavenly spheres in much the same way as the medieval Kabbalists describe their system of *sephiroth,* and it was this type of occultism that continued to inspire the best minds in the West well past the fall of the Roman Empire and served as a foundation for modern-day astrology.

When astrology was still quite new to Europe, many Greek philosophers were doubtful of the accuracy of its forecasts. Carneades, before the advent of the Roman Empire, posed the question, "Are all the men that perish together in a battle born at the same moment because they have the same fate?" Of course, there was also the argument concerning the destinies of twins. The Chaldeans were able to answer all of the objections to their science, noting the effect of the Sun on the seasons of the year, the effect of the Moon on the ocean's tides, not to mention the more complicated evidence revealed in natal horoscopy. Nobody could refute this logic, and because their testimony proved true year after year and their personality analysis quite exact, astrology conquered the West with little difficulty. The skeptics refused to accept it, rejecting it along with all other learning. The Stoics, who believed in the omnipotence of fate, accepted astrology wholeheartedly. By the end of the second century anyone who would dare contest the validity of sidereal divination would have been considered idiotic.

To the early Christians, though, excluding those wonderfully bizarre Gnostic sects, astrology was undeniably interwoven with the paganism they abhorred. Polemics against the science were launched, using the language of the Greek dialecticians who had argued against the art when it first entered the Hellenic sphere. The same arguments that had been proved false by the early stellar prophets were used, but in the frenzy of Christian conversion the astrologers were condemned along with the rest of European paganism. The library at Alexandria, containing many thousands of astrological textbooks, was burned to the ground; the ancient monuments were destroyed or turned into Christian churches. In the fourth century of the Christian Era (the Piscean Age), Theodosius the Great outlawed all forms of paganism under penalty of death. A bloodbath, resembling the horrible autos-da-fé of the later Inquisition, ensued. Thousands of Roman citizens fled their native lands because of the terrible cruelty of their new "enlightened" rulers. Many went to India, where a cultural flowering occurred, signaling the beginning of the Indian golden age.

With the reign of Theodosius and the forbidding of the traditional European forms of religion as well as the Asian cults, the ghastly thousand-year journey of the Dark Ages began. It is at this point that the history of astrology in the West comes predominantly under the sphere of the Arabs. In Rome the papacy rejected astrology as a pagan (i.e., evil) practice. In Byzantium, however, it was recognized to some degree that astrology and Christianity were not incompatible, for many accepted Scriptures implied a belief in stellar significance ("And God said, Let there be lights in the firmament of the heaven to divide the day from the night; and let them be for signs, and for seasons, and for days, and years" [Genesis 1:14]. There are numerous Kabbalistic/astrological references all through the Old and New Testaments, primarily in the ultimate book, Revelation.). St. Augustine had declared that astrology was a fraud and that even if its predictions were accurate, they were obviously made under the influence of evil spirits.

With the appearance of Islam and the sudden emergence of the Arab empire in the seventh century A.D., astrology was saved from a state of ignominy. Damascus became a center of occult learning. Al-Mansur established a grand observatory in Baghdad. In the ninth century

Albumazar wrote *Introductorium in Astronomiam*, a textbook of astrological theory. By way of Spain, Arab scientific knowledge revived the faltering European educational centers.

Throughout the Middle Ages in Europe there was a raging controversy about whether astrology should be accepted as a science or as a "black art." By the thirteenth century, following the example of St. Thomas Aquinas, academicians generally accepted that the stars were the cause of all that took place on earth. The University of Bologna established a chair of astrology in the year 1125. Dante found astrology to be a source of inspiration in the writing of *The Divine Comedy* in the fourteenth century—for example, when the poet hero visits the angels of the planetary spheres.

By the fifteenth century even the papacy was using astrology to make important decisions. Pope Sixtus IV was himself an astrologer of repute, and Julius II recognized the need for astrological counsel. Johann Müller drew up horoscopes for the pope, established the first European observatory in Nuremberg, and published a thirty-year ephemeris on his own printing press. Copernicus (1473–1543), renowned for his discovery that the Earth is not the center of the solar system, was an astrologer. It is peculiar that modern anathemas against astrology use his discovery as a tool for contradicting astrological theory, but the founder of modern astronomy himself proclaimed that stellar divination was not in the least affected by his then-controversial deductions.

Michel de Notredame (Nostradamus) was one of the foremost astrologers of his time and the author of a book called *Centuries,* a collection of prophecies that remains popular to this day. In 1556 he was hired to compute the horoscopes of the royal children of the French court. Queen Catherine de Médici's honored him all his life after she discovered that his interpretations concerning the fate of her children were correct.

The Danish astrologer Tycho Brahe, the Englishman Francis Bacon, and the Italian Tommaso Campanella all helped to keep astrology alive through the sixteenth and seventeenth centuries. The Elizabethan court astrologer John Dee (1527–1608) was also a professional alchemist and magician. It was he who believed he had conversed with angels, leading him to discover a system of "Enochian" keys, or calls, that could unlock the worlds of the five elements and the thirty aethyrs. After experimentation with these magical methods, he was forced to retract what he had declared concerning their sanctity, for the content of the visions they produced clearly ran counter to the Christian code of ethics.

It remained for Aleister Crowley in the twentieth century to take up the thread of Dee's magical (or psychological) research by invoking the thirty aethyrs in the desert of North Africa. Crowley left behind a record of spiritual achievement unparalleled in the rationalistic West, entitled *The Vision and the Voice*. Within these "aethyrs," or psychic substrata, exist various combinations of astrological "powers," though it is difficult to say whether they are objective astral phenomena or subjective dreamlike experiences.

In the seventeenth century Johannes Kepler and William Lilly were representative of their age's astrological thought. The former, a mathematician, had definite doubts about the accuracy of astrological delineation as he knew it but expressed a belief that an authentic science of the stars could be developed if serious-minded men put it to the test. The latter, Lilly, was a prodigious writer and a leading horoscope maker in England. He predicted the Great Fire of London in 1666.

In more recent years Alan Leo and Dane Rudhyar both have tried to bring their chosen profession into line with current scientific trends, giving it a new, more intellectual framework. During World War II Karl Ernst Krafft was employed by the Nazis to translate the teachings of Nostradamus, which, it was felt, could be used profitably as propaganda. On the British side, Louis de Wohl was convinced that the Germans were using astrology in their effort to win and that the British should use the same means. The government agreed, and de Wohl became the official astrological mouthpiece of the Allies.

While the West has been growing ever more divorced from its mystical beginnings, the East (namely, India and its neighboring countries) has retained its age-old belief in astrology and, in many instances, the primitive magic associated with it. In the non-Communist countries of the Far East, astrological practices have remained virtually unchanged. The Buddhist priests of Sri Lanka perform a ceremony with the intention of invoking planetary forces in the curing of disease, fever, and poverty; Chandra (the Moon), Buddha (Mercury), Shukra (Venus), Kuja (Mars), Guru (Jupiter), Shani (Saturn), Rahu (North Node), and Ketu (South Node) all represent spiritual powers which, when adverse, produce diseases and misfortune analogous to the Westerner's analysis of each planet's negative effects.

In present-day Europe and America astrology is once again gaining a place in the universities, and surprisingly enough, psychology is investigating its uses in therapy. Sigmund Freud, ever loath to lend any credence to astrology, stated shortly before his death that he did hold a masked interest in the occult. Carl Jung, the most influential psychologist since Freud, used horoscopes to aid him in diagnosing the causes of his patients' illnesses. His studies have done much to validate astrology's claim to be a science, not a parlor game for the superstitious.

The theories of sidereal effects have become more sophisticated with the passing of the centuries. Radiation, cosmobiological impulses, subatomic conscious forces (a euphemism for "gods") have all been put forth as explanations of astrological accuracy. Perhaps the most convincing argument presented by modern science is that of Carl Jung. He propounded a theory that divinatory arts such as astrology, the tarot, and the *I Ching* are examples of a universal principle that he called "acausal synchronicity." The significance of this hypothesis is that it states, in effect, that there are no influences whatsoever acting upon the daily life of humanity originating in the position of the planets but rather that the planets portray a pattern of events synchronized to the life of the individual or group of individuals (such as a nation). This seems much more suitable than the theory of cosmic radiation, for no matter how much radiation exists in the earth's atmosphere, it cannot account for all the aspects of human life that astrology can accurately predict.

Acausal synchronicity does, to some extent, account for psychological analysis by the way of the natal chart, but many predictions would be impossible according to this theory. It may account for changes within the individual organism, but it is difficult to explain how planetary vibrations can cause events to happen to an individual, events that could be accurately predicted by ordinary horoscopy. To recognize the fact that every aspect of the universe acts in conformity with the remainder of the universe is only to extend the concept of ecology one step further. One can find significance in every aspect of the physical world. Astrology happens to be the most logical, mathematically determined divinatory science we have developed thus far. The fact is that the stars do not have a *causal* effect on the Earth, but a connection between the planets and individuals that is rooted in astrological meaning does much to alleviate it from the age-old objections to its validity.

As for the spiritualistic theory of cosmic effects, there is no evidence to support it which cannot be explained by more practical hypotheses. This does not mean that it is necessarily false, but it lowers the probability of its being true. The theory of acausal synchronicity presents a cleaner, more efficient astrological theory and explains how the planets can actually describe every detail of human experience without being the direct cause. They are an abstraction of our daily activities. If the spiritualistic theory were, in fact, true, then the *causal* arts of magic (i.e., the omnipotence of the magician in controlling his universe through controlling spiritual noumena) must be granted. Here one begins to fall into the trough of uncertain, difficult, and pretentious metaphysics—difficult to prove and impossible to integrate with the truths of physical existence. It may be that astrology and magic are examples of psychic causality. If so, everything we know is *wrong*! Not only that, but natural laws are thrown topsy-turvy, *psychological facts are disgraced as mere fables*, and we become the victim of a rampaging solipsism. In the years to come, we may see science turn its attention to problems such as these, and the outcome may be very surprising.

PERSONALITY TRAITS FOR CANCER

Your Place in the Sun. You are the nourisher of the zodiac. Yours is the fourth sign of the natural horoscope—ruling the house of home and psychological roots. You folks are nurturing, protective, and domestic—with much sympathetic feeling for those in your immediate circle. Being a water sign, you are also emotional and intuitive. You follow your instincts rather than logic and prefer a fluid, adaptable, and nonintellectual approach to life. As a cardinal sign, you like to initiate projects and then take charge and direct others. This you do mostly on an emotional level, however. Your deep feelings are powerful agents for influencing people, and you have considerable tenacity and defensive energy with which to protect yourself.

The Significance of Your Ruling Planet. Your ruler is the Moon—symbol for the subconscious, which stores memories and impressions. Under its influence, you are sentimental and fond of the good old days. You're also attuned to the habits and rhythms of your early conditioning and, thus, are fluctuating in your emotional response—like the waxing and waning Moon. Other traits are sensitivity and response on the feeling level—equipping you for occupations such as child care, social work, teaching, healing, counseling, acting, and art. You do well in business, for you are shrewd and have "a feel" for what the public wants. Catering, hotel management, real estate, antique dealing, and work with home-related products are all possibilities.

The Meaning of Your Symbol. The crab is Cancer's symbol. This shows your capacity for containment and alludes to the soft interior hidden beneath your tough outer shell. Like the crab, you also move toward your goals in a sidelong, indirect manner. You're not generally the pushy type and tend to yield and flow around opposition rather than meeting it head-on. You have a great deal of negative strength in the form of patience and endurance. In dealings with others, you are a master of passive resistance. As the crab alternates between sea and land, so do you alternate between extroversion and introversion. You love your private world, but you also need stimulation from the outside.

Qualities to Stress. You have a strong creative and inspirational side and should take time to develop it. Music, dance, painting, poetry, creative writing—all of these provide constructive channels for your powerful emotions and imagination. You should also be sure to employ your soft, sensitive nature in some sort of useful social activity lest you merely become hypersensitive and overly concerned for yourself. Your greatest challenge is mastery of your emotions; any course of study explaining the mechanism of the subconscious, which triggers these, could be highly useful. Once you have curbed the tempestuous sea of feeling within you, your outward behavior will reflect more readily the beautiful intuitions you feel.

Weaknesses to Overcome. Your chief problem is moodiness. You are too much governed by your subconscious impulses and subject to intense bouts of energy-wasting emotionalism. You also tend to live in the past and spend too much time in daydreams and memories. Many of you are clannish, insular, obsessed with family matters, too fond of tradition. Your mind can be of the tribal variety that frowns on innovation and individualism. Perhaps your greatest weakness, though, is your approach to others. You are far too touchy, timid, and reactive and will always have problems until you achieve a degree of detachment and impersonality. You're especially smothering in close relations and must eventually learn that to love is to let go.

SUN SIGNS
AROUND THE ZODIAC

The Sun stands at the center of the zodiac, as the focal point of our charts. Just as the heart pumps lifeblood throughout our bodies, so, too, is the sun the life-force energy that ignites our beings, expressing itself as our identities, how we define ourselves in the world. The Sun also describes our conscious self-expressions, what we know ourselves to be and how we project that to others. It is the creative thrust of energy that moves us forward. Placement and aspects to the Sun describe the issues we struggle with on our path to fulfilling the map laid out by our charts. How we solve these challenges is the free-will aspect of astrology, as we ourselves determine exactly how our Sun Sign energy gets expressed.

It is said that the Sun is the soul or the self, that aspect of us central to our being which involves the smooth running of our inner and outer lives. Our ability to take hold of whatever thought, desire, or wish we have and move it into a conscious place is described by our Sun Sign. How we take the inner pieces of our personality and integrate them and then reflect them to others—creatively and interpersonally—is another function of that core part of us.

Our purpose in life is also signified by the Sun Sign under which we were born. Understanding our Sun Sign can help us define our mission, issues, aims, goals, and life task as well. The Sun represents that central place inside us from which is shed the light of consciousness on other parts, struggles, and pieces. In defining some of our obstacles, clarity and growing self-awareness enable us to overcome barriers to expressing our inner strength and essence.

Finally, the Sun represents our joy in life, the path which by its right nature in our lives successfully leads us to "follow our bliss." In turning in toward a center of ourselves that we know feels right, we can move out into the world in the best way possible. Then, contributing our greatest talents, we make it a more joyful and fulfilling place for those around us as well, extending as far as the heart can see.

The more successful we are in finding and fulfilling ourselves, the more readily, easily, and helpfully we can reach out and shine the light on the paths of others. Our Sun stands symbolically as that beacon, illuminating our own path to self-understanding and self-mastery.

Aries

Aries is the first sign of the zodiac and as such is associated with leadership, the head, and being first. Aries individuals are known for their spontaneity and assertiveness and, unless negatively aspected, a certain natural leadership ability. Idealism, too, is part of the Aries heritage. With the energy and motivation to stand up for matters of principle, Aries is the champion of the fight for individual freedom for the self and of the fight for others.

Aries is motivated by action, by taking charge in a situation and moving forward in it. This core of inner self therefore often involves a life of removing obstacles to the expression of an overt and straightforward energy. In the struggle to assert themselves, Aries people are often involved with dealing with issues of anger and aggression, learning how to channel or even make a career of those characteristics—as criminal lawyers, boxers, politicians, or warriors on the path to peace, truth, or justice.

A sense of humor is often the trademark of such individuals, who have been through the school of hard knocks long enough to realize that the head is often smarter and faster than the hand. The wise Aries learns that a quick quip can do much more than a clenched fist to forward his or her aims.

Taurus

Taurus is reputed to be the most stubborn, determined, and stable sign because it is associated with the earth and money, as well as with creativity, sensual pleasure, and fertility. These characteristics all relate to the material or physical aspects of life, of which Taureans are notoriously aware and to which they are quite sensitive.

Comfort is a basic aspiration of such members of the zodiac. Taurus is very much aware of basic needs and what feels good. Sensualists and even hedonists, Taureans are no less practical when it comes to seeing to it that all the necessities are taken care of before the pleasure begins.

The energy of creativity made manifest in some tangible form often leads Taurus people into the field of art or some related endeavor. Expressing a unique aesthetic sensibility, these materially minded artists often find lucrative outlets for their talents.

With a particularly acute sense of timing, Taurus is able to attune to knowing exactly when and how to get a job done and then brilliantly see it through to completion. Security is the impetus that keeps Taurus' nose to the grindstone. Otherwise she or he surely would be dissolved somewhere in a puddle of sensual delight.

Gemini

Gemini is the sign most directly expressing our basic duality as human beings: how every issue has two sides (at least) and how each moment of life has a myriad of possibilities for action, passivity, philosophical distance, and emotional reaction. The complexity of this awareness makes Gemini the first of the mental signs, and communication and thought are keys to the Gemini personality. Writing and study are some of the skills applied in making the bridges that Gemini builds between the self and others.

Gemini is also known for a great diversity of charms and talents, taking on a plethora of projects and commitments and a multileveled and reflective awareness that makes for a rather self-contradictory quality evident in interactions. When directed, the energy of the Sun Sign person can be brilliant and productive, often in the field of literary endeavors or the media.

The awareness that members of this sign have of the many details that constitute existence results in a fascinating personality, an inspiring conversationalist, and an interesting companion. Life is incredibly entertaining to Gemini, and as much as you are a part of his or her audience, you are also part of the show.

Cancer

Cancer is the Sun Sign most clearly associated with the home, nurturing, and that inner part of ourselves that is still a child in sensitivities and needs to be taken care of. Most often this need does not get directly expressed and instead emerges as a very mothering, directive energy—often by a Cancer who has walled off an incredibly deep vulnerability that goes wanting inside.

Developing emotional security and finding a place of safety in life are the driving forces of this Sun Sign individual. Often Cancer people use money or intellect—or neurotic worry—as shields against their fantastic psychic attunements to the feelings of others, reflecting their own sensitive selves.

The quality of knowing intuition can make Cancer individuals a success in just about any field chosen. The driving emotional needs, however, make monetary success or even fame too often an unsatisfying substitute for that deeper striving to be truly nurtured that is sought throughout their lives.

The most secure, rewarding, and emotionally fulfilling

employment this sign can undertake involves taking care of others—neighborhood police surveillance work, perhaps—or attaining a level of expertise in a field where compassion, understanding, and nurturing are needed.

Leo

Leos shine when happy and then reflect to others their own finest qualities, encouraging and inspiring them with tireless enthusiasm. On the other hand, keeping a Leo happy takes a lot of energy and usually requires an entire audience of admirers.

This need for attention is expressed in negative ways, however, only when there isn't a creative outlet, an arena in which Leo is known to stand out. This lack can make for a whiny, self-centered, narrowly focused, and dominating character with little to share but complaints.

Leo may as a child have been deprived of the love and recognition that one needs to develop into a secure, confident adult. Dignity can become overly dramatic histrionics and a sense of confidence can degenerate into an overbearing pride when Leo has not learned to bolster self-esteem so that each sensation of vulnerability need not be so devastating.

The ego must be honed to keep Leo on his or her best behavior. Skills and talents need to be cultivated so that there is always a place for Leo to go that feels like a platform for well-deserved adulation. Once in the comfortable position of leading and advising others, Leo can move on to lend that golden glow to the rest of a fun-filled, creative, and loving life.

Virgo

These hardworking and most sensitive members of the zodiac know just what they can do to serve you, and most often they deliver that promise modestly, completely, and well. Virgos are ever alert to any physical needs that are as yet unfulfilled, and their well-developed gifts—especially those involving the use of the hands or particular analytical or other mental abilities—are always efficiently directed.

The almost driving perfectionism of members of the sign, however, needs to be tempered by an acceptance and toleration for what is—for their own and others—human limitations. Otherwise, a sadly cynical, frustrated, and/or depressed person is the result. A more fruitful direction for the discriminating talents of Virgo is the purification in some way of the environment or some system that connects to the betterment of our physical world for us all to live healthier and simpler lives.

An overwhelming sensitivity—to others, to allergens, to disorder, tension, pain, etc.—drives Virgo into a kind of intellectual retreat or one that involves the manipulation of others in order to avoid revealing a deeper side of self, although a wealth of tender responsiveness is there for the asking by the right person, at the correct time, in the appropriate way.

Libra

Libra is the only sign represented by neither an animal nor a human symbol. Instead, the scales represent the rather abstract quality of Librans. Equality, justice, and a sense of fairness are what members of this sign are driven by in arriving at and fulfilling their life purposes. As such, they need to find a balance between their own needs and those of others, their desires and direction in life—as opposed to the ones they have been following in order to please or pacify others. Problems can develop when Librans give with the expectation of getting, rather than just seeing to it that their own needs are taken care of before giving anything of themselves to others.

Librans are always involved in some kind of relationship, so that they can see the mirrors of their own inner selves in others. Partnership can be quite crucial to them because they have trouble defining themselves alone or apart from others.

Above all, Librans seek harmony, usually manifested in a sensitivity to the aesthetic surroundings in which they live and work. The deeper peace they seek, however, lies within themselves, where they struggle with anything that gets in the way of experiencing serenity. Once in touch with their own inner beauty, however, they easily bring it out in others.

Scorpio

Scorpio is the sign that governs transformation—that is, conscious change, acknowledging and taking responsibility for some inner negativity and turning it into a constructive force. It may seem to members of this sign that life is filled with task after task of this kind. Indeed, emotional challenges of the most arduous variety are often Scorpio's lot in life. Surviving and moving through such difficulties, however, result in a highly developed character, furthered through a concentration of positive power.

Within the psyche of these magnetic and strong individuals is an indomitable strength which, when not correctly channeled, can become an unscrupulous force for domination and even brutality over others. The driving nature of a Scorpio who has not come to terms with a great inner power can be manifested in destructiveness to the self and to others or in the cultivation of disease.

Once Scorpio has discovered the miraculous power of turning that negativity around and making it part of everyday life, healing on all levels becomes one of many precious gifts the Scorpio individual possesses—to be performed on the self as well as conveyed to others. A profession aligned with the positive expression of such energies satisfies the Scorpio soul, helps others, and turns the energy around.

Sagittarius

Sagittarians are often known as the wanderers of the zodiac because they may never really seem to land or plant themselves firmly anywhere—in a relationship, career, or home—for very long. Should you find a happy Sagittarian who has seemingly given up that overt striving for freedom, you may have found one who knows the true secret of the sign: that life is but a journey to be lived out, the process being even more important than the goal, how you love and work as much as who and what and how much.

Sagittarians are philosophical travelers with an insatiable curiosity and zest for life. They thrive on the new and, with lively enthusiasm, bring great joy and excitement into the lives of others. All people are potential friends to a Sagittarian, who is a citizen of the world, at home everywhere.

Sagittarians get into quandaries about what direction to take—they are easily diverted—when other parts of their personalities demand fulfillment. The answer lies in seeing even a life-binding commitment as but a deeper path to explore, enjoy, and move along down the path of life.

Good careers for Sagittarians range from judges to space explorers, philosophers, teachers, or writers. Any profession undertaken is pursued with joy and satisfaction so long as it involves the exploration of life and being with people.

Capricorn

Capricorn is traditionally that hardworking sign of the zodiac that takes responsibility for all that goes on, sees to it that everything necessary gets completed successfully and well, and has a rather serious view of life. This typically describes the early attitude of members of this sign, who have usually emerged from childhoods that leave them deprived of some significant aspect of youth and mature before their time. Responsible to a fault, they often enter adulthood motivated mostly by a fear for their own survival and for that of those in their charge as well.

Capricorns derive a sense of purpose and satisfaction from taking good care of either a large number of people or a significant area of expertise or materials of some value. Always up for a good challenge, they can be strong adversaries and staunch supporters of others, their ideas, their work—whatever serves the well-being of the group.

Usually because they have taken strict good care of their physical selves throughout their lives, Capricorns live long and relatively healthy lives, active and employed well into old age. With arduous lives behind them, their later years are often dotted with the delight of a childlike and life-loving existence they didn't get to enjoy when young.

Aquarius

Aquarius is a rather challenging sign, with issues and struggles that all of us in this Aquarian Age are now learning about.

Aquarians especially are dealing with coming to terms with the scientific and the artistic needs within us all, allowing for full expression of both. Another way of viewing this dilemma is the need to reconcile the dreamer (Aquarians are filled with magnificent and sometimes grandiose ideas for the future) with the pragmatist, knowing that the priority is to get things done now so that the greatest number of people can immediately benefit.

Many Aquarians feel the pull of these conflicting drives their entire lives, while others sacrifice one aspect of their natures for another. The larger truth that can serve to help the Aquarian fulfill his or her purpose is that he or she heeds the guiding intuitive voice within that can lead him or her to a successful and peaceful integration of those various parts of self.

Members of this sign are especially successful in

professions in which they can channel their uniqueness and talent into helping others recognize their own gifts and cultivate self-sufficiency in them. Because they thrive on being of service, they automatically do well.

Pisces

As members of the last sign of the zodiac, Pisceans are in touch with the temporal nature of reality, with the fact that everything is finite and that nothing endures. Pisceans do not find themselves attached to the future, to plans or to material gain—let alone to any profession that seeks to structure or organize resources, people, or time to the destruction of the human spirit. Pisces thrives on a creative flow that involves spontaneity, artfulness, and the ability to tap into an abundant emotional and spiritual reservoir within. Conflicts Pisceans experience often involve a choice between acting toward something new and staying with the known; all their lives involve building bridges, most often between the inner selves and the outer world of others.

With the gift of magically understanding the value of every human and other sentient being, each moment and every feeling, Pisceans fulfill themselves often by being there for others and by supporting friends and family, clients and customers through the travails of everyday life. Pisceans possess a magnificent intuitive ability to extend the self as needed, when needed in just the right way to be of help to others.

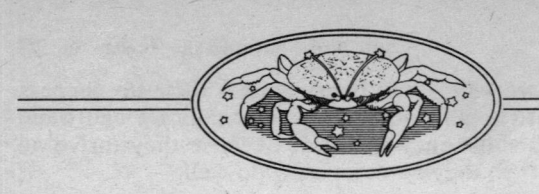

HOW TO MAINTAIN GOOD HEALTH

If you were born from June 22 to July 2, the Moon rules your decan. Your emotions have a great influence on your physical well-being, particularly your stomach and digestive processes. Therefore, never eat when upset, and consume your nourishment in as peaceful surroundings as possible. Being overweight can be a problem for you if you eat because you are unhappy or stressed out; it is best to only eat when you are truly hungry. To make matters worse, you also tend toward water retention. To help keep bodily fluids in balance, cut down on salt, coffee, sugar, and alcohol, because these substances can greatly lower your potassium level. Instead, eat potassium-rich foods such as citrus fruits, tomatoes, green leafy vegetables, and bananas. Exercise is also essential for keeping your weight down. Sit-ups for flattening the tummy are recommended.

If you were born from July 3 to July 13, Mars and Pluto rule your decan. You are intensely emotional but you tend to bottle up your feelings, which can lead to constipation and gastrointestinal ulcers. Try to express your emotions, especially anger, instead of letting them fester to the point of doing internal damage. Don't eat overly spicy foods, since they can irritate the delicate stomach lining. In addition, avoid medications like aspirin, which can cause bleeding of the stomach walls. Milk helps neutralize harmful acids which can build up in the stomach. A daily helping of bran mixed with prunes, or some other fruit, helps control constipation. Exercise is also a must to promote regularity and reduce tension. Belly dancing allows you to express your strong sexuality while also strengthening and trimming your stomach area.

If you were born from July 14 to July 23, Neptune rules your decan. Your health can be somewhat delicate, especially if your lymphatic system, which helps ward off illness, becomes sluggish. To strengthen your resistance against disease, it is imperative to get a good amount of rest. However, sleeping pills, and medication in general, are not advised because they can reduce the efficiency of the immune system and make you more susceptible to infection. Likewise, avoid or drastically reduce your alcohol consumption. Stay away from junk foods and switch to foods high in riboflavin, such as broccoli, dried apricots, beef, cheese, and eggs. A regular routine of moderate exercise helps keep you energetic and strong. Meditative activities such as yoga and swimming are especially beneficial.

YOUR GUIDE TO FRIENDS AND LOVERS

How You Relate

Because you are deeply sensitive, strong emotional ties are very important to you. This prompts you to form lasting, meaningful relationships. Fiercely loyal, you treat friends as members of your own family. With your lover, you tend to be extremely possessive, demanding complete devotion.

Cancer with Aries: Your Aries friend can bring excitement into your life, but it can be hard to keep up with the hectic pace. You are turned on by your Aries lover's sexiness and confidence. However, this somewhat selfish individual can run roughshod over your feelings. Therefore, for this relationship to work, you have to develop a thicker skin.

Cancer with Taurus: This can be a wonderful friendship, because your Taurus companion and you share the same emotional and material values. Your Taurus lover is romantic, passionate, and looking for a commitment you are only too happy to give. Warmth and understanding abound in this ideal relationship.

Cancer with Gemini: While it's not always easy to understand your Gemini friend, this versatile companion can expand your interests and lighten your moods. You are very different from your Gemini lover, who enjoys gadding about town, while you prefer quiet, romantic evenings at home. This relationship needs work in order to succeed.

Cancer with Cancer: On the same emotional wavelength as you, your Cancer friend is a warm and caring companion. You need to nurture and be nurtured, and your Cancer lover fits the bill perfectly. Home and family are on top of both your agendas. Even though you understand each other's moods, if you happen to get into a bad mood at the same time, communication can break down.

Cancer with Leo: Even though you are as temperamentally different from your Leo friend as night is from day, this upbeat individual can brighten your darker moods, while you can deepen the other's sensitivity. However, your Leo lover, although romantic and affectionate, may be too self-involved to fully understand the depth of your feelings. A common ground that can unite you is your love of children.

Cancer with Virgo: You have a great understanding of your Virgo friend, who can be as shy and retiring as you are. But you will have to make the first move to start things humming with your Virgo lover. Once you are committed, you appreciate each other's homemaking abilities and thrifty eye toward money management. This helps assure domestic security.

Cancer with Libra: Even though there are many differences between you and your Libra friend, you both are gentle souls who need a harmonious environment for your well-being. However, there can be many problems in your relationship with a Libra lover. Although romantic and loving to you, flirtatious Libra likes to charm others as well. Libra's extravagance can make you feel financially uneasy.

Cancer with Scorpio: You have a faithful friend in Scorpio because you understand each other's needs and feelings. The same holds true with your Scorpio lover, which makes for a very passionate and powerful combination. Except for an occasional flare-up of jealousy, this can be an ideal blend.

Cancer with Sagittarius: Although you don't see eye to eye with your Sagittarius friend, this optimistic individual can lift you out of your darkest moods. The problems intensify with your Sagittarius lover. You enjoy staying close to home, while Sagittarius thrives on traveling far and wide. And your possessive attitude can only make freedom-loving Sagittarius travel farther and wider.

Cancer with Capricorn: Even though you are zodiacal opposites, you both choose traditional values, which helps cement your friendship. You fit together with your Capricorn lover like a hand in a glove. You feel secure and protected by Capricorn's strength and drive for success. In return, Capricorn welcomes your nurturing.

Cancer with Aquarius: A friendship with an Aquarius can be confusing because you like to live in the past, while Aquarius is future-oriented. A love relationship with an Aquarius can also be disheartening because you are sentimental and emotional, while Aquarius is detached and rational. You concentrate on personal interests, Aquarius focuses on universal concerns. Common goals are needed.

Cancer with Pisces: There is a psychic link between you and your Pisces friend because you are on the same emotional wavelength. Your intuitive Pisces lover gives you the romance and devotion you need to make you feel emotionally secure. However, in order to feel financially secure with this sometimes impractical individual, you should handle the money.

CAREER-WEALTH POTENTIALS

Are You in the Right Job? Three houses of a birth-chart are significant in determining your career potentials—the tenth (general field of work), the third (mental skills and aptitudes), and the sixth (capacity for work; conditions related to employment; relationshps with coworkers, employees, etc.). You will be happiest in a job where there is both security and potential for advancement. As Cancer is a cardinal water sign, you are highly ambitious—but also very self-protective, especially in matters related to security. You are not inclined to project yourself obviously into the limelight, but you usually manage to be at least on the fringe of it, pulling a few strings here and there "offstage." Aries on your solar tenth house is the sign of new beginnings, and you don't at all mind taking a few calculated risks for a job which you intuitively feel is going to get you in on the ground floor of a successful enterprise. Virgo on your solar third house can make you meticulous in handling the details of your work and also enables you to express your thoughts in a concise and practical way. With Sagittarius on your solar sixth house, you would be well liked by your coworkers or employees and have the ability to make your job environment comfortable and hospitable. The blend of your Cancer Sun-Sign with these signs on your solar third, sixth, and tenth houses shows that you would be at your best in the fields of surgery, hairdressing (or wig making or selling), tool or machinery manufacture, dentistry (Aries); writing, selling, teaching, accounting

(Virgo); law, publishing, travel, or work related to a philanthropic organization (Sagittarius). Your Cancer Sun-Sign has given you traits of sympathy, understanding, and compassion, which add to your potential job fields social service, counseling, geriatrics, and personnel work.

Are You Aware of Your Wealth Potentials? In a birth-chart, the second house signifies personal property, possessions, financial connections, investments, ability to increase income, valuable ideas, monetary prowess, ambitions, personal belongings, earnings, and all forms of money (gold, jewels, bonds, securities, stocks, etc.). Leo, your money house, has the Sun as its ruler. But Aquarius, whose ancient ruler is Saturn, opposes this house. This is not considered good for money matters in that it creates some kind of unhappiness regarding funds or material prospects. However, your financial house being in between the houses of the Moon (ruler of Cancer) and Mercury (ruler of Virgo), you stand good chances to inherit property. Generally, the Sun and Mercury are likely to be in conjunction. This will mean a conjunction of the ruler of the money house with the ruler of the solar twelfth house—Gemini (the house of expenses and losses). This is not considered good, as it will make you a spender as well as an earner. Your spending may be generally for prestige. Even if you are born into a rich family, you are not likely to be happy moneywise. Your ability to earn will probably match your spending. Your ego attached to money may be the probable cause of your spending. You will have cordial relations with fellow workers as well as superiors and subordinates. You are likely to have good credit facilities, and the way you work will be appreciated. You do possess a potential to overcome difficulties in your way of making money. You possess courage and determination, and your imagination knows no bounds. These attributes indicate that you are likely to be very successful in your business, and your attitude will probably be to earn by honest means and with grace and foresight. With so much on your side, you should be able to conquer obstacles and put yourself on a sound course, one that will lead to ample financial returns. The manner in which you conduct your work and the efficient way in which you handle your duties and responsibilities are bound to lead to promotions. Your credit standing should be good, and the contacts you make with people in high positions will stand you in good stead.

HOBBIES FOR FUN AND PROFIT

What do you do with your leisure time? Many psychologists say that from the answer to this question they can tell more about your personality than they can from even complete knowledge of your vocation. Although most people have far fewer hours to spend on hobbies than they must give to daily routine, the way those free hours are spent reveals much concerning the individual's chance for happiness and progress.

No matter how many avocations you choose to follow, you will see each through to successful completion. Your friends know your competence, and you may often be asked to help in initiating a leisure-time program for other people. It is a joy to you to give this aid.

Hospitality is so much an innate part of your nature that it is likely that you will take part in many organizations in which you can play the part of host. Nothing gives you greater pleasure than to entertain in your own home. Appropriate hobbies for you, therefore, would include anything in the way of home decoration or furnishing. The preparation of unusual foods is also fun.

The fact that Cancer is a water sign explains your natural interest in anything which has to do with that element. Swimming, boating, and fishing offer means of enjoyable relaxation in your leisure hours. You many want to have an aquarium or make a collection of sea pictures, miniature boats, or stories of people whose lives are bound up with the sea. Shells may be gathered and made into attractive objects which will delight your friends.

You are bound to have an interest in the costumes and furniture of past generations. Collecting and refinishing antiques would, consequently, be a satisfying activity. Hooking rugs, converting old vases into lamps, or making reproductions of any old objects would be pleasurable and profitable. In this regard, there are possibilities in constructing replicas of old historical buildings or dressing dolls to show the changing styles of the years.

A telescope could give you a lot of enjoyment, for you would be able to study the phases of the Moon, a subject in which you have an interest through cosmic influences. Gathering together legends and pictures of this fascinating body would also be a source of great inspiration for you.

Your spare-time activities should be chosen with cosmic influences in mind if you are to derive the most satisfaction and relaxation for yourself. Wise use of leisure also enables you to give the maximum pleasure and help to your associates. The position of the Sun at the time of your birth inclines your choice of hobbies in certain directions. To ignore these forces and swim against the tide, so to speak, is to hold yourself back from development— emotionally and spiritually, often even physically.

STELLAR TIPS FOR PARENTS

Fire, Earth, Air, or Water Element. While an element has a common mold, each sign falling under it has individual characteristics. The fire signs are Aries (March 21–April 20), Leo (July 24–August 23), and Sagittarius (November 23–December 21); the earth signs are Taurus (April 21–May 21), Virgo (August 24–September 23), and Capricorn (December 22–January 20); the air signs are Gemini (May 22–June 21), Libra (September 24–October 23), and Aquarius (January 21–February 19); the water signs are Cancer (June 22–July 23), Scorpio (October 24–November 22), and Pisces (February 20–March 20). Here is the way to place children in their own particular environment.

Cancer Parents with Fire Children. You have a tough time keeping up physically with fire-sign children, yet are stimulated by the spontaneity, exuberance, high-spiritedness, and enthusiasm for life these children exhibit. Temperamentally, you tend to be on the moody side, but don't let negative emotions dampen these youngsters' spirits. Above all, prevent these children from coming to the mistaken conclusion that they are somehow responsible for the mood swings to which you may be susceptible. Fire-sign children can be guilty of hurting others simply through careless behavior or hasty words. Use your sensitive emotional nature in a positive way, by teaching them to be aware of the feelings of others. These youngsters are eager to experience physically all that life has to offer, an approach that is largely responsible for a constant round of activities and numerous friends. Once you understand that this is a primary part of their nature, you won't feel rejected when these offspring seem to neglect home and hearth in order to pursue their many interests.

Cancer Parents with Earth Children. In comparison to your extremely emotional, sentimental nature, earth-sign children can appear to lack feelings. Weighing everything according to its practical value, these children are at times difficult for you to understand. To elicit cooperation when you make a request, your first instinct may be to appeal to these offspring on an emotional level. This method may work when they are young, but once they gain some maturity (and earth-sign children mature at a very young age), you may lose respect with this approach unless it is accompanied by some sound practicality. Do not allow your wavering emotions to interfere with establishing a very firm, structured, organized family life, for that is what earth-sign children require in order to function happily in the world. If you issue a directive, be prepared to stand behind it and not be swayed by stubborn behavior on the part of these youngsters; they may very well try to outlast you in the hope that you'll give in.

Cancer Parents with Air Children. As a Cancerian parent, you may exhibit too much possessiveness to suit the temperament of air-sign children. You have to find a way to show your affection and pride in their accomplishments without becoming so emotional that as these youngsters get older they begin to feel smothered. Your natural tendency to worry to excess can also be a source of difficulty. Here again you must be able to demonstrate your concern without going so far as to make these children feel overprotected. Once you establish a lighter, freer, less inhibiting atmosphere in your home, these youngsters will relax and learn from your sensitive understanding of life and its various experiences. When these offspring fail at a project or are disappointed by the behavior of others, do not project your own hurt feelings into the situation; you'll only make matters worse. These children are more apt to shrug the problem off unless you indicate something else should be happening, in which case they will try to feign hurt in order to please you.

Cancer Parents with Water Children. You can enjoy a close bond with water-sign children because of similarities in temperament and personality. These offspring will exhibit the same sensitivity to life and its experiences as you. This will help foster a strong parent-child relationship. Excess emotionalism can wipe out practicality and reason, however, qualities that must be demonstrated in your household in order to give these children the tools needed to deal effectively with the real world. When a situation gets too emotional, stop and let things calm down before trying to reach a solution. To offset so much emotion, you need to establish a firm, structured family life, yet at the same time allowing some room for flexibility. By exhibiting strength of character, you can be the role model these youngsters need to keep from being destroyed by introversion.

YOUR BIRTHDAY'S PLANETARY RULER

Planetary Rulerships. The system of planetary rulership of the days was evolved by the Egyptians, under Greek influence. The system spread over the entire then-known world and resulted in the days of the week being named after the planetary rulers. The planetary ruler of the day you were born exerts a powerful influence on your life. You can determine the planetary ruler on your birth day using the tables on pages 39–40. Find the year in question on Table 1. On the same line, to the right, note the key number under the month you were born. Add the key number to your date of birth (i.e., the day of the month); find the total in Table 2. On that line, to the left, will be found the day of the week you were born.

Born on Sunday/the Sun. You're daring, with a strong sense of romance and adventure. You're well liked by others and are social. Though confident, you have an inner need to live up to the best of your potentials. You give a lot to life and expect a lot in return. Arrogance could lead to problems.

Born on Monday/the Moon. You know how to get along with others but can be moody and self-centered. At times you hurt people without realizing it. You love home but may feel confined by domesticity. Nervous tension may interfere with your fulfilling your potentials, though these are great, especially in art.

Cancer JUNE 22–JULY 23

Born on Tuesday/Mars. You have strong desires and are a fighter. Undoubtedly you will do your own thing, come what may. Individuality brings you success, but you need more tact and consideration for others. Your energy often keeps the midnight oils burning, for you keep going longer than most.

Born on Wednesday/Mercury. You have many irons in the fire but may only skim the surface. You're too often quick to abandon a project if success isn't immediate. Restlessness can interfere with study, which you need to be successful. Be less judgmental. Your versatility leads to achievement in such areas as medicine, writing, science, and theater.

Born on Thursday/Jupiter. You'd make a good fighter for a cause. You're quite independent in your outlook on life and have your own definition of honor. A love of ideas can make you overlook the human factor. Luck is with you, but don't overplay your hand. Though personable, you appear detached.

Born on Friday/Venus. You like life's finer things and spend freely on what you want. Though anxious to please others, you're not always considerate of their feelings. An artistic or professional career can lead you to popularity with the masses. Your sex appeal will bring you many admirers.

Born on Saturday/Saturn. You're ambitious but do better on your own among strangers than in the family milieu. You must like your work for you to succeed. You can easily rise to the heights, though you may resent authority. You need to learn when to be passive and when to be aggressive in timing in order to fulfill your potentials. Patience is your ally.

TABLE 1

Year	Year	Year	Jan.	Feb.	Mar.	Apr.	May	June	July	Aug.	Sept.	Oct.	Nov.	Dec.
1918	1946	1974	2	5	5	1	3	6	1	4	0	2	5	0
1919	1947	1975	3	6	6	2	4	0	2	5	1	3	6	1
*1920	*1948	*1976	4	0	1	4	6	2	4	0	3	5	1	3
1921	1949	1977	6	2	2	5	0	3	5	1	4	6	2	4
1922	1950	1978	0	3	3	6	1	4	6	2	5	0	3	5
1923	1951	1979	1	4	4	0	2	5	0	3	6	1	4	6
*1924	*1952	*1980	2	5	5	2	4	0	2	5	1	3	6	1
1925	1953	1981	4	0	0	3	5	1	3	6	2	4	0	2
1926	1954	1982	5	1	1	4	6	2	4	0	3	5	1	3
1927	1955	1983	6	2	2	5	0	3	5	1	4	6	2	4
*1928	*1956	*1984	0	3	4	0	2	5	0	3	6	1	4	6
1929	1957	1985	2	5	5	1	3	6	1	4	0	2	5	0
1930	1958	1986	3	6	6	2	4	0	2	5	1	3	6	1
1931	1959	1987	4	0	0	3	5	1	3	6	2	4	0	2
*1932	*1960	*1988	5	1	2	5	0	3	5	1	4	6	2	4
1933	1961	1989	0	3	3	6	1	4	6	2	5	0	3	5
1934	1962	1990	1	4	4	0	2	5	0	3	6	1	4	6
1935	1963	1991	2	5	5	1	3	6	1	4	0	2	5	0
*1936	*1964	*1992	3	6	0	3	5	1	3	6	2	4	0	2
1937	1965	1993	5	1	1	4	6	2	4	0	3	5	1	3
1938	1966	1994	6	2	2	5	0	3	5	1	4	6	2	4
1939	1967	1995	0	3	3	6	1	4	6	2	5	0	3	5
*1940	*1968	*1996	1	4	5	1	3	6	1	4	0	2	5	0
1941	1969	1997	3	6	6	2	4	0	2	5	1	3	6	1
1942	1970	1998	4	0	0	3	5	1	3	6	2	4	0	2
1943	1971	1999	5	1	1	4	6	2	4	0	3	5	1	3
*1944	*1972	*2000	6	2	3	6	1	4	6	2	5	0	3	5
1945	1973	2001	1	4	4	0	2	5	0	3	6	1	4	6

1901 1902 1903 *1904 1905 1906 1907 *1908 1909 1910 1911 *1912 1913 1914 1915 *1916 1917

*Leap Year.

39

TABLE 2

Sunday	1	8	15	22	29	36
Monday	2	9	16	23	30	37
Tuesday	3	10	17	24	31	
Wednesday	4	11	18	25	32	
Thursday	5	12	19	26	33	
Friday	6	13	20	27	34	
Saturday	7	14	21	28	35	

YOUR MOON SIGN

Moon. The Moon in your horoscope rules your emotional life. It is your desires, as opposed to willpower and ego; your emotional needs, as opposed to what expediency or reason dictates. It indicates how you are likely to react to the various situations and experiences you encounter. To a certain extent it rules your body's physical and mental functions as well as the functions and routine of daily life. When you are emotionally troubled, all these normal functions will be correspondingly interrupted. The Moon also indicates your actual residence and all aspects of your domestic life. It indicates your relationships with babies and young children in your life, and it rules women in general and your mother in particular.

Moon in Aries. You want to turn your feelings into physical experiences. When you want something (or someone), you don't always stop to think whether it's practical or whether it will involve a deeper or longer emotional commitment than you're willing to give. You are an eager participant in life and will soon lose interest in people who don't demonstrate the same passionate enthusiasm that you do. Your adventurous spirit can make it hard to settle down and accept responsibilities and daily routine unless you have other outlets that keep you happy and stimulated. You are easily insulted but can just as easily be persuaded to forget an incident if you receive an apology. A quick temper can get you into trouble at times, but fortunately you are also quick to forget your anger. You are meant to be master of your own successes or failures. You may relish this kind of challenge or may be all too willing to blame mistakes on everyone else. Resentful of authority, you may find it difficult to take direction or advice from anyone. Though you are capable of being self-indulgent, overconfident, and just plain foolhardy, your courageous and dynamic spirit can turn you into an inspired leader. Others will greatly admire your passion and tireless efforts. Magnanimous generosity wins you many friends, though this generosity can be diminished by your sometimes careless disregard for the feelings of others. Women with an Aries Moon may be unflatteringly aggressive in romance, but they are emotionally well suited to conquer many other types of situations that would destroy less hardy types. Men with an Aries Moon expect too much and give too little in romance but are emotionally well suited to pursue other matters with an enterprising, often clever and original approach.

Moon in Taurus. You require tangible proof of affection from others. Though there is a conservative element in your nature, you have very strong physical appetites and don't hesitate to gratify desires. Material comforts and the advantages material wealth can bring are important to you, and in pursuit of such things you can become overly concerned with social status. You need the solid structure of home and family, but you are not necessarily a homebody and can spend a lot of time on other pursuits instead of taking care of routine household or family chores. It is likely that you have artistic or musical talent, certainly an appreciation of beauty in all forms, and a desire for an attractive, well-decorated home. You don't like to be rushed or forced into emotional commitments. However, once you have made a commitment, you doggedly hang on forever. You have a great sense of humor about most things but can get very upset with people who do not keep their promises to you or prove unreliable in other matters. It is hard for you to accept when things go wrong, and it may take you a long time to make necessary changes or adjustments. Your calm temperament has a stabilizing influence on others, but it can also give you an aura of self-containment that makes you appear too proud or aloof. Your memory may be excellent, but sometimes it is too long for your own good and you waste time bearing grudges that should have been forgotten. Women with a Taurus Moon are independent and self-reliant. They often gain materially through marriage. Men with a Taurus Moon are diplomatic in social relationships and sensual romantic partners. Though hedonistic, they are usually unselfishly devoted to their children.

Moon in Gemini. You may give the impression of emotional coolness because of your analytical approach to emotional experiences. Sometimes this intellectual approach goes too far and robs you of the actual physical enjoyment of things. You are very talkative, alert, and innately curious about everything. You have a wide range of interests and may have trouble limiting yourself to one thing at a time. Always looking for intellectual stimulation, you are easily bored. You love intrigue and gossip and sometimes pay too much attention to what everyone else is doing instead of tending to your own business. News and information seem to come to you, and to others it appears you always know what's going on. As eager to share information as you are to receive it, you are very good in all areas of teaching and communication; however, you don't always take the time to get all the facts straight before repeating them. You instinctively understand what others want to hear and how to please them, but you can be very secretive about your own feelings. An emotional duality in your character allows you to say or do one thing even though you really think or feel something else. Though outwardly bright and optimistic, you can harbor an inner loneliness that others don't suspect. To keep happy and productive, you need a variety of tasks and a frequent change of scene. Women with a Gemini Moon are often skilled with their hands. Though they can be very efficient and organized, they are usually not very domestic. Men with a Gemini Moon are charming, with a wide variety of interests and many friends. They are not particularly suited to sustained passion in themselves or to putting up with emotional hysteria in others.

44 ♋ Cancer JUNE 22–JULY 23

Moon in Cancer. You need to feel there is depth to your emotional involvements or at least that there is the potential for a real commitment. You are intuitive, though at times it gets entangled with self-serving needs. Creative and talented, you are vulnerable to the influence of those with whom you spend the most time, and it is sometimes hard to tell when you are expressing your own opinions or reflecting those of someone else. You can be extremely passive even in unhappy situations. Though you may eventually take on a more satisfying relationship, emotional insecurity can make you possessive and unwilling to let go of the unhappy relationship. You hate to throw anything away, whether material possessions or relationships, and if you are not careful, your life can become cluttered with useless things. Lack of motivation can seriously sabotage your personal growth and success since it can result in laziness, disorganization, and sloppiness. There are contradictory elements in your emotional makeup. For instance, you can be quite shy but also very aggressive, very warm and loving but also selfish and demanding. A nurturing instinct makes you hospitable and philanthropic. You have strong identification with home and family and domestic skills that can make you an excellent cook or gardener. You tend to treat everyone as family and often use this as a successful ploy in gaining the cooperation of others. Women with a Cancer Moon are vulnerable and emotionally dependent while at the same time intuitive and clever; much depends on their backgrounds. Men with a Cancer Moon are domestic and usually have a close relationship with their mother or a physical resemblance to her. It is hard for men with a Cancer Moon to act with emotional certainty or sustained aggressiveness.

Moon in Leo. You are magnanimous and passionate with a strong need for instant physical gratification. Your enthusiasm and tendency for exaggeration are great in some circumstances but can lead to being what others may consider insincere. Aroused by the excitement of a particular moment, you may later forget what you said or promised in your enthusiasm even though you were being sincere at the time. Stubborn pride is often your downfall, and your unwillingness to admit when you are wrong can put a severe strain on relationships. It's hard for you to separate emotions from ego, and your ego prompts you consciously or subconsciously to dominate relationships. Though you can be extremely stubborn, you can also demonstrate such inspired purpose and determination that it makes you a natural leader. Your people-oriented personality wins many friends and can make you an excellent fund-raiser as well as extremely effective in public relations. Strongly idealistic, you are capable of great personal sacrifice. You are very assertive when it comes to protecting not only your own freedom but also the rights and freedom of others. In romantic attachments you can be jealous though you may not be particularly possessive. You are likely to have artistic talent or at least a great interest in art, architecture, and design. Women with a Leo Moon have forceful emotional natures. If disappointed in love, they are not anxious to repeat an unflattering failure. They can be too materialistic and preoccupied with status, but they accept responsibilities as a matter of pride. Men with a Leo Moon can be braggarts who always need to have the last word. They actively seek the good things in life, but their emotional natures also include a willingness to share their good fortune generously.

Moon in Virgo. You are guarded about your feelings and consciously or subconsciously put up invisible barriers, perhaps tangible impediments, for those who want a relationship with you. In most cases, however, you really hope others will view these barriers as a challenge to be overcome. It is difficult for you to lose inhibitions. Though not lacking in passion, you lean more to compassion, which makes you a victim in relationships you would like to terminate but feel guilty about ending lest you hurt your partner's feelings. You have a good sense of humor, but your critical eye can direct your humor toward sarcasm. Though serious-minded with common sense about most things, you can be surprisingly unrealistic at times. Your creativity has a practical element, and if you are a writer or an artist, you usually stick to what you know best. You know what it takes to make others feel better, and your sympathetic nature makes you valuable as a friend but also makes you vulnerable to exploitation. You are fond of books and writing, and your intellectual curiosity gives you a penchant for gathering information, a tendency that can develop into serious research or turn out to be an indulgence for gossip. You are mentally and emotionally stimulated by travel, communication in all forms, and the idea that what you do serves a definite and helpful purpose, not only for your own good but for the good of others. Women with a Virgo Moon may encounter sorrow through marriage or marry men with serious problems. They can be dreadful nags or themselves victims of nagging spouses. Men with a Virgo Moon tend to idealize their wives but not be very passionate toward them. Their quiet emotional natures tend toward domesticity but often hide desires for intrigue and flamboyancy.

Moon in Libra. In spite of a certain analytical detachment in emotional situations, you are loving and loyal in relationships. You have a romantic nature, if not an overly passionate approach. Hurt when emotionally compromised, you would prefer not to hang on to a relationship if your partner is unwilling. However, when you are guilty of an emotionally compromising situation, you may rationalize why such deception was necessary since above all, you hate confrontation and hurting the feelings of others. You are disinclined to live alone, preferring attachment of some sort, even if it is not marriage. Your accomplishments are often motivated by (and even dependent upon) stimulation you get from interaction with others, so it is in your best interests to be out in public. You are better at planning maneuvers than at carrying them out. It isn't that you are not capable of carrying them out; it's just that you can rely on your considerable ability to enlist the cooperation of others, and it is they who perform the actual execution of projects while you step back to supervise the job. Though you can be quite good at planning and problem solving, you can be very impractical about personal matters. You are apt to have aesthetic tastes, which can be seen in a fondness for dressing well, an interest in art and music, and a desire for an attractive home. Women with the Moon in Libra have temperaments more suited to finances, gaining social status, and pursuing intellectual matters than to raising children or taking care of mundane household chores. Men with a Libra Moon have a streak of domesticity that may show up as an interest in cooking, home design or furnishings, and gardening. If their mates are unable to keep them mentally stimulated, their attentions tend to wander.

Moon in Scorpio. Your actions are primarily led by strong emotional needs, but you may not be open about revealing those needs to others. You have powerful sexual energy that can be sublimated into attaining many goals having nothing to do with sex. A Scorpio Moon in the horoscope often indicates wide mood swings, which, with maturity, you can learn how to control properly. Though you don't like being forced into emotional commitments, once they are made, you hang on forever. You have a keen competitive spirit that can make you a formidable opponent. There is almost nothing you can't accomplish if you develop your incredible willpower and amazing ability to overcome all kinds of adversity. Just when everyone thinks you're down, you'll find a way to come back better and stronger than ever. Intense concentration is another factor in your success, but one mistake you can make is being so intent on controlling others that you never learn self-control. Though secretive yourself, you have a keen interest in others because of a genuine interest in human nature and also because it gives you an emotional advantage, a conscious or subconscious sense of being in control. When you develop undesirable habits, the stubborn quality of your nature makes it difficult to break them. Your relationships suffer from jealousy and possessiveness whether on your part or that of your partner's. Women with a Scorpio Moon can be shrewdly ambitious. Their ambition is not so much wanting to acquire greath wealth as a desire to gain positions of power. Men with a Scorpio Moon can be

48 ♋ Cancer JUNE 22–JULY 23

driven to distraction by situations that offer no solution and by people who refuse to tell them anything. Their emotional natures are best suited to dealing with resources, especially human resources.

Moon in Sagittarius. You are idealistic and romantic. Your risk-taking, adventurous spirit and magnanimous generosity are a curse as well as a blessing. They can leave you vulnerable to those who exploit your generosity, but they are also the combination needed for success, especially in enterprises that more cautious people would avoid. Your open, honest personality, while appreciated by some and certainly by those who know you well, can nevertheless be too candid at times, making you seem rude or tactless rather than merely truthful. Impatience can be your biggest stumbling block to success unless you learn to control it. Knowledge will play a significant role in your destiny. No matter how scholarly you may or may not be, you will be required to have increasing knowledge and expertise in your particular field, and that is what makes you successful. A duality in your nature can make you fickle and emotionally insecure but also readily adaptable to changing circumstances and stable relationships. Social and business associations with powerful and educated people are the way you are likely to approach learning and personal advancement, two of your main goals in life. If this approach is taken too far, however, you may become pseudointellectual and an incurable snob. For you, the best opportunities are likely to involve writing, teaching, performing, or any area dealing with sales, entertainment, art, education, and communication. Women with a Sagittarius Moon often make better friends than lovers, though their restlessness may lead to sexual adventures. Friendship is very important to them. Their natures are not well suited to domestic life. Men with a Sagittarius Moon are inveterate chasers of the ideal woman. Their natures tend toward selfishness and personal freedom, but they have a sense of loyalty and a prophetic intuition.

Moon in Capricorn. Practical by nature and fearing rejection, you do not spontaneously act on your emotions or openly declare your feelings unless you feel you're on solid ground. Your outward formality or reticence can be deceiving since in private you can be a very passionate sexual partner. Though willing to fulfill responsibilities connected with relationships, you may be unable or unwilling to understand what others actually want or need. It is hard for you to relate to those who do not share your views or values. Capricorn's influence on your Moon is demonstrated in your constant worry and in your desire for formality and structure. Anything vague or unspecified, whether in business or personal relationships, makes you feel insecure; you must know where you stand. Ambitious and strong-willed, you are more than capable of accomplishing a lot for others, though you are primarily directed to seek your own advancement. You have a great respect for knowledge and are probably quite bright. You are apt to be given or voluntarily to assume heavy family responsibilities, in the care of your children or your parents when they are older. A tendency to harbor anger and resentment inside can result in physical maladies or mental depression or both. It is hard to confide emotional problems, though you are interested in and very helpful dealing with the problems of others. Female relationships are likely to be problematical and inhibited in some way. Women with a Capricorn Moon can be ambitious at the expense of their emotional lives. However, they are interested in preserving traditional family structures and are excellent administrators. Men with a Capricorn Moon are often rugged individualists who demand attention and respect. They are apt to be either too close to or too distant from their mothers.

Moon in Aquarius. You are sympathetic without being sentimental. If you are rarely beset with moodiness (as is likely), you may fail to pay attention to it in others, giving the impression you don't care. You are idealistic, optimistic, and friendly. Your highly social nature attracts many friends, and as far as you're concerned, it's the more, the merrier since it is hard to focus your attention on one person. Your orientation to people makes you a good social mixer or organizer. Even if you are a bit eccentric or erratic, or perhaps because of it, you have a calming effect on those who are mentally disturbed or hysterical. Although you don't like being rushed into emotional commitments, once you have made them, you are extremely loyal and will doggedly pursue, protect, and hang on to relationships. Strong individualism can make marriage difficult especially if your spouse is not as strong as you, and if, in addition, you both have to make determined efforts to make the relationship successful. Once you have formed attitudes, interests, and behavior patterns, marriage and raising a family are not likely to change anything. You tend to remain independent in views and attitudes, which may turn out to be fairly traditional. You are likely to have talent for or a very strong interest in art, entertainment, or public relations. Your unflappable nature is not often surprised or repelled by what others consider strange or abnormal. In fact, you may deliberately say or do bizarre things for their shock value. Women with an Aquarius Moon are better companions than mothers to their children. Men with an Aquarius Moon display little possessiveness in romance, which is sometimes interpreted by their parents as lack of love. Their mental abilities are keener than their interest in material wealth.

Moon in Pisces. You need to establish solid relationships and values that can provide you with an underlying strength you do not naturally possess. It may be very difficult for you to see the reality of many situations especially if you are emotionally involved in any way, and it may be even harder for you to accept reality if it happens to disagree with your concept of how things should be. Shy and vulnerable to the influence of others, you can be an easy prey to the demands of stronger personalities. Easily wounded, you do not do well in relationships with those who are emotionally independent and demand personal freedom. You may do very well if your home is near the ocean or some other body of water. Romantic and idealistic, you have a vivid imagination. Your remarkable sensitivity can make you a gifted writer, actor, musician, or illustrator. These traits may also be demonstrated in a gift for promotion, though you may not always be aware of how much actual substance is in your various schemes. Yours is an addictive nature, if you do not exercise great care from an early age, you may find yourself waging a lifelong battle against overindulgence of every kind. While your analytical abilities can be remarkably imaginative and farsighted, your major flaw is either lack of practicality or clarity or both. Women with a Pisces Moon are psychic, likely to be artistic, and prone to anxiety complexes. Their emotional natures are well suited to the comfort of domestic life, though they may not be efficient householders. Men with a Pisces Moon are vulnerable to victimization in their own relationships, while at the same time they still manage to have strength and wisdom to handle the affairs of others ably.

Your Moon Sign Nature

How to Find Your Moon's Sign and Degree

This is the simplest and briefest table that has been devised for getting the Moon's place on any date over a great many years, and if you follow carefully the directions below, you will have a part of your individual horoscope that heretofore has been available only to those who knew how to use an ephemeris or were able to have individual charts drawn up for them. If you follow the simple directions, you get not only the sign occupied by the Moon but also the actual degree, correct within 1½ degrees, for any hour of any date between 1880 and 2000 inclusive.

HOW TO FIND YOUR MOON'S PLACE

1. Note your birth year in the tables (pages 56–79).
2. Run down the left-hand column and see if your date is there.
3. IF YOUR DATE IS IN THE LEFT-HAND COLUMN, move across on this line till you come to the column under your birth year. Here you will find a number. This is your BASE NUMBER. Write it down, and go directly to the part of the directions below, under the heading "What to Do with Your Base Number."
4. IF YOUR BIRTH DATE IS NOT IN THE LEFT-HAND COLUMN, get a pencil and paper. Your birth date falls between two numbers in the left-hand column. Look at the date closest *after* your birth date; move across on this line to your birth year. Write down the number you find there, and label it "TOP NUMBER." Having done this, write directly beneath it on your piece of paper the number printed just above it in the table. Label this "BOTTOM NUMBER."
   Subtract the bottom number from the top number. If the top number is smaller, add 360 to it and then subtract. The result is your DIFFERENCE.

5. Go back to the left-hand column and find the date next *before* your birth date. Determine the number of days between this date and your birth date by subtracting. Write this down, and label it "INTERVENING DAYS."
6. In the Table of Difference below, note which group your DIFFERENCE (found through Step 4) falls in.

Difference	Daily Motion
80–87	12°
88–94	13°
95–101	14°
102–106	15°

Note: If you were born in leap year *and* use the difference between February 26 and March 5, use the special table following:

Difference	Daily Motion
94–99	12°
100–108	13°
109–115	14°
116–122	15°

Write down the DAILY MOTION corresponding to your place in the proper Table of Difference above.
7. Multiply this daily motion by the number labeled "INTERVENING DAYS" (found through Step 5).
8. Add the result of Step 7 to your BOTTOM NUMBER (under 4). The result of this is your BASE NUMBER. If it is more than 360, subtract 360 from it and call the result your BASE NUMBER. Now turn to the table of Base Numbers on page 55.

53

WHAT TO DO WITH YOUR BASE NUMBER

LOCATE YOUR BASE NUMBER in the table on page 55. At the top of the column you will find the SIGN your MOON WAS IN. At the left you will find the DEGREE (°) your Moon occupied at: 7:00 A.M. of your birth date if you were born under eastern standard time, 6:00 A.M. of your birth date if you were born under central standard time, 5:00 A.M. of your birth date if you were born under mountain standard time, 4:00 A.M. of your birth date if you were born under Pacific standard time.

IF YOU DON'T KNOW THE HOUR OF YOUR BIRTH, accept this as your Moon's sign and degree.

IF YOU DO KNOW THE HOUR OF YOUR BIRTH, get the exact degree as follows:

If you were born *before* 7:00 A.M., EST (6:00 A.M. CST, etc.), determine the number of hours before that time that you were born. Divide this by two. *Subtract* this from your base number, and the result in the table will be the exact degree and sign of the Moon on the year, month, date, and hour of your birth.

If you were born *before* 7:00 A.M., EST, (6:00 A.M. CST, etc.), determine the number of hours before that time that you were born. Divide this by two. *Subtract* this from your base number, and the result in the table will be the exact degree and sign of the Moon on the year, month, date, and hour of your birth.

TABLE OF BASE NUMBERS

	♈	♉	♊	♋	♌	♍	♎	♏	♐	♑	♒	♓
0°	0	30	60	90	120	150	180	210	240	270	300	330
1°	1	31	61	91	121	151	181	211	241	271	301	331
2°	2	32	62	92	122	152	182	212	242	272	302	332
3°	3	33	63	93	123	153	183	213	243	273	303	333
4°	4	34	64	94	124	154	184	214	244	274	304	334
5°	5	35	65	95	125	155	185	215	245	275	305	335
6°	6	36	66	96	126	156	186	216	246	276	306	336
7°	7	37	67	97	127	157	187	217	247	277	307	337
8°	8	38	68	98	128	158	188	218	248	278	308	338
9°	9	39	69	99	129	159	189	219	249	279	309	339
10°	10	40	70	100	130	160	190	220	250	280	310	340
11°	11	41	71	101	131	161	191	221	251	281	311	341
12°	12	42	72	102	132	162	192	222	252	282	312	342
13°	13	43	73	103	133	163	193	223	253	283	313	343
14°	14	44	74	104	134	164	194	224	254	284	314	344
15°	15	45	75	105	135	165	195	225	255	285	315	345
16°	16	46	76	106	136	166	196	226	256	286	316	346
17°	17	47	77	107	137	167	197	227	257	287	317	347
18°	18	48	78	108	138	168	198	228	258	288	318	348
19°	19	49	79	109	139	169	199	229	259	289	319	349
20°	20	50	80	110	140	170	200	230	260	290	320	350
21°	21	51	81	111	141	171	201	231	261	291	321	351
22°	22	52	82	112	142	172	202	232	262	292	322	352
23°	23	53	83	113	143	173	203	233	263	293	323	353
24°	24	54	84	114	144	174	204	234	264	294	324	354
25°	25	55	85	115	145	175	205	235	265	295	325	355
26°	26	56	86	116	146	176	206	236	266	296	326	356
27°	27	57	87	117	147	177	207	237	267	297	327	357
28°	28	58	88	118	148	178	208	238	268	298	328	358
29°	29	59	89	119	149	179	209	239	269	299	329	359

♈ Aries
♉ Taurus
♊ Gemini

♋ Cancer
♌ Leo
♍ Virgo

♎ Libra
♏ Scorpio
♐ Sagittarius

♑ Capricorn
♒ Aquarius
♓ Pisces

MOON SIGN TABLES

	1880	1881	1882	1883	1884	1885	1886	1887	1888	1889
Jan. 1	144	294	67	190	315	105	238	359	127	276
8	240	32	152	278	52	202	323	89	224	12
15	341	116	239	18	151	286	49	190	321	96
22	67	202	342	113	236	13	153	284	46	185
29	154	302	77	198	325	113	248	8	136	285
Feb. 5	250	41	161	286	63	211	331	97	235	20
12	349	124	248	29	159	295	58	200	329	104
19	75	212	351	122	244	24	161	293	59	196
26	163	311	86	207	334	122	257	16	144	294
Mar. 5	275	49	170	294	88	218	340	105	260	28
12	10	133	257	38	180	303	69	209	350	112
19	94	222	359	132	264	34	169	302	74	205
26	185	320	95	215	356	133	265	25	166	305
Apr. 2	286	57	179	303	98	226	349	114	270	36
9	18	141	267	47	189	311	79	217	359	120
16	102	232	7	141	272	43	178	311	83	214
23	194	331	103	224	4	143	273	34	175	315
30	297	65	187	312	108	235	357	124	279	45
May 7	28	149	278	54	198	319	89	225	8	128
14	111	241	17	149	281	52	108	319	92	223
21	202	342	111	233	13	154	281	43	184	325
28	306	73	195	323	117	243	5	155	288	54
June 4	37	157	288	63	207	327	99	234	17	137
11	119	250	27	158	291	60	199	327	101	231
18	211	352	119	241	22	164	289	52	194	335
25	315	82	203	333	126	252	13	145	296	63

MOON SIGN TABLES

July 2	46	165	297	72	216	336	108	244	26	146
9	129	258	37	165	299	69	209	335	110	240
16	220	2	127	250	32	173	298	59	204	343
23	323	91	211	344	134	261	21	155	304	72
30	54	174	306	82	224	345	117	254	34	156
Aug. 6	138	267	48	174	309	78	219	343	119	250
13	231	11	136	258	43	181	307	68	215	352
20	331	100	220	354	142	270	30	165	313	80
27	63	184	314	93	232	355	125	265	42	165
Sept. 3	147	276	58	182	317	88	228	352	127	260
10	242	19	145	266	54	190	316	76	226	359
17	340	109	229	3	152	278	40	173	323	88
24	70	193	323	103	239	4	134	275	50	174
Oct. 1	155	286	67	191	325	99	237	1	135	271
8	252	27	154	274	64	198	324	85	236	8
15	350	117	238	11	161	286	49	181	332	96
22	78	202	332	113	248	12	144	284	58	182
29	163	297	75	200	333	110	245	10	143	282
Nov. 5	262	36	163	263	74	207	332	94	245	18
12	359	124	248	19	171	294	59	190	342	104
19	87	210	342	122	257	20	154	292	67	190
26	171	308	83	208	341	120	253	18	152	292
Dec. 3	271	45	171	293	82	216	340	104	253	27
10	10	132	257	28	181	302	67	199	351	112
17	95	218	353	130	265	28	165	300	76	198
24	179	318	91	217	351	130	262	26	162	301
31	279	55	179	302	89	226	348	113	261	37

57

MOON SIGN TABLES

	1890	1891	1892	1893	1894	1895	1896	1897	1898	1899
Jan. 1	49	170	298	87	220	340	109	258	30	149
8	132	259	37	183	303	69	209	352	114	240
15	221	2	131	266	32	174	301	76	203	335
22	323	94	215	357	135	265	25	169	305	76
29	58	178	307	96	229	348	117	268	39	157
Feb. 5	141	267	47	190	312	78	219	359	122	249
12	230	12	140	274	42	162	310	84	214	353
19	332	103	223	7	143	274	34	179	314	84
26	67	187	315	106	236	357	125	278	46	168
Mar. 5	150	276	72	198	321	87	243	8	130	259
12	241	20	161	282	52	190	331	92	225	1
19	340	113	244	17	152	283	55	188	323	93
26	75	196	337	117	244	6	148	289	54	177
Apr. 2	159	285	81	206	329	97	252	17	138	269
9	251	28	170	290	63	198	340	100	235	9
16	350	121	253	25	162	291	64	196	333	101
23	83	204	346	127	252	15	157	299	62	185
30	167	295	89	215	337	108	261	25	146	280
May 7	261	36	179	299	73	207	349	109	244	19
14	0	129	262	33	172	299	73	204	344	108
21	91	213	355	137	261	23	167	308	71	193
28	174	307	98	224	345	119	269	34	155	291
June 4	271	46	188	308	81	217	357	119	253	29
11	11	137	272	42	182	307	82	213	354	117
18	99	221	6	146	269	31	178	316	80	201
25	183	317	106	233	353	129	277	43	164	300

MOON SIGN TABLES

July 2	278	56	195	317	89	227	5	128	261	39
9	21	145	281	51	192	315	91	223	3	125
16	108	229	17	154	278	39	189	324	89	209
23	192	327	115	241	2	138	286	51	173	309
30	287	66	203	327	99	237	13	138	269	49
Aug. 6	31	153	289	62	201	324	99	234	11	134
13	117	237	28	162	287	48	200	332	97	219
20	201	336	124	250	12	147	296	59	183	317
27	295	76	211	336	108	247	21	146	279	58
Sept. 3	39	162	297	72	209	333	107	245	19	143
10	125	246	38	171	296	57	209	341	105	228
17	211	344	134	257	22	155	305	67	193	326
24	305	86	220	345	118	256	29	155	290	67
Oct. 1	47	171	305	83	217	341	116	256	27	151
8	134	256	47	179	304	67	218	350	113	238
15	220	352	144	265	31	164	315	75	202	335
22	315	94	228	352	128	264	39	162	301	75
29	55	179	314	94	225	350	125	266	36	160
Nov. 5	142	265	56	189	312	77	226	359	121	248
12	229	2	153	274	40	173	324	84	210	346
19	327	102	237	0	139	272	47	171	311	82
26	64	188	323	103	234	358	135	275	45	167
Dec. 3	149	275	63	198	320	86	235	9	129	257
10	237	12	162	282	47	184	332	93	218	356
17	338	110	246	9	149	280	56	179	321	91
24	72	196	333	112	243	5	145	282	54	175
31	158	284	72	208	328	95	244	18	138	265

MOON SIGN TABLES

	1900	1901	1902	1903	1904	1905	1906	1907	1908	1909
Jan. 1	280	55	188	308	76	227	358	119	246	39
8	21	149	272	37	179	320	82	208	350	129
15	112	234	2	141	270	43	174	311	81	213
22	195	327	101	234	353	138	273	44	164	309
29	288	66	196	317	83	238	6	128	255	50
Feb. 5	31	158	280	46	188	328	89	219	359	138
12	121	241	12	149	279	51	184	319	89	221
19	204	335	111	242	2	146	283	52	173	317
26	296	76	204	326	92	248	13	136	264	59
Mar. 5	40	166	288	57	211	334	98	229	21	147
12	130	249	22	157	300	59	194	328	110	230
19	213	344	121	250	24	154	293	59	195	325
26	305	86	212	334	116	258	22	144	288	69
Apr. 2	49	175	296	68	219	345	106	240	29	156
9	138	258	31	157	309	69	202	338	118	239
16	222	352	132	258	33	163	304	68	204	334
23	315	96	220	342	127	267	31	152	299	77
30	57	184	304	78	227	354	114	250	38	164
May 7	177	268	40	177	316	78	210	348	126	249
14	231	1	142	266	42	172	313	76	212	344
21	325	104	229	350	138	275	40	160	310	85
28	65	193	313	87	236	3	124	259	47	172
June 4	155	277	48	187	324	88	219	358	134	259
11	239	11	151	275	50	182	322	85	220	355
18	336	112	238	359	149	283	48	169	320	93
25	74	201	322	96	245	11	133	267	57	180

MOON SIGN TABLES

July 2	163	286	57	197	333	97	228	8	142	267
9	248	21	160	283	58	193	330	94	228	6
16	347	121	247	7	159	291	57	178	330	102
23	84	209	332	105	255	19	143	276	66	188
30	171	295	66	206	341	105	239	17	151	275
Aug. 6	256	32	168	292	66	204	338	103	237	17
13	357	130	255	17	168	301	65	188	339	111
20	94	217	341	113	265	27	152	285	76	196
27	179	303	77	215	350	113	250	25	160	283
Sept. 3	264	43	176	301	75	215	346	111	246	27
10	6	229	263	27	176	310	73	198	347	121
17	103	225	350	123	274	35	161	294	85	206
24	188	311	88	223	358	122	261	33	169	292
Oct. 1	273	53	185	309	85	224	355	119	256	36
8	14	149	271	36	185	320	81	207	356	130
15	113	233	359	133	283	44	169	305	93	214
22	197	319	99	231	7	130	271	42	177	301
29	283	62	194	317	95	233	5	127	266	44
Nov. 5	22	158	279	45	193	329	89	216	5	139
12	121	242	6	144	291	53	177	316	101	223
19	206	328	109	239	15	140	281	50	185	311
26	293	70	203	325	105	241	14	135	276	52
Dec. 3	31	167	288	54	203	338	98	224	15	147
10	129	251	14	155	299	61	185	327	109	231
17	214	338	118	248	23	149	289	59	193	322
24	303	78	213	333	115	249	23	143	286	61
31	41	176	296	61	213	346	107	232	26	155

61

MOON SIGN TABLES

	1910	1911	1912	1913	1914	1915	1916	1917	1918	1919	1920
Jan. 1	168	289	57	211	337	100	228	23	147	270	39
8	252	20	162	299	61	192	332	110	231	5	143
15	346	122	251	23	158	293	61	193	329	103	231
22	84	214	334	119	256	23	145	290	68	193	316
29	175	298	65	221	345	108	237	32	155	278	49
Feb. 5	259	31	170	308	69	203	340	118	249	16	150
12	356	130	260	32	167	302	70	203	338	113	239
19	94	222	344	128	266	31	154	298	78	201	325
26	184	306	75	231	353	116	248	41	164	286	60
Mar. 5	267	42	192	317	77	214	2	127	248	26	172
12	5	140	280	41	176	311	89	212	346	123	259
19	105	230	5	136	276	39	176	308	87	209	346
26	192	314	100	239	2	124	273	49	173	294	85
Apr. 2	276	52	200	326	86	223	10	135	257	35	181
9	13	149	288	51	184	321	97	232	355	133	267
16	115	238	14	146	286	48	184	318	96	218	355
23	201	322	111	247	11	132	284	57	181	303	96
30	285	61	208	334	96	232	19	143	267	43	190
May 7	21	160	296	60	192	331	105	231	4	142	275
14	124	246	22	157	294	56	192	329	104	227	3
21	209	331	122	255	20	141	294	66	190	312	105
28	294	69	218	342	106	240	29	151	277	51	200
June 4	30	170	304	69	202	341	114	249	14	151	284
11	132	255	30	167	302	65	200	340	112	235	11
18	218	340	132	264	28	151	304	74	198	322	114
25	304	78	228	350	115	249	59	159	286	60	209

MOON SIGN TABLES

July 2	40	179	312	78	212	349	122	248	25	159	293
9	140	264	38	178	310	74	209	350	120	244	21
16	226	349	141	273	36	161	312	84	206	332	123
23	314	87	237	358	125	258	48	168	295	70	218
30	51	187	321	86	223	357	131	256	36	167	302
Aug. 6	148	272	48	188	319	82	219	359	129	252	31
13	234	359	149	282	44	170	320	93	214	342	131
20	323	96	246	6	133	268	57	177	303	81	226
27	62	195	330	94	234	5	140	265	46	175	310
Sept. 3	157	281	57	198	328	90	229	8	138	260	41
10	242	9	158	292	52	180	329	102	222	351	140
17	331	107	255	15	141	279	65	186	312	91	234
24	73	204	339	103	244	13	149	274	56	184	319
Oct. 1	166	289	68	206	337	98	239	17	148	268	51
8	250	18	167	301	61	189	338	111	231	359	150
15	339	118	263	24	149	290	73	195	320	102	242
22	83	212	347	113	254	22	157	284	65	193	326
29	176	296	78	214	346	106	250	25	157	276	61
Nov. 5	259	27	177	309	70	197	348	119	240	7	161
12	347	129	270	33	158	300	81	203	329	112	250
19	91	221	355	123	262	31	164	295	73	202	334
26	185	305	88	223	355	115	259	34	165	285	70
Dec. 3	268	34	187	317	79	205	359	127	249	16	171
10	356	138	279	41	168	310	89	211	340	120	259
17	99	230	3	134	270	40	172	305	81	211	343
24	194	313	97	232	4	124	267	44	173	294	78
31	277	42	198	325	87	214	9	135	257	25	181

63

MOON SIGN TABLES

	1921	1922	1923	1924	1925	1926	1927	1928	1929	1930
Jan. 1	194	317	80	211	5	127	250	23	176	297
8	280	41	177	313	90	211	349	123	260	22
15	4	141	275	41	175	312	86	211	346	123
22	101	239	3	127	272	51	172	297	83	221
29	203	325	88	222	13	135	258	34	184	306
Feb. 5	289	49	187	321	99	220	359	131	269	31
12	14	149	284	49	185	320	95	219	356	131
19	110	249	11	135	281	59	181	305	93	230
26	211	334	96	233	21	144	266	45	191	314
Mar. 5	297	58	197	343	107	230	8	153	276	41
12	23	157	294	69	194	328	105	238	6	139
19	119	258	19	157	292	68	189	327	104	238
26	219	343	104	258	29	153	275	70	199	323
Apr. 2	305	68	205	352	115	239	16	163	284	51
9	33	166	303	77	204	337	114	247	14	149
16	130	266	28	164	303	76	198	335	115	246
23	227	351	114	268	38	161	285	79	208	331
30	313	78	213	1	123	250	25	172	292	61
May 7	42	176	313	85	212	348	123	255	23	160
14	141	274	37	173	314	84	207	344	125	254
21	236	359	123	277	47	169	295	88	217	339
28	321	88	222	11	131	259	34	181	301	70
June 4	50	186	321	94	220	358	131	264	31	171
11	152	282	45	182	324	92	215	354	135	263
18	245	7	134	285	56	177	305	96	226	347
25	329	97	232	20	139	268	44	190	310	78

MOON SIGN TABLES

July 2	58	197	329	103	229	9	139	273	40	181
9	162	291	54	192	333	101	223	4	144	272
16	254	15	144	294	65	185	315	104	236	355
23	338	106	242	28	148	276	54	198	319	87
30	67	208	337	112	238	20	147	282	49	191
Aug. 6	171	299	62	202	341	110	231	15	152	281
13	264	24	153	302	74	194	324	114	244	4
20	347	114	253	36	157	284	65	206	328	95
27	76	218	345	120	248	29	156	290	59	200
Sept. 3	179	309	70	213	350	119	239	25	161	290
10	273	32	162	312	83	203	332	124	252	13
17	356	122	264	44	166	293	75	214	337	105
24	86	227	354	128	258	38	165	298	70	208
Oct. 1	188	318	78	223	358	128	248	35	169	298
8	281	41	170	322	91	212	340	134	260	23
15	5	132	274	52	175	303	85	222	345	115
22	97	235	8	136	269	46	174	306	81	216
29	196	327	87	233	7	137	257	44	179	307
Nov. 5	289	50	178	332	99	221	349	144	268	31
12	13	142	283	61	183	313	93	231	353	126
19	107	243	12	144	279	54	183	315	91	225
26	206	335	96	241	17	145	266	52	189	314
Dec. 3	297	59	187	343	106	230	359	154	276	39
10	21	152	291	70	190	324	101	239	1	137
17	117	252	21	153	289	63	191	324	99	234
24	216	343	105	249	28	152	275	59	199	322
31	305	67	197	352	115	237	9	162	285	47

65

MOON-SIGN TABLES

	1931	1932	1933	1934	1935	1936	1937	1938	1939	1940
Jan. 1	61	196	346	107	231	8	156	277	41	181
8	162	294	70	193	333	104	240	5	145	275
15	257	20	158	294	68	190	329	105	239	0
22	342	108	255	32	152	278	67	202	323	88
29	68	207	353	116	239	19	164	286	50	191
Feb. 5	171	302	78	203	342	113	248	15	153	284
12	267	28	168	302	78	198	339	113	248	8
19	351	116	266	40	161	286	78	210	332	96
26	77	217	2	124	248	29	172	294	59	200
Mar. 5	179	324	86	213	350	135	256	24	161	306
12	276	48	177	311	87	218	348	123	257	29
19	1	137	277	48	170	308	89	218	340	119
26	87	241	10	132	258	53	180	302	70	223
Apr. 2	187	334	94	223	358	144	264	34	169	314
9	285	57	185	321	95	227	356	133	265	38
16	9	146	287	56	179	317	99	226	349	128
23	96	250	19	140	268	61	189	310	80	231
30	196	343	102	232	7	153	273	43	179	323
May 7	293	66	193	332	103	237	4	144	272	47
14	17	155	297	65	187	327	108	235	357	139
21	107	259	28	148	279	69	198	318	90	240
28	205	351	111	241	17	161	282	52	189	331
June 4	301	75	202	343	111	246	13	154	281	56
11	25	165	306	73	195	337	117	244	5	150
18	117	267	37	157	288	78	207	327	99	248
25	215	0	120	250	28	169	291	60	200	339

MOON-SIGN TABLES

July	2	309	83	211	353	119	254	23	164	289	64
	9	33	176	315	82	203	348	125	253	13	160
	16	126	276	46	165	297	87	216	336	108	258
	23	226	8	130	258	39	177	300	69	210	347
	30	318	92	221	2	128	262	33	173	297	72
Aug.	6	41	187	323	91	211	359	133	261	22	171
	13	135	285	54	175	306	97	224	346	117	269
	20	237	16	139	267	49	185	309	78	220	355
	27	326	100	232	10	136	270	44	181	307	80
Sept.	3	50	197	331	100	220	9	142	270	31	180
	10	144	296	62	184	314	107	232	355	125	279
	17	246	24	147	277	58	194	317	89	228	4
	24	335	108	243	18	145	278	55	189	316	89
Oct.	1	59	206	341	108	229	17	152	278	40	188
	8	152	306	70	193	323	117	240	4	135	288
	15	255	32	155	287	66	203	325	100	236	13
	22	344	117	253	27	154	287	65	198	324	98
	29	68	215	351	116	239	26	162	286	50	196
Nov.	5	161	316	78	202	332	126	248	12	145	297
	12	264	41	163	298	74	212	333	111	244	22
	19	353	126	262	36	162	297	74	208	332	108
	26	77	223	1	124	248	34	172	294	59	205
Dec.	3	171	325	87	210	343	135	257	20	156	305
	10	271	50	171	309	82	220	342	121	253	30
	17	1	135	271	46	170	306	81	217	340	118
	24	87	231	11	132	257	43	181	302	66	215
	31	182	333	95	218	354	143	266	28	167	313

MOON SIGN TABLES

	1941	1942	1943	1944	1945	1946	1947	1948	1949	1950
Jan. 1	326	88	212	353	135	258	23	165	305	70
8	50	176	316	86	220	348	126	256	29	163
15	141	276	50	169	312	87	220	340	123	261
22	239	12	133	259	52	182	303	69	224	354
29	334	96	221	2	143	256	33	174	314	78
Feb. 5	57	186	324	95	227	358	134	265	37	173
12	150	285	58	178	321	96	228	349	132	271
19	250	20	142	267	62	190	312	78	234	2
26	342	104	231	11	152	274	43	182	323	86
Mar. 5	65	196	332	116	236	8	142	286	46	182
12	158	295	67	199	329	107	236	10	140	282
19	261	28	150	290	72	198	320	102	243	10
26	351	112	242	34	162	282	53	204	332	94
Apr. 2	74	205	340	125	245	17	152	294	55	191
9	166	306	74	209	337	118	244	19	148	292
16	270	36	158	300	81	206	328	112	252	19
23	0	120	252	42	170	290	64	212	340	103
30	83	214	351	133	254	25	163	302	64	199
May 7	175	316	82	218	346	128	252	28	158	302
14	279	45	166	311	89	215	336	123	260	28
21	9	128	262	50	179	299	73	222	349	112
28	92	222	1	141	263	34	173	310	74	207
June 4	184	326	91	226	356	137	261	36	168	310
11	287	54	174	322	98	224	345	134	268	37
18	17	138	271	60	187	308	81	231	357	122
25	102	231	12	149	272	42	183	318	83	217

MOON SIGN TABLES

July 2	194	335	99	234	7	145	270	44	179	318
9	296	63	183	332	106	233	353	144	276	45
16	25	147	279	70	196	318	90	241	5	132
23	111	240	21	157	281	52	192	327	91	227
30	205	343	108	242	18	153	278	52	190	327
Aug. 6	304	72	192	342	115	241	3	153	287	53
13	33	156	288	80	203	327	99	251	13	141
20	119	250	30	165	289	63	201	336	99	238
27	216	351	117	251	29	162	287	61	200	335
Sept. 3	314	80	202	351	125	249	13	162	296	61
10	41	166	297	90	211	336	108	260	21	149
17	127	261	39	174	297	74	209	345	107	249
24	227	0	125	260	39	171	295	71	210	344
Oct. 1	323	68	211	359	135	257	23	170	306	69
8	49	174	306	99	220	344	119	269	30	157
15	135	272	47	183	305	85	217	353	116	259
22	236	9	134	269	47	180	303	81	217	353
29	334	95	221	7	144	265	31	179	315	78
Nov. 5	58	182	317	107	229	352	130	277	39	165
12	143	283	55	192	314	94	226	1	126	269
19	244	18	142	280	55	190	311	91	226	3
26	343	104	229	17	153	274	39	189	323	86
Dec. 3	67	190	328	114	237	0	140	285	47	174
10	153	292	64	200	324	103	235	9	136	277
17	252	28	149	289	64	199	319	100	234	12
24	352	112	237	27	162	282	47	199	332	95
31	76	198	338	123	246	9	150	293	57	180

MOON-SIGN TABLES

	1951	1952	1953	1954	1955	1956	1957	1958	1959	1960
Jan. 1	193	335	115	237	5	146	285	47	178	317
8	296	66	198	331	106	237	8	143	277	47
15	29	150	293	70	199	320	104	241	9	131
22	113	239	35	161	283	51	207	351	93	222
29	204	344	123	245	16	154	284	54	188	325
Feb. 5	304	75	207	340	115	245	17	152	287	55
12	37	159	301	80	207	329	112	252	17	140
19	122	249	45	169	291	61	216	339	101	233
26	214	352	132	253	27	162	303	65	199	333
Mar. 5	313	96	216	349	125	265	27	180	297	75
12	45	180	309	90	215	351	121	248	25	161
19	130	273	53	178	299	86	224	348	109	258
26	225	14	141	261	37	185	311	72	308	255
Apr. 2	323	104	225	357	135	273	36	168	307	83
9	53	189	319	100	223	359	131	271	33	169
16	137	284	62	186	307	96	232	357	117	269
23	234	23	150	270	45	194	319	81	216	5
30	334	111	235	6	145	281	45	157	317	91
May 7	62	197	329	109	222	7	141	279	42	177
14	146	295	70	195	316	107	240	5	127	279
21	243	32	158	280	54	203	327	91	224	14
28	344	120	244	15	155	289	54	187	326	99
June 4	70	205	340	117	241	15	152	287	51	185
11	154	305	78	204	325	117	249	14	136	288
18	251	42	166	290	62	213	335	100	233	24
25	363	128	252	25	164	298	62	197	334	108

MOON SIGN TABLES

July	2	79	213	351	125	250	24	163	295	59	194
	9	164	315	87	212	335	125	258	22	146	296
	16	260	52	174	299	71	223	344	110	243	33
	23	2	137	260	36	172	307	70	208	342	117
	30	88	222	1	133	258	33	173	304	68	204
Aug.	6	173	323	97	220	345	134	268	29	156	305
	13	269	61	182	307	81	232	352	118	253	42
	20	10	145	269	47	180	316	79	219	350	126
	27	97	231	11	142	266	43	182	313	75	214
Sept.	3	183	331	107	228	354	142	277	38	165	314
	10	280	70	191	316	92	240	1	126	264	50
	17	18	154	277	58	188	324	88	229	359	134
	24	105	241	20	152	274	53	190	323	84	225
Oct.	1	192	340	116	236	3	152	286	46	174	323
	8	290	78	200	324	105	248	10	134	275	58
	15	26	162	286	68	197	332	98	238	8	142
	22	112	252	26	161	270	63	190	332	92	235
	29	201	350	125	245	11	162	295	35	182	334
Nov.	5	301	86	208	332	113	256	19	143	285	66
	12	35	170	296	76	206	340	108	246	17	150
	19	121	262	36	170	290	73	208	341	100	244
	26	209	0	153	254	19	172	302	64	190	344
Dec.	3	312	94	217	341	123	264	27	153	293	74
	10	45	178	307	84	216	348	119	254	26	158
	17	129	271	45	179	299	81	217	349	109	252
	24	217	11	140	263	27	183	310	73	198	252
	31	321	103	225	352	132	273	34	164	302	355

71

MOON-SIGN TABLES

	1961	1962	1963	1964	1965	1966	1967	1968	1969	1970
Jan. 1	96	217	350	128	26	27	163	298	76	197
8	179	315	89	217	350	126	260	27	161	297
15	275	53	179	302	86	225	349	112	257	36
22	18	141	263	65	189	311	74	207	359	122
29	105	225	1	135	275	35	173	307	85	206
Feb. 5	189	323	98	225	0	134	270	35	171	305
12	284	64	187	310	95	234	357	121	267	45
19	26	149	272	46	197	320	81	218	7	130
26	113	234	11	144	283	45	182	314	93	156
Mar. 5	198	331	109	245	9	142	280	54	180	313
12	293	73	195	332	105	244	5	142	277	53
19	34	159	280	71	204	329	90	243	15	139
26	122	243	19	166	291	54	190	338	101	226
Apr. 2	208	340	119	253	19	151	290	63	189	323
9	304	82	204	340	114	252	14	150	288	61
16	42	167	289	81	213	337	99	252	23	147
23	130	253	28	176	299	64	198	347	109	235
30	216	349	128	261	26	161	298	71	197	333
May 7	315	90	212	348	127	260	23	158	299	70
14	51	176	298	91	222	345	109	261	31	155
21	137	263	36	185	307	74	207	357	117	245
28	225	359	136	270	35	172	306	81	205	344
June 4	325	98	222	355	137	268	31	168	309	78
11	60	184	308	99	231	353	119	270	42	163
18	146	272	45	195	315	82	217	6	126	253
25	233	10	144	279	43	183	315	89	214	355

MOON SIGN TABLES

July 2	336	106	230	6	147	276	40	178	318	87
9	70	191	318	108	241	1	129	278	51	171
16	154	281	54	204	324	91	227	14	134	261
23	241	21	153	288	52	193	323	98	223	335
30	345	115	239	16	156	286	47	188	327	97
Aug. 6	79	200	327	116	250	10	138	288	60	180
13	163	289	66	212	333	99	238	22	144	270
20	250	32	161	296	61	203	331	106	233	14
27	353	124	246	27	164	295	55	199	335	106
Sept. 3	88	208	336	126	259	19	147	297	68	189
10	171	297	77	220	342	108	249	30	152	279
17	259	41	170	304	72	212	340	114	243	22
24	1	134	254	37	173	304	64	208	344	114
Oct. 1	97	217	345	136	267	28	155	308	76	198
8	181	306	88	228	351	117	259	38	161	289
15	270	50	179	312	82	220	349	122	254	31
22	10	143	262	47	182	313	72	217	353	123
29	105	226	352	146	275	37	163	318	84	207
Nov. 5	189	315	97	237	359	127	268	47	168	299
12	281	58	188	320	93	228	358	130	264	39
19	19	151	271	57	191	321	82	225	3	131
26	113	235	1	157	282	45	173	308	92	215
Dec. 3	197	326	105	245	7	138	276	55	176	310
10	291	66	197	329	102	237	7	139	273	47
17	30	159	280	63	202	329	91	234	13	139
24	121	243	11	166	291	53	183	337	101	223
31	205	336	113	254	14	148	284	64	185	319

73

MOON SIGN TABLES

	1971	1972	1973	1974	1975	1976	1977	1978	1979	1980
Jan. 1	335	108	246	7	147	279	56	179	318	90
8	71	198	332	107	243	6	144	278	54	176
15	158	283	69	207	328	93	240	18	139	263
22	244	20	169	292	54	192	339	102	224	4
29	344	117	255	17	156	288	64	189	327	99
Feb. 5	81	204	342	115	253	14	153	287	63	184
12	167	291	79	216	337	101	251	26	147	271
19	252	30	177	300	62	203	347	110	233	14
26	353	126	263	27	164	297	72	199	334	109
Mar. 5	91	224	351	124	262	34	162	296	72	204
12	176	312	60	224	346	122	262	34	156	293
19	261	55	184	309	72	226	356	118	244	37
26	1	149	270	37	172	320	80	208	343	130
Apr. 2	100	233	359	134	270	43	170	307	80	213
9	184	320	101	232	354	131	273	42	164	302
16	271	64	194	317	82	235	5	126	254	45
23	9	158	278	47	181	329	88	217	352	139
30	109	242	8	145	278	52	178	318	88	222
May 7	193	329	111	240	3	140	282	50	173	312
14	281	73	203	324	92	243	14	134	264	54
21	19	167	287	55	191	337	97	226	3	147
28	117	251	16	156	286	61	187	328	96	231
June 4	201	339	120	249	11	151	291	59	180	323
11	291	81	153	333	102	251	23	143	273	63
18	29	176	296	64	201	346	106	234	13	155
25	125	260	25	167	294	69	196	338	105	239

MOON-SIGN TABLES

July 2	209	350	129	257	19	162	299	68	188	334
9	300	90	222	341	111	261	32	152	282	72
16	40	184	305	72	212	354	115	243	23	163
23	133	268	5	176	307	78	206	347	104	248
30	217	0	137	267	27	172	308	77	197	344
Aug. 6	309	99	230	350	120	271	40	161	290	83
13	51	192	314	81	222	2	124	252	33	171
20	172	276	45	185	312	86	217	356	123	256
27	225	10	146	276	36	62	317	86	206	353
Sept. 3	317	109	238	0	128	281	48	170	299	93
10	61	200	322	90	232	10	132	262	43	180
17	151	284	56	193	321	94	228	4	132	264
24	234	20	125	284	45	191	326	94	215	2
Oct. 1	325	120	246	9	137	291	56	179	308	103
8	70	238	330	101	241	19	140	273	51	189
15	160	292	36	201	330	102	238	12	140	273
22	243	28	165	292	54	199	336	102	225	10
29	334	130	254	17	146	301	64	187	318	112
Nov. 5	79	217	338	112	249	27	148	284	59	197
12	169	301	76	210	339	111	247	21	148	282
19	253	36	175	300	63	207	347	110	234	18
26	344	139	262	25	156	310	73	195	329	120
Dec. 3	86	226	346	122	257	36	157	294	67	206
10	177	310	83	220	347	121	255	31	156	292
17	261	45	185	308	12	216	356	118	242	28
24	355	148	271	33	167	318	81	203	340	128
31	95	228	354	132	265	44	166	303	76	217

75

MOON SIGN TABLES

	1981	1982	1983	1984	1985	1986	1987	1988	1989	1990
Jan. 1	227	350	128	261	36	162	299	72	206	333
8	315	88	225	346	126	260	36	156	297	71
15	52	188	309	73	225	358	120	243	37	168
22	149	273	35	176	319	82	206	347	130	252
29	235	0	136	270	44	172	307	81	214	343
Feb. 5	324	98	234	355	134	269	44	165	305	82
12	63	196	318	81	236	6	128	252	47	176
19	157	281	45	184	328	90	217	355	139	260
26	242	10	144	280	52	181	316	90	222	352
Mar. 5	332	108	243	15	142	280	52	186	313	93
12	74	204	327	103	246	14	137	275	57	184
19	166	289	55	207	337	98	227	18	148	268
26	251	19	153	301	61	190	325	111	231	0
Apr. 2	340	119	251	24	150	291	60	195	321	103
9	84	212	335	113	255	23	145	286	68	193
16	176	296	65	216	346	106	237	26	157	276
23	259	28	164	309	70	198	336	119	240	8
30	348	129	259	33	159	301	68	203	331	113
May 7	93	221	343	124	263	32	152	296	74	202
14	185	305	75	224	355	115	246	35	165	285
21	268	36	174	317	79	206	347	127	249	17
28	357	139	267	42	169	311	77	211	341	122
June 4	101	230	351	135	271	41	161	307	82	211
11	194	313	83	234	4	124	254	45	173	295
18	277	44	185	325	88	215	357	135	258	27
25	8	149	275	50	180	319	86	219	352	130

MOON-SIGN TABLES

July 2	109	239	359	145	280	50	169	317	91	220
9	202	323	92	244	12	133	262	55	181	304
16	286	53	195	333	96	225	7	144	266	37
23	18	157	285	58	191	328	95	227	3	138
30	118	248	8	154	289	58	178	326	101	168
Aug. 6	210	332	100	254	20	142	271	66	189	313
13	294	63	205	342	104	235	15	152	274	48
20	29	165	294	66	201	336	104	236	13	147
27	128	257	17	163	299	66	188	334	111	236
Sept. 3	218	341	109	264	28	151	281	75	198	321
10	302	74	213	351	112	246	23	161	282	59
17	39	174	302	75	181	345	112	245	22	156
24	138	267	27	171	309	74	197	342	121	244
Oct. 1	226	349	119	274	36	159	291	84	206	329
8	310	85	221	0	120	257	31	170	291	69
15	49	183	311	84	220	354	120	255	30	166
22	148	272	36	180	319	82	206	351	130	252
29	235	357	130	282	45	167	302	92	215	337
Nov. 5	319	95	229	8	129	267	40	178	300	78
12	57	193	318	94	228	4	128	265	38	175
19	158	280	44	189	329	90	184	1	139	261
26	244	5	141	290	54	175	313	100	224	345
Dec. 3	328	105	238	17	139	276	49	186	310	87
10	65	203	326	103	236	14	136	274	47	185
17	167	289	52	200	337	99	222	12	147	270
24	252	13	151	298	62	184	323	108	232	355
31	337	113	248	24	149	284	59	194	320	95

MOON SIGN TABLES

	1991	1992	1993	1994	1995	1996	1997	1998	1999	2000
Jan. 1	110	243	16	145	280	53	185	317	92	224
8	206	326	107	243	16	137	278	55	186	307
15	290	54	209	338	100	225	21	148	270	36
22	18	158	300	62	190	329	111	231	2	139
29	118	252	24	154	289	62	194	325	101	232
Feb. 5	214	335	115	254	24	146	286	66	194	316
12	298	63	219	346	108	235	30	156	278	47
19	28	166	309	70	200	336	120	239	12	147
26	127	261	332	163	299	71	203	334	111	240
Mar. 5	222	356	123	265	32	167	294	76	202	337
12	306	87	228	354	116	259	39	165	286	71
19	39	188	318	78	210	359	129	248	21	170
26	137	281	42	171	309	91	212	342	121	260
Apr. 2	230	5	132	275	40	175	304	86	210	345
9	314	98	236	4	124	270	47	174	294	82
16	48	197	327	87	219	8	137	257	30	180
23	148	289	51	179	320	98	221	350	132	268
30	239	13	142	284	49	183	315	94	219	353
May 7	322	108	244	13	132	280	55	182	303	92
14	57	197	335	96	227	18	145	267	38	190
21	158	297	60	188	330	106	230	0	141	277
28	247	21	153	292	58	191	326	102	228	1
June 4	331	118	253	21	141	290	64	191	312	101
11	65	217	343	105	235	28	153	276	47	200
18	168	305	68	198	339	115	238	10	150	285
25	256	29	164	300	67	199	336	111	237	10

MOON SIGN TABLES

July 2	340	128	262	29	151	299	193	199	321	110
9	73	227	351	114	244	38	161	285	56	210
16	177	314	76	209	348	124	246	21	158	294
23	265	38	175	309	75	208	346	119	245	19
30	349	136	272	37	160	307	83	207	331	118
Aug. 6	83	237	359	123	254	48	169	293	67	218
13	186	322	84	220	356	133	254	32	166	303
20	274	47	184	318	83	218	355	129	253	29
27	359	145	282	45	170	316	93	215	340	127
Sept. 3	93	246	8	131	265	56	178	301	78	226
10	194	331	92	231	4	141	263	43	174	311
17	282	57	193	327	92	228	4	138	261	39
24	8	153	292	53	178	325	103	223	348	137
Oct. 1	104	255	17	139	276	64	187	309	89	234
8	202	340	102	241	13	150	273	52	183	319
15	290	67	201	337	99	238	12	148	269	49
22	16	163	301	62	186	335	111	232	356	147
29	115	262	26	147	287	72	195	318	99	243
Nov. 5	211	348	111	249	22	158	283	60	193	327
12	298	76	210	347	107	247	21	157	278	58
19	24	173	309	71	194	346	119	240	4	158
26	125	270	34	157	297	80	204	328	108	251
Dec. 3	221	356	121	257	32	165	293	68	202	335
10	306	85	219	356	116	255	31	166	286	66
17	32	184	317	79	202	357	127	250	13	169
24	134	279	42	166	305	89	212	338	116	260
31	230	4	131	265	41	173	303	77	212	343

79

YOUR UNIQUE SUN AND MOON PORTRAIT

Since the luminaries are the most important bodies in any chart, the positions of the Sun and Moon, and their relationship to each other, furnish an important key to the understanding of human nature. The following exploration of these factors reveals the manner in which the individuality (Sun) is expressed through the personality (Moon).

Sun in Cancer—Moon in Aries: The Moon in Aries denotes an aggressive, restless, and adventure-loving personality. With self-control, you may go far in the field of personal accomplishment. However, you will probably resent any discipline, whether you exercise it on yourself or someone else tries to impose it on you. The Sun in Cancer implies sensitiveness to potential danger, while Aries is combative. You often resort to attack as a method of defense. The urge for protection, manifesting through an aggressive personality, not only seeks but strives toward its ends. If you are under stress, you may attack, even though the danger is only imagined. You may appear temperamental, being good-natured at one time, touchy and quick to take offense at another. You may lead or be a pioneer in your chosen profession, conscious of your power to break ground for others and to protect them from any of the hardships you yourself have had to face.

Sun in Cancer—Moon in Taurus: With the Moon in Taurus, you are courteous and reflective but somewhat fixed in your opinions. The Moon is well placed in this sign, however, since Taurus adds needed strength and stability to the lunar temperament. The Sun in Cancer makes a very comfortable combination with the Moon in Taurus. The Cancerian need for protection and the Taurean urge for possessions combine to achieve and maintain for you a comfortable, if not wealthy, position in life. Your assets may be derived from real estate, mines, or other Cancerian concerns. You have active emotions, often expressed through pronounced likes and dislikes. If you are interested in intellectual pursuits, you will undertake your studies with a great deal of feeling. For this reason, you may find it difficult, sometimes, to form coldly logical and accurate conclusions. You have a great love of beauty, as well as artistic inclinations. You naturally attract friends, and you will express and demonstrate a love for humanity. You may be somewhat of a philanthropist with your money. Your attitudes will tend to be optimistic and good-natured.

Sun in Cancer—Moon in Gemini: With the Moon in Gemini, changeability and restlessness are emphasized in your nature. This position of the Moon presupposes a versatile and investigative mentality. With the Sun in Cancer, emotions and intellect are blended to produce the faculty of imagination. Cancer indicates a sensitivity to trouble, while Gemini affirms mental activity. The mind, therefore, could picture trouble where it does not exist. In some cases, you should make a successful builder or organizer, for you would be able to protect your work against any potential danger. However, you may be inclined to worry over fancied slights, to be oversensitive to your environment. You should undertake some intellectual study in order to force your attention away from your immediate concerns. Creative writing may be an outlet for your active imagination. You may be associated with some kind of institution—such as a hospital, jail, asylum, etc.—or you may suffer from a confining situation or condition at some time in your life.

Sun in Cancer—Moon in Cancer: The Moon in Cancer signifies a sympathetic, emotional, meditative personality. The Moon is Cancer's ruling planet. Therefore, the personality is apt to be dominant. With the Sun in this sign also, the characteristics of Cancer are intensified. It may be rather difficult to become acquainted with you, unless first your trust is gained, for the crablike shell protecting your overly sensitive feelings will be present. However, though you may appear hard, callous, or cold, you are really emotional, tender—and sometimes very lonely. Cancer rules the home, parents, country, real estate, mines, and matters of defense—anyone or anything operating as a protector. With both luminaries in Cancer, you will be concerned with some or all of these affairs. You will show a certain aggressiveness and initiative. You should accomplish a great deal, for you have imagination and caution as well as initiative.

Sun in Cancer—Moon in Leo: With the Moon in Leo, the changeable nature of the luminary is stabilized and illuminated. You will be tolerant and generous, with a great pride in your own personality. With the Sun in Cancer, a very powerful combination is formed, for here the Sun is in the Moon's sign and the Moon is in the Sun's sign—a case of mutual reception. Your sensitive emotions find some degree of protection behind the pride in the personal self. Leo's urge is to shine. Yet the Cancer sensitivity demands a more adequate protection than mere pride and show. You will, therefore, be moved toward some accomplishment in order to justify your pride. This combination of Sun and Moon would make you an excellent teacher, lecturer, or writer of works relating to the past or having to do with the retention or protection of past knowledge. This combination is also good for anyone connected with a bank or other financial or commercial organization. You may have an intuitive knowledge about financial affairs, coupled with a fine organizational ability.

Sun in Cancer—Moon in Virgo: With the Moon in Virgo, you will be practical, sympathetic, and analytical. You will have considerable awareness of detail and great love of perfection. With the Sun in Cancer, you can count on a favorable combination with the Moon in Virgo. The emotional sensitivity of Cancer finds its protection in the alert mentality of Virgo. You will not be aggressively ambitious—you probably never strive for name or fame—rather, you will be quietly efficient, perhaps an excellent homemaker or a superior office assistant. You are uniquely adapted for work related to the preservation of records or the gathering of statistics. Cancer indicates active emotions; Virgo, a practical and intellectual mentality. You can thus achieve a fine balance between your emotional nature and your intellect. This enables you to harness your inspirations and put them to practical and profitable purposes. You are idealistic but express your ideal in a practical way—in a clean, moral, and upright life. You are active and inquiring, with an interest in many subjects. You should be able to express your thoughts with accuracy and clarity. Because you are both careful and accurate, you would make a good stenographer. This combination of the Sun and Moon is also good if you are interested in writing on historical subjects.

Sun in Cancer—Moon in Libra: With the Moon in Libra your disposition is affectionate and agreeable. You weigh matters very carefully in your attempt to reach a balanced conclusion. In some cases, however, this may present the problem of indecision. With the Sun in Cancer, this kind of sensitivity tends to be emphasized. You could have too much dependence on others and, at the same time, some suspicion in regard to their motives. The winning manner of Libra, coupled with a reluctance to be confidential (the "shell" of Cancer), sometimes produces an impression either of superiority or condescension. You may seem mysterious in some way or appear incapable of being understood by others. With this combination of Sun and Moon, you could be unusually sensitive about your appearance (Libra rules clothes). A fastidious attitude in this respect provides you with an excellent protective shell. You may tend to overdress (or underdress), be given to loud mannerisms, or tend to be a show-off. Behind this front—this awkward shell—however, there hides a shy, timid, sometimes actually retiring soul. You should make a good mediator or matchmaker, for you feel that the best way to achieve protection lies in the resolution of conflict, the bringing of people together. You may also have unusual diplomatic ability.

Sun in Cancer—Moon in Scorpio: With the Moon in Scorpio, you are endowed with enterprise, courage, and force. Hence, your personal emotions are sometimes active to the point where their expression becomes a dominant urge. With the Sun in Cancer, your emotional nature is increased. You are capable of getting a great deal of happiness—or sorrow—out of life. The inner Cancerian sensitivity may be completely hidden behind an emotional intensity and drive that carries everything before it. Constructive channels should be found for the expression of this intensity, for your first reaction to a potential threat to yourself, your home, your loved ones, or your country is often to annihilate the enemy. You tend to strike swiftly and with deadly purpose. You should contemplate any matter quietly and thoroughly before you act. When your energies are turned to some wholesome creative activity, you can experience a surge of power that will make life a joy to you. This combination of Sun and Moon is an excellent one if you are interested in becoming an author, especially if you have a desire to write of the secrets of the past or delve into the mystery of hidden treasure. You have much executive ability and would do well in command of others. You would make an excellent construction manager, especially of housing, for Scorpio would provide the necessary element to drive the activity homeward. Your dramatic ability should be useful and profitable in expressing your emotions.

Sun in Cancer—Moon in Sagittarius: The Moon in Sagittarius presupposes personal optimism and farsightedness. Your mind will be alert and active; yet your interests may tend to be superficial unless depth of purpose can be developed. With the Sun in Cancer, the Moon in Sagittarius forms a combination which indicates a basic condition of mental and emotional restlessness. You will probably feel that your protection can come only from a knowledge of law, religion, or philosophy. You may seek to be informed along one or more of these lines. This feeling may find expression in a deep religious conviction, a faith in the unseen God as the Great Protector. You have the potential to be able to comprehend the fundamental laws "protecting" universal existence. In some cases, this combination may indicate an overemphasis upon rules. You may advocate rigid morals and ethics but find it difficult to live up to your admonitions, your emotions dictating your own action at a lower level. This combination of Sun and Moon could make you a good lawyer, teacher, or salesperson—and it is especially helpful if you want to deal in real estate or corporate matters. You will have a detailed awareness of the fundamental laws which ensure protection of health, though you may suffer from illnesses occasioned by apprehension and fear for your own welfare.

Sun in Cancer—Moon in Capricorn: With the Moon in Capricorn, you are practical, ambitious, and have an austere personality. Personal happiness is rare, but a capacity for leadership is predicted. With the Sun in Cancer, the urge for active accomplishment tends to be stressed—since it is in achievement, in the mastery of obstacles, that you find your fullest realization of protection. This combination of Sun and Moon is a good one for the builder of a home to protect and shelter the family or of an organization or corporation for the protection of a business venture or idea. If you are fearful and apprehensive about your relations with the public, you may build a kind of wall around yourself, enclosing your sensitivity behind a hard, cold personality. You may be miserly, the Capricorn industry expressing in the collection of possessions in order to fortify yourself in one way or another. However, you will find that you can secure happiness only in a forgetfulness of self, in turning your practical talents to the building of walls of protection for others. This combination is not a happy omen for relationships with others unless you have great patience and are morally and spiritually advanced.

Sun in Cancer—Moon in Aquarius: With the Moon in Aquarius, you are tolerant, friendly, independent, and interested in the unusual. The Sun in Cancer gives you a deep desire to "mother" humanity in one way or another. The protective instinct of Cancer, combined with a love of humanity, often manifests in the urge to provide protection for helpless or needy persons. Cancer implies a potentially active imagination; Aquarius, originality of thought. Thus, you will possess an active and original imagination. Your phobias and fears and your great desire to be different should be noted by you early in life and severely curbed. Aquarius is a student of human nature; Cancer, the nurturing, protecting mother. Hence, you will desire to succor and protect humanity in some way. Matters concerning birth and death, legacies, gifts, and taxes will be outstanding in your life.

Sun in Cancer—Moon in Pisces: With the Moon in Pisces, you tend to have a romantic, idealistic, and psychic temperament. You are sensitive to any disharmony in your environment and may easily become discouraged if there is such a situation. With the Sun in Cancer, the emotions are doubly stressed, though you will probably remain idealistic. You are not ambitious, as a rule, since you are essentially sympathetic and considerate. Under the protection of another person or of some institution, you will be at your best. If left to your own devices, you soon achieve some kind of protective shell for yourself or discover some other method of escape from your problems. This combination of Sun and Moon is excellent for the development of the inner mind or the psychic senses. You often seem to possess a kind of fountain of inner contentment and happiness. You are often able to make others happy, too, possibly through your writings, poetry, music—or merely by your sympathy and kindness.

YOUR RISING SIGN AND SUN-SIGN COMBINATION

Your Sun-Sign describes that core identity you possess, that source of your sense of self and the purpose that guides you through life. Your ascendant is the way in which that self gets expressed, the filter through which you see the world, and through which the world sees you. Not only is each combination different, but every person has a unique way of manifesting it. As the length of days and nights varies in different latitudes, the guidelines below may be less than accurate, so try reading the message before or after the one suggested, to see if it is more helpful in deepening your understanding of how you manifest your unique self in the world.

If you were born between 4:00 A.M. and 6:00 A.M., your ascendant is the same as your Sun-Sign, Cancer. As such, the Moon is an influential part of your chart, noting the importance of security—both emotional and physical—to you, as well as having a safe place for your deep and sensitive feelings to be expressed. Because of your heightened sensitivities, you may be extraordinarily self-protective, armoring yourself either intellectually or by creating distances between yourself and others to safeguard your vulnerability. It would be wise for you to find a career or avocation in which you would deliver to others the compassionate and generous caretaking you yourself would like to receive from others.

If you were born between 6:00 A.M. and 8:00 A.M., your ascendant is Leo, ruled by the fiery, light-giving Sun. You

88 ♋ Cancer JUNE 22–JULY 23

are quite blessed in that you possess a deeper kind of sensitivity that reaches and helps other people, as well as the kind of personality that enables you to put forth such gifts and talents with a confidence and optimism that is inspiring to others. Be careful to avoid getting caught up in the ego satisfaction of guiding the lives of others; should you lose sight of your purpose and merely bask in the glory of performance, you'll end up being less helpful than you'd like—and less popular as well.

If you were born between 8:00 A.M. and 10:00 A.M., your ascendant is Virgo. Mercury rules this sign, imparting a natural affinity for detail as well as an instinctive desire to be of service to others. You are a marvel in the helping professions, or any field allied with healing and counseling others; you readily make a success of any talents you possess. You tend to be a bit of a perfectionist, though your gentler, more compassionate side helps you learn to temper this tendency with self-awareness and empathy for the human qualities we all possess. You also have a great gift for timing—knowing exactly when to approach people with certain questions; be sure to use it.

If you were born between 10:00 A.M. and noon, your ascendant is Libra. Ruling this sign is the planet of relationships and beauty, Venus. Coupled with your Cancer Sun-Sign, this makes for a personable negotiator, creating compromises and seeing to it that everyone's ruffled feathers are soothed. You'd make a marvelous diplomat and most likely use that skill unofficially all the time. You may have a tendency, however, to think more about pleasing others than taking care of your own needs in any given situation. Instead of being embittered by the neglect of others, be more assertive in putting out exactly what you need to get the satisfaction you deserve and want.

If you were born between noon and 2:00 P.M., your ascendant is Scorpio, ruled by the planet of great power, renewal, and transformation, Pluto. Emotions run deep in your life, and are often a motivating force in what you do,

Your Rising Sign and Sun-Sign Combination ☉ 89

which career you choose, and how you go about your business. You sometimes overreact to situations in which you feel others are trying to control or manipulate you, and instead of directly confronting them, you withdraw or seek some form of indirect revenge. Try to create situations in which you feel safe, and take care not to treat others in the way you yourself would not want to be treated; manipulation and control on either side needs to be dealt with immediately and directly.

If you were born between 2:00 P.M. and 4:00 P.M., your ascendant is Sagittarius. The jovial, philosophical influence of Jupiter is felt here, with a certain enlivening effect on your personality. You tend to be very outgoing and entertaining with others, inspiring laughter and even tears with stories you tell that bring people together in a common recognition of their humanity. Befriending all you meet, you are also able to intuit just how to make others feel at ease with you in whatever social situations you find yourself. Beware a tendency to overextend yourself and make promises you can't follow up on. Realize that often your presence is enough of a gift to others—without the need to say you'll do more.

If you were born between 4:00 P.M. and 6:00 P.M., your ascendant is Capricorn, the sign opposite your Sun-Sign, Cancer. With Saturn's influence here, you tend to be even more self-protective and less outgoing with your feelings. You may shield your vulnerability by taking on a professional role with others that allows you to serve and connect with them without revealing any personal aspects of yourself that you are uncomfortable sharing with less than intimate friends. Your outlook on life is somewhat cautious, as you temper any expectations or hopes you have about yourself, others, or the future, with a certain realism; your attitude is always affected by practical and material concerns and fluctuations.

If you were born between 6:00 P.M. and 8:00 P.M., your ascendant is Aquarius. Uranus, the planet ruling the common person, sudden change, and unpredictability, makes it hard to determine just how its influence will affect you. Your attitude toward others will most likely be erratic, in that you may react differently to the same situation at different times, and even find yourself responding to people in an inconsistent manner. You are certainly a stimulating person to be around, as you have a unique perspective on life, and can share with others your appreciation of aspects of the future that others may not be able to imagine. Your wild fantasies can be exciting, inspiring, and fun.

If you were born between 8:00 P.M. and 10:00 P.M., your ascendant is Pisces. You are possessed of a great sensitivity, as Neptune, ruler of your rising sign, bestows upon you keen awareness of the emotional undercurrents that surround you and an increased psychic receptivity. You tend to absorb the vibrations of everything that goes on around you, and need to make sure that you find a process for yourself that helps you release some of the emotional overload that could otherwise get you down. Your fantastic creativity and ability to intuit the feelings of others could lead you either into some kind of counseling, caretaking, or creative field of professional endeavor.

If you were born between 10:00 P.M. and midnight, your ascendant is Aries. With Mars the planet ruling your rising sign, you assert directly what you feel and put forth your desires to others without hesitation or a need for protection. You have a kind of warrior consciousness, meaning that you are able to stand up for what you believe and even in the face of opposition, remain true to your ideals— bolstered by an intuitive inner sense of what is right. You can be an enlightened leader, utilizing the compassion of your Cancer Sun-Sign, and motivated by the strength of your Aries ascendant, knowing just how to inspire people to take the steps they need to move closer to their goals.

If you were born between midnight and 2:00 A.M., your ascendant is Taurus. The influence of Venus, ruler of

Taurus, on you makes for a rather materialistic approach to life, with a great emphasis on security—in your home, your work, and your relationships. You may be less trusting of your intuitions and rely more on your experiential sense in knowing things, as the earthiness of your sign puts you in touch with what goes on around you in a very here-and-now factual way. You respond to situations slowly and conservatively, giving things thought and measuring others' opinions against your own experience—which you know to be the master of your final decision in any given situation.

If you were born between 2:00 A.M. and 4:00 A.M., your ascendant is Gemini. Mercury, ruling your rising sign, imparts a certain flexibility and ambivalence to your attitude in most situations. You approach the world seeing both sides of every issue, with compassion for either end of a dilemma. Decision making is therefore hard for you, as you find it hard to take any consistent action in one direction. The master of self-expression, however, you are so gifted in verbalizing feelings that you make it easier for others to see their own emotions clearly, helping them to communicate what they want. Forging emotions on an emotional level is harder, however, due to a certain evasive quality in your interactions and personality.

MERCURY: MIND OVER MATTER

Mercury is the planet governing the connections we make in the world. Communication is a part of how we reach out to other people. This includes our approach to putting ourselves forward in relationships. Our beliefs, attitudes, and all that governs just how we make that move to connect our inner world with what is going on around us are the domain of this planet.

Whether we choose to open up to others with words or some kind of nonverbal gesture, whether we find a strictly intellectual or formal way of making ourselves known or wait for others to notice, the varying styles of communication can be better understood by knowing the sign in which Mercury is placed in our charts.

Thinking is another aspect of ourselves that involves making connections—in this case, synthesizing the various parts of ourselves that make up the whole. What we think, how we think about ourselves, our attitudes toward others, and our beliefs about the world determine just what we want to put forward into it and how.

In a way Mercury acts as a filter through which we understand what is all around us. How we perceive and process what others put out to us affects our feelings, our interpretations, and our acts in relationships. The connections we make in our minds between events that occur influence our sense of self as well.

In other words, this little planet represents just how we connect all the diverse parts of our mind, impacting on not only the way we reach out but also the quality of our bond with others.

Mercury: Mind Over Matter

Sharing the knowledge, information, and feelings we have makes us part of a larger whole, more than just ourselves, now a small piece of the larger universe. Mercury points the way to how we deal with the human recognition that we are not alone in the world and to exactly what we do about this. The first inkling of a relationship starts with gestures and words and, even before that, the thoughts we have about others. So begin communication and the relations people forge with one another.

Mercury governs our understanding of and way of making that connection. As we read about our particular placement of Mercury in the chart, we are better able to see how the impact of our attitudes and thoughts affects other people and how we create some of the interactions and relationships we have in our everyday lives.

Mercury in Aries adds a lively, active tone to communications. The individual with this placement of Mercury is likely to take the lead in a conversation, even start one up without any kind of hesitancy or self-consciousness, and exudes a certain directness in ensuing dialogues. There may also be a serious flirtatiousness to interactions because the sign of Aries tends toward a passionate and directly sexual manner of engaging members of the opposite sex.

On the other hand, an Aries Mercury individual is often expressive in a rather combative way. Finding it easy to provoke disharmony, such a person could unintentionally start verbal arguments with others that lack any resolution or completion.

Lack of follow-through may be a bit frustrating in conversing with a Mercury in Aries individual. Many ideas will be communicated, and feelings conveyed, often without any sense of closure or even reciprocity. This person may be prone to asking questions and then not waiting until they are answered, starting a story and then interrupting himself or herself with another one, or perhaps just cutting someone off to say something that pops up and needs to be expressed immediately.

The thought processes and connections of this individual are intuitive, quick, and somehow magically provoked. An impatience about disclosure is expressed in a tendency to want to say things quickly. A marvelous wit and humor, however, take the edge off an omnipresent aggressiveness.

Mercury in Taurus denotes a certain deliberate, thoughtful, and cautious manner of expression and intellectual digestion of ideas and information. The almost scholarly seriousness with which even the most mundane conversation is received reflects the careful and conservative pacing of the Taurus Mercury individual's mind. A certain bluntness and conciseness are reflective of the Taurean respect for time and efficiency, moderation in using just the right number of words, and measured sensibility about communication in general.

These individuals are usually not the ones to initiate conversations, nor are they known for any particular adeptness in keeping one going. Their manner of conveying information is most often nonverbal—particularly physical—for words are not where Mercury in Taurus individuals feel most at home.

The thought processes of such people lend themselves to methodical and systematic presentation of ideas and even feelings. Frustration is in store for individuals seeking more philosophical or emotional exchanges because of the seeming lack of interaction that goes on. The truth is that Taurus Mercury people need time to take in fully what another person is telling them and then more time to formulate a response that is completely and concisely satisfying. Humor is a quality that presents itself almost as an antidote to the rather slow and serious manner of receiving and reacting to information.

Mercury in Gemini is quite a lively influence on one's manner of thought, understanding, and interaction with others. At home in its own sign, Gemini rules the communications aspect of the personality, which in such an individual may be dominant. Gemini Mercury people thrive on much interaction with others and may have serious issues

Mercury: Mind Over Matter ☉ 95

about communication that need to be dealt with throughout life. Highly communicative, these people know just how to keep conversations going—not just leading or dominating them but facilitating equal participation.

Gemini individuals make connections everywhere they go—especially in the vicinity of their homes—with the mailman, the grocer, the sanitation worker, the gardener, learning all sorts of interesting tidbits about the way others live, think, work, and feel. This information is then readily shared with others, as Mercury in Gemini individuals forge links among people.

Gemini Mercury people are quick and adept at processing a lot of information at once. Alert to any small changes, these individuals bring their awarenesses to bear in almost every situation, sharing those awarenesses with others. If it seems there are always other things distracting these people while you converse with them, it's true. They always have thoughts pouring through them and, while in constant verbal motion, are simultaneously processing information and creating more.

Mercury in Cancer lends an emotional tone to an individual's manner of taking in and putting forth information, feelings, and ideas. With a pronounced lunar influence, feelings dominate the intellectual processes; the person may react emotionally to what is being said even before the words are fully understood. Responding to the tone rather than the message of another, such an individual knows exactly what you are really asking at the level beneath the actual question and may therefore have trouble responding directly to you.

The sensitivity of Mercury Cancer is matched only by their intuitive awareness. Communication with them is a double-edged sword. You can learn about the impact of your communication style on others by their reactions and profit from the wisdom of their intuitions. If you offend them, however, they tend to withdraw. As sharp communicators with strong psychic/intuitive edges, they may lead others out in conversation without really involving themselves in a personal way.

Thinking and feeling are closely aligned for Mercury in Cancer individuals. Despite the apparent detachment some of them cultivate as a defense, almost all that they say has some kind of emotional investment for them. They take in all levels of what you are saying in conversation and respond accordingly.

Mercury in Leo gives a dazzle and a shine to communications as well as a certain one-sidedness to interactions. The excitement of a Mercury in Leo individual's sharing some idea about which he or she is enthusiastic sparks the intellectual and emotional sensibilities. Sometimes, however, one may tire of hearing of the achievements of such an individual or any story that is so filled with excessive self-congratulatory airs that seem almost to negate the accomplishments of others. A certain inflexible, didactic, and dogmatic way of expression alternates with an entertaining, charming, and totally winning style that one could listen to and enjoy endlessly.

A fun sense of life—as well as language—makes for some remarkable and intriguing conversations with Leo Mercury people. Extroverts by nature, they may take a bit of time to warm up to new situations. Once into them, however, these individuals certainly know how to provide warmth, entertainment, and even inspiration to those with whom they interact.

The mental processes of Leo individuals usually start with "Well, what does this have to do with me?" in order to measure the worth of any interaction and just how much of the self Leo Mercury people need to invest in understanding and responding to it. These focused, purposeful individuals find a great satisfaction in the completion and appreciation of their thoughts and conversations as well as goals.

Mercury in Virgo indicates an awareness of and interest in the details that make up a situation, conversation, or thought. Though these individuals may seem a bit slow in responding to or comprehending what you say, they are really picking up on aspects even more exacting and de-

Mercury: Mind Over Matter 97

tailed in what you are expressing than you yourself are likely to notice. You get a very thorough response when you ask these people questions.

As the ruler of the sign Mercury is at home in Virgo, where little things take on an importance all their own. These people truly believe that every particular aspect of life deserves attention, an attitude that centers them in the present, in the physical world to serve others best.

Virgo Mercury communicators may get mired in the practical aspects of reality, be less prone to go off on tangents, and be more likely to get into the how-to of things than most other individuals. Their awareness and ability to deal with mechanical things can be astounding— and quite a lifesaver—for fitting things together is part of the analytical nature of this kind of mind.

Those born with Mercury in Virgo use words with such exactitude that there is little ambiguity about their meaning. The only problem arises when you don't apply the same rules of perfection to your own communications.

Mercury in Libra denotes individuals whose prime concern in communication is making connections that foster harmony in relationships. Too often these may be people who let deeper feelings and truths slip by for that higher priority of peace in interaction. A conciliatory attitude or any kind of evasion of fact needs to be monitored. There is a sense of fairness in that they seldom dominate conversations. They may be too polite when *you* do to say so, but they are always able to hold their own. They often seem to have something nice or at least inoffensive to say which keeps the conversational ball rolling.

Libra Mercury individuals also tend to use words to make things better, lovelier, or easier to take. There is a kind of gentleness to the tones of those with this placement of Mercury, a way in which interaction is used truly to strengthen and beautify the bonds people have toward each other in relationships. The intent of these individuals is almost always, first, to promote good feelings between people, second, to communicate ideas or feelings.

The thought patterns of a Libra Mercury individual

may seem somewhat calculating in that they stem from the intention of propagating harmony among people. But with such positive motivation, what is the harm of a little bit of fiction mixed with fact?

Mercury in Scorpio can be an intensifying influence on the individual, manifested in a sharp, scathing, highly focused mentality. Interactions are very rarely of a light nature, nor are they usually detached or purely factual. The Scorpio influence on Mercury makes for a strongly felt undercurrent in interactions, so that even when the conversation seems to have little, if any, emotional content, something is going on under the surface.

There is rarely anything superficial going on in the mind of Mercury in Scorpio people—even concerning matters that don't seem to have much deeper significance. The seriousness and focus brought to bear upon ideas and interactions are matched only by the ability to penetrate the meaning of a situation and discern what is really being said underneath the words. Conversations with these people, therefore, are rarely boring and almost always impart some deeper insight to their listeners—about themselves, the Mercury in Scorpio people, or what is being discussed.

The mentality of these individuals brings a level of complexity, depth, and meaning to even the most superficial of subjects. Another aspect of Mercury in Scorpio people, aside from a scathing sense of black humor that even frightens some people away, is the power of Scorpio's silence.

Mercury in Sagittarius imparts a versatility and expansiveness to the mentality. The connections made are often general and perhaps superficial ones—offered to anyone who responds—with some philosophical ramifications which almost always engage someone in conversation. Spreading ideas is one of the activities at which these individuals feel most at home, so sharing information with others comes as second nature, as does putting others at ease in conversation. One may grow a bit tired of long-winded stories, but jokes, tidbits of juicy facts, humorous anecdotes, and assorted other ways of verbal sharing and fun are the forte of Sagittarius Mercury people. The ease and joy they impart in relating to others stem from their own enjoyment of friendly connections.

There may be a kind of slapdash quality, however, to how even important information is conveyed. Not the most organized of thinkers, Sagittarius Mercury types often miss a vital fact here or there—with such charm and wit that it is hard to pin them down to taking responsibility.

The mental outlook of these individuals is usually broadly philosophical. They take great delight in thinking and sharing, and their enthusiasm is readily imparted to their listeners. Mercury in Sagittarius people make great teachers, public speakers, or orators.

Mercury in Capricorn gives direction to the interactive focus of individuals, making for goal-oriented, factual, and dry manners of presentation. Small talk would be rather difficult for these people unless there were a lot of factual detail attached to a story that made it something solid to communicate, because real-life issues are the most comfortable subjects for conversation with Capricorn Mercury people. A certain seriousness pervades such interactions as well, the practical nature of the sign influencing how words get expressed, which are chosen, and what subjects will be discussed. You can totally rely on information from Mercury in Capricorn individuals, however, because they would be reluctant to impart less than accuracy, truthfulness, or verifiable information of a practical nature. You will not find a lot of emotional content in their interactions unless you are willing to look harder or plumb deeper. It's hard for these individuals even to touch on anything of an emotional nature because their factual, to-the-point natures often protect the deep and sensitive feelings hidden deep within.

The thinking process of a Capricorn in Mercury type is one of weeding out inessential thoughts so that there is little clutter, nothing to get in the way of the essentials of an interaction.

Mercury in Aquarius lends a touch of the offbeat to conversations and makes for fascinating interactions in which the focus is on other people. The Aquarian propensity for drawing others out and inspiring them to recognize their uniqueness is part of the motivation in any connections with an Aquarian Mercury type. Topics introduced range from factual situations or information to the most personal of emotional disclosures. These individuals are open to cultivating a conversation on any topic—as more of a supporter than participant, busy creating an environment wherein one feels that special attention one needs to recognize one's own particular importance and self-worth. As listeners Aquarians have an uncanny ability to focus. As communicators they can pick up on the most obscure aspects of an issue and elicit information or hold forth on it in most unusual ways.

The thought processes of Aquarians are erratic. At times they can match the depth of any other thinkers and even add to it with a particular gift of intuition. At other times their scan of a situation is rather superficial, catching all the details of a situation but missing the essential meaning, thereby distorting the whole thing. Emotional communication is difficult for Mercury in Aquarius individuals, as are comfortably knowing and experiencing their own negativity.

Mercury in Pisces imparts a magical quality to any interactions with such an individual. The intuitive way in which you are approached by this person meets you exactly where you are at that moment, drawing out whatever you need to say or share, putting you at ease with yourself, the conversation, and the person as well. It is often just the presence of the person that emanates a nonverbal acceptance and appreciation of your most sensitive inner self, allowing you to be and express any level of who you are.

A more difficult aspect of this placement of Mercury in Pisces is the individual's tendency to stick more to a global or inner truth about the temporal nature of reality than to the facts. In other words, despite an underlying consistency somewhat incomprehensible to the listener, on the surface of things this person seems constantly to change his or her mind. Though it may be the overwhelming emotional sensitivities of the Piscean Mercury person that makes for shifting awareness of what is important from moment to moment, there is difficulty in relying on any consistent opinion or reaction from one time to another.

This flexibility verging on variability of this person's mental focus is part of what causes the seeming inconsistencies in interactions. The mind of Pisces extends much farther than the bounds of any conversation, far beyond the facts and parameters of the present situation.

How to Find the Place of Mercury in Your Chart

Find your birth year in the left-hand column and read across the chart until you find your birth date. The top of that column will tell you where Mercury lies in your chart.

PLACE OF MERCURY—1880–1891

	ARIES	TAURUS	GEMINI	CANCER	LEO	VIRGO	LIBRA	SCORPIO	SAGITT.	CAPRI.	AQUAR.	PISCES
1880	3/5–5/1	5/12–5/27	5/28–6/10	6/11–6/27	6/28–9/3	9/4–9/19	9/20–10/7	10/8–10/29 11/25–12/12	1/10 10/30–11/24 12/13–	1/11–1/30	1/31–2/16	2/17–3/4
1881	4/16–5/4	5/5–5/18	5/19–6/2	6/3–6/28 7/10–8/10	6/29–7/9 8/11–8/26	8/27–9/11	9/12–10/1	10/2–12/7	1/3 12/8–12/26	1/4–1/21 12/27–	1/22–2/8	2/9–4/15
1882	4/10–4/26	4/27–5/10	5/11–5/28	5/29–8/3	8/4–8/18	8/19–9/4	9/5–9/27 10/23–11/10	9/28–10/22 11/11–11/30	12/1–12/19	–1/14 12/20–	1/15–2/1 2/26–3/17	2/2–2/25 3/18–4/9
1883	4/3–4/17	4/18–5/2	5/3–7/10	7/11–7/26	7/27–8/10	8/11–8/29	8/30–11/4	11/5–11/23	11/24–12/12	–1/7 12/13–	1/8–3/15	3/16–4/2
1884	3/26–4/8	4/9–4/30 5/13–6/13	5/1–5/12 6/14–7/2	7/3–7/16	7/17–8/2	8/3–8/25	8/26–9/16 10/10–10/27	9/17–10/9 10/28–11/15	11/16–12/4	–1/1 1/21–2/14 12/25–	1/2–1/20 2/15–3/7	3/8–3/24
1885	3/17–4/1	4/2–6/9	6/10–6/24	6/25–7/8	7/9–7/27	7/28–10/2	10/3–10/19	10/20–11/8	11/9–11/30 12/17–	2/29 12/1–12/16	2/10–2/28	3/1–3/16
1886	3/9–5/15	5/16–6/1	6/2–6/15	6/16–7/1	7/2–7/28 8/7–9/8	7/29–8/6 9/9–9/24	9/25–10/12	10/13–11/1	–1/12 11/2–	1/13–2/3	2/4–2/20	2/21–3/8
1887	3/3–3/22 4/18–5/9	5/10–5/24	5/25–6/7	6/8–6/26	6/27–9/1	9/2–9/17	9/18–10/5	10/6–10/29 11/14–12/11	–1/7 10/30–11/13 12/12–12/31	1/8–1/26	1/27–2/13	2/14–3/2 3/23–4/17
1888	4/14–4/30	5/1–5/14	5/15–5/30	5/31–8/7	8/8–8/22	8/23–9/8	9/9–9/28	9/29–12/4	12/5–12/23	1/1–1/19 12/24–	1/20–2/5	2/6–4/13
1889	4/7–4/22	4/23–5/6	5/7–5/28 6/16–7/12	5/29–6/15 7/13–7/30	7/31–8/14	8/15–9/1	9/2–9/27 10/9–11/8	9/28–10/8 11/9–11/27	11/28–12/16	–1/10 12/17–	1/11–1/30 2/12–3/17	1/31–2/11 3/18–4/6
1890	3/31–4/13	4/14–4/30	5/1–7/1	7/2–7/22	7/23–8/6	8/7–8/26	8/27–11/1	11/2–11/19	11/20–12/9	–1/4 12/10–	1/5–3/12	3/13–3/30
1891	3/22–4/5	4/6–6/13	6/14–6/29	6/30–7/13	7/14–7/30	7/31–10/7	10/8–10/24	10/25–11/12	11/13–12/2	–1/1 1/7–2/13 12/3–	1/2–1/6 2/14–3/5	3/6–3/21

PLACE OF MERCURY—1892-1905

1892	3/13–3/30 4/20–5/15	3/31–4/19 5/16–6/5	6/6–6/20	6/21–7/4	7/5–7/25 8/30–9/9	7/26–8/29 9/10–9/29	9/30–10/16	10/17–11/4	1/3–1/13 11/5	2/8–2/25	2/26–3/12
1893	3/6–5/12	5/13–5/28	5/29–6/11	6/12–6/28	6/29–9/5	9/6–9/21	9/22–10/9	10/10–10/30 11/30–12/12	10/31–11/29 12/13–12/31	1/10 1/11–1/30	1/31–2/17	2/18–3/5
1894	4/17–5/5	5/6–5/20	5/21–6/3	6/4–6/26 7/18–8/10	6/27–7/17 8/11–8/28	8/29–9/13	9/14–10/2	10/3–12/8	1/1–1/4 12/9–12/28	1/5–1/23 12/29	1/24–2/9	2/10–4/16
1895	4/12–4/27	4/28–5/11	5/12–5/28	5/29–8/5	8/6–8/20	8/21–9/5	9/6–9/27	9/28–10/27 11/12–12/1	10/28–11/11 12/2–12/21	1/15 12/22	1/16–2/27 3/4–3/16	2/3–3/3 3/17–4/11
1896	4/4–4/18	4/19–5/3	5/4–7/10	7/11–7/26	7/27–8/10	8/11–8/29	8/30–11/4	11/5–11/23	11/24–12/12	12/13	1/9–3/15	3/16–4/3
1897	3/27–4/9	4/10–4/29 5/22–6/12	4/30–5/21 6/13–7/4	7/5–7/18	8/4–8/25 9/22–10/11	8/26–9/21 10/11–10/28	10/29–11/16	11/17–12/6	1/25–2/14 12/7	1/2–1/24 2/15–3/9	3/10–3/26
1898	3/19–4/2	4/3–6/10	6/11–6/25	6/26–7/10	7/11–7/27	7/28–10/4	10/5–10/21	10/22–11/9	11/10–11/30 12/22	2/10 12/1–12/21	2/11–3/1	3/2–3/18
1899	3/11–5/15	5/16–6/3	6/4–6/17	6/18–7/2	7/3–7/26	7/27–8/14 9/10–9/26	8/15–9/9 9/27–10/13	10/14–11/2	11/3	1/13	1/14–2/4	2/5–2/22	2/23–3/10
1900	3/4–3/29	3/30–4/16 5/11–5/25	4/17–5/10 5/26–6/8	6/9–6/26	6/27–9/2	9/3–9/18	9/19–10/6	10/7–10/29 11/19–12/12	10/30–11/18 12/13	1/8 1/9–1/28	1/29–2/14	2/15–3/3
1901	4/16–5/3	5/4–5/17	5/18–6/1	6/2–8/9	8/10–8/25	8/26–9/10	9/11–9/30	10/1–12/6	1/2 12/7–12/25	1/3–1/20 12/26	1/21–2/6	2/7–4/15
1902	4/9–4/24	4/25–5/9	5/10–5/28 6/26–7/12	5/29–6/25 7/13–8/2	8/3–8/17	8/18–9/3	9/4–9/27 10/16–11/10	9/28–10/15 11/11–11/29	11/30–12/18	1/13 12/19	1/14–2/1 2/19–3/18	2/2–2/18 3/19–4/8
1903	4/2–4/16	4/17–5/2	5/3–7/10	7/11–7/25	7/26–8/9	8/10–8/29	8/30–11/3	11/4–11/22	11/23–12/11	1/6 12/12	1/7–3/14	3/15–4/1
1904	3/24–4/7	4/8–6/13	6/14–7/1	7/2–7/15	7/16–8/1	8/2–8/27 9/8–10/8	8/28–9/7 10/9–10/26	10/27–11/14	11/15–12/4	1/1 1/14–2/14 12/5	1/2–1/13 2/15–3/6	3/7–3/23
1905	3/16–4/1 4/29–5/15	4/2–4/28 5/16–6/8	6/9–6/22	6/23–7/7	7/8–7/26	7/27–10/1	10/2–10/18	10/19–11/7	11/8–12/1 12/10	2/28 12/2–12/9	2/9–2/27	2/28–3/15

103

PLACE OF MERCURY—1906-1917

	ARIES	TAURUS	GEMINI	CANCER	LEO	VIRGO	LIBRA	SCORPIO	SAGITT.	CAPRI.	AQUAR.	PISCES
1906	3/8–5/14	5/15–5/31	6/1–6/14	6/15–6/30	7/1–9/7	9/8–9/23	9/24–10/11	10/12–11/1 12/7–12/12	11/2–12/6 12/13 ⤴1/12	1/13–2/1	2/2–2/19	2/20–3/7
1907	3/4–3/13 4/18–5/8	5/9–5/22	5/23–6/6	6/7–6/26 7/27–8/12	6/27–7/26 8/13–8/30	8/31–9/15	9/16–10/4	10/5–12/10	12/11–12/30 ⤴1/6	1/7–1/25 12/31 ⤴	1/26–2/11	2/12–3/3 3/14–4/17
1908	4/13–4/29	4/30–5/13	5/14–5/29	5/30–8/6	8/7–8/21	8/22–9/11	9/8–9/28 11/2–11/11	9/29–11/1 11/12–12/13	12/4–12/22	12/23 ⤴1/18	1/19–2/4	2/5–4/12
1909	4/6–4/20	4/21–5/5	5/6–7/12	7/13–7/29	7/30–8/13	8/14–8/31	9/1–11/7	11/8–11/26	11/27–12/15	12/16 ⤴1/9	1/10–3/16	3/17–4/5
1910	3/29–4/12	4/13–4/30 6/2–6/11	5/1–6/1 6/12–7/6	7/7–7/21	7/22–8/5	8/6–8/26 9/29–10/11	8/27–9/28 10/12–10/31	11/1–11/18	11/19–12/8	12/9 ⤴1/3 1/31–2/15	1/4–1/30 2/16–3/11	3/12–3/25
1911	3/21–4/4	4/5–6/12	6/13–6/28	6/29–7/12	7/13–7/30	7/31–10/6	10/7–10/23	10/24–11/11	11/12–12/2 12/28 ⤴2/12	12/3–12/27	2/13–3/4	3/5–3/20
1912	3/12–5/16	5/17–6/4	6/5–6/18	6/19–7/3	7/4–7/25 8/21–9/10	7/26–8/20 9/11–9/27	9/28–10/15	10/16–11/4	11/5 ⤴1/14	1/15–2/6	2/7–2/24	2/25–3/11
1913	3/5–4/7 4/14–5/11	5/12–5/27	5/28–6/10	6/11–6/27	6/28–9/3	9/4–9/19	9/20–10/8	10/9–10/30 11/24–12/12	10/31–11/23 12/13 ⤴1/9	1/10–1/29	1/30–2/15	2/16–3/4 4/8–4/13
1914	4/17–5/4	5/5–5/18	5/19–6/2	6/3–8/10	8/11–8/26	8/27–9/12	9/13–10/1	10/2–12/7	12/8–12/27 ⤴1/3	1/4–1/22 12/28 ⤴	1/23–2/8	2/9–4/16
1915	4/11–4/26	4/27–5/10	5/11–5/28	5/29–8/3	8/4–8/18	8/19–9/4	9/5–9/27 10/21–11/11	9/28–10/20 11/12–11/30	12/1–12/19	12/20 ⤴1/14	1/15–2/1 2/24–3/19	2/2–2/28 3/20–4/10
1916	4/2–4/16	4/17–5/2	5/3–7/10	7/11–7/25	7/26–8/9	8/10–8/28	8/29–11/4	11/5–11/22	11/23–12/11	12/12 ⤴1/7	1/8–3/14	3/15–4/1
1917	3/25–4/8	4/9–6/14	6/15–7/2	7/3–7/17	7/18–8/2	8/3–8/26 9/15–10/9	8/27–9/14 10/10–10/27	10/28–11/15	11/16–12/5	1/10–2/14 12/6–12/31	1/2–1/17 2/15–3/8	3/9–3/24

PLACE OF MERCURY — 1918–1931

1918	3/17–4/2	4/3–6/9	6/10–6/24	6/25–7/8	7/9–7/27	7/28–10/2	10/3–10/20	10/21–11/8	11/9–12/1 12/16	1/1–2/9 12/2–12/15	2/10–2/28	3/1–3/16
1919	3/9–5/15	5/16–6/1	6/2–6/15	6/16–7/1	7/2–9/8	9/9–9/25	9/26–10/12	10/13–11/2	11/3 1/13	1/14–2/3	2/4–2/21	2/22–3/8
1920	3/3–3/19 4/18–5/8	5/9–5/23	5/24–6/6	6/7–6/26 8/3–8/9	6/27–8/2 8/10–8/31	9/1–9/16	9/17–10/4	10/5–10/30 11/11–12/10	10/31–11/10 12/11–12/30	1/8–1/27 12/31	1/28–2/13	2/14–3/2 3/20–4/17
1921	4/14–4/30	5/1–5/14	5/15–5/30	5/31–8/7	8/8–8/23	8/24–9/8	9/9–9/29	9/30–12/4	12/5–12/23	1/18 12/24–12/31	1/19–2/4	2/5–4/13
1922	4/7–4/22	4/23–5/6	5/7–5/30 6/11–7/13	5/31–6/10 7/14–7/31	8/1–8/14	8/15–9/1	9/2–9/30 10/25–11/8	10/1–10/4 11/9–11/27	11/28–12/16	1/11 12/17	1/12–2/1 2/9–3/17	2/2–2/8 3/18–4/6
1923	3/31–4/14	4/15–4/30	5/1–7/8	7/9–7/22	7/23–8/7	8/8–8/27 10/4–10/11	8/28–10/3 10/12–11/1	11/2–11/20	11/21–12/9	2/7–2/13 12/10	1/5–2/6 2/14–3/12	3/13–3/20
1924	3/22–4/5	4/6–6/12	6/13–6/29	6/30–7/13	7/14–7/30	7/31–10/6	10/7–10/24	10/25–11/11	11/12–12/2	12/3–12/31	2/14–3/4	3/5–3/21
1925	3/14–4/1 4/16–5/16	4/2–4/15 5/17–6/6	6/7–6/20	6/21–7/5	7/6–7/25 8/27–9/10	7/26–8/26 9/11–9/29	9/30–10/16	10/17–11/3	1/1–1/13 11/6	1/14–2/6	2/7–2/25	2/26–3/13
1926	3/6–5/12	5/13–5/29	5/30–6/11	6/12–6/28	6/29–9/5	9/6–9/21	9/22–10/9	10/10–10/30 11/28–12/13	10/31–11/27 12/14	1/10 1/11–1/30	1/31–2/17	2/18–3/5
1927	4/18–5/5	5/6–5/20	5/21–6/4	6/5–6/28 7/14–8/11	6/29–7/13 8/12–8/28	8/29–9/13	9/14–10/2	10/3–12/8	12/9–12/28	1/4 1/5–1/23 12/29	1/24–2/9	2/10–4/17
1928	4/11–4/26	4/27–5/10	5/11–5/28	5/29–8/4	8/5–8/19	8/20–9/5	9/6–9/27 10/25–11/10	9/28–10/24 11/11–12/1	12/2–12/20	1/16 12/21	1/17–2/2 2/29–3/17	2/3–2/28 3/18–4/10
1929	4/4–4/18	4/19–5/3	5/4–7/11	7/12–7/27	7/28–8/11	8/12–8/29	8/30–11/5	11/6–11/23	11/24–12/13	1/7 12/14	1/8–3/15	3/16–4/3
1930	3/27–4/10	4/11–4/30 5/17–6/14	5/1–5/16 6/15–7/4	7/5–7/18	7/19–8/3	8/4–8/26 9/20–10/10	8/27–9/19 10/11–10/29	10/30–11/16	11/17–12/6	1/1 1/23–2/15 12/17	1/2–1/22 2/16–3/9	3/10–3/26
1931	3/19–4/3	4/4–6/10	6/11–6/26	6/27–7/10	7/11–7/28	7/29–10/4	10/5–10/21	10/22–11/9	11/10–12/1 12/20	2/11 12/2–12/19	2/12–3/2	3/3–3/18

105

PLACE OF MERCURY—1932–1943

	ARIES	TAURUS	GEMINI	CANCER	LEO	VIRGO	LIBRA	SCORPIO	SAGITT.	CAPRI.	AQUAR.	PISCES
1932	3/10–5/15	5/16–6/2	6/3–6/16	6/17–7/1	7/2–7/27 8/10–9/8	7/28–8/9 9/9–9/25	9/26–10/13	10/14–11/2	11/3 ↰1/14	1/15–2/4	2/5–2/22	2/23–3/9
1933	3/3–3/25 4/18–5/9	5/10–5/25	5/26–6/8	6/9–6/26	6/27–9/1	9/2–9/17	9/18–10/6	10/7–10/29 11/16–12/11	10/30–11/15 12/12 ↰1/7	1/8–1/27	1/28–2/13	2/14–3/2 3/26–4/17
1934	4/15–5/2	5/3–5/16	5/17–5/31	6/1–8/9	8/10–8/24	8/25–9/9	9/10–9/30	10/1–12/5	12/6–12/25 ↰1/1	1/2–1/19 12/26 ↰	1/20–2/6	2/7–4/14
1935	4/9–4/24	4/25–5/8	5/9–5/29 6/21–7/13	5/30–6/20 7/14–8/1	8/2–8/16	8/17–9/2	9/3–9/28 10/13–11/9	9/29–10/12 11/10–11/28	11/29–12/17	12/18 ↰1/12	1/13–1/31 2/15–3/18	2/1–2/14 3/19–4/8
1936	3/31–4/14	4/15–4/30	5/1–7/8	7/9–7/23	7/24–8/7	8/8–8/27	8/28–11/1	11/2–11/20	11/21–12/9	12/10 ↰1/3	1/6–3/12	3/13–3/30
1937	3/23–4/6	4/7–6/13	6/14–6/30	7/1–7/14	7/15–7/31	8/1–10/7	10/8–10/25	10/26–11/13	11/14–12/3	12/4 ↰1/1 1/18–2/13	1/2–1/17 2/14–3/6	3/7–3/22
1938	3/15–4/1 4/24–5/16	4/2–4/23 5/17–6/8	6/9–6/22	6/23–7/6	7/7–7/26 9/3–9/10	7/27–9/2 9/11–9/30	10/1–10/18	10/19–11/6	1/7–1/12 11/7 ↰	1/13–2/8 ↰1/6	2/9–2/26	2/27–3/14
1939	3/7–5/14	5/15–5/30	5/31–6/13	6/14–6/29	6/30–9/6	9/7–9/22	9/23–10/10	10/11–10/31 12/3–12/13	11/1–12/2 12/14 ↰1/11	1/12–2/1	2/2–2/18	2/19–3/6
1940	3/4–3/7 4/17–5/6	5/7–5/21	5/22–6/4	6/5–6/26 7/21–8/11	6/27–7/20 8/12–8/28	8/29–9/13	9/14–10/2	10/3–12/9	12/10–12/28 ↰1/5	1/6–1/24 12/29 ↰	1/25–2/11	2/12–3/3 3/8–4/16
1941	4/12–4/28	4/29–5/12	5/13–5/29	5/30–8/5	8/6–8/20	8/21–9/6	9/7–9/27 10/30–11/11	9/28–10/29 11/12–12/2	12/3–12/21	12/22 ↰1/6	1/17–2/3 3/7–3/15	2/4–3/6 3/16–4/11
1942	4/5–4/20	4/21–5/4	5/5–7/12	7/13–7/28	7/29–8/12	8/13–8/30	8/31–11/6	11/7–11/25	11/26–12/14	12/15 ↰1/9	1/10–3/16	3/17–4/4
1943	3/28–4/11	4/12–4/30 5/26–6/13	5/1–5/25 6/14–7/5	7/6–7/20	7/21–8/4	8/5–8/26 9/25–10/11	8/27–9/24 10/12–10/30	10/31–11/18	11/19–12/7	1/28–2/15 12/8 ↰1/2	1/3–1/27 2/16–3/10	3/11–3/27

PLACE OF MERCURY—1944–1958

1944	3/19–4/3	4/4–6/10	6/11–6/26	6/27–7/10	7/11–7/28	7/29–10/4	10/5–10/21	10/22–11/9	11/10–12/1 12/23	↓2/12 12/22–12/22	2/13–3/2	3/3–3/18
1945	3/11–5/16	5/17–6/3	6/4–6/18	6/19–7/3	7/4–7/26 8/18–9/9	7/27–8/17 9/10–9/27	9/28–10/13	10/14–11/3	↓1/13 11/4–12/31	1/14–2/4	2/5–2/22	2/23–3/10
1946	3/4–4/1 4/17–5/11	5/12–5/26	5/27–6/9	6/10–6/27	6/28–9/3	9/4–9/19	9/20–10/7	10/8–10/29 11/21–12/12	↓1/9 10/30–11/20 12/13	1/10–1/28	1/29–2/15	2/16–3/3 4/2–4/16
1947	4/16–5/3	5/4–5/18	5/19–6/2	6/3–8/10	8/11–8/26	8/27–9/10	9/11–10/1	10/2–2/7	↓1/1 12/8–12/26	1/2–1/20 12/27	1/21–2/7	2/8–4/15
1948	4/9–4/24	4/25–5/8	5/9–5/27 6/29–7/11	5/28–6/28 7/12–8/2	8/3–8/16	8/17–9/3	9/4–9/26 10/17–11/9	9/27–10/16 11/10–11/29	11/30–12/18	↓1/13 12/19	1/14–2/1 2/20–3/17	2/2–2/19 3/18–4/8
1949	4/2–4/16	4/17–5/1	5/2–7/9	7/10–7/24	7/25–8/8	8/9–8/28	8/29–11/3	11/4–11/21	11/22–12/11	↓1/5 12/12	1/6–3/13	3/14–4/1
1950	3/25–4/7	4/8–6/14	6/15–7/2	7/3–7/16	7/17–8/1	8/2–8/27 9/10–10/9	8/28–9/9 10/10–10/26	10/27–11/14	11/15–12/4	↓1/1 1/15–2/14 12/5–12/31	2/10–2/28 2/15–3/7	3/8–3/24
1951	3/17–4/2 5/2–5/15	4/3–5/1 5/16–6/9	6/10–6/24	6/25–7/8	7/9–7/27	9/8–9/23	8/28–9/9 10/10–10/26	10/20–11/8	11/9–12/1 12/13	↓1/1 12/2–12/12	2/10–2/28	3/1–3/16
1952	3/8–5/14	5/15–5/31	6/1–6/14	6/15–6/30	7/1–9/7	9/8–9/23	9/24–10/11	10/12–11/1	11/2 ↓1/13	1/14–2/3	2/4–2/20	2/21–3/7
1953	3/3–3/15 4/18–5/8	5/9–5/23	5/24–6/6	6/7–6/26 7/29–8/11	6/27–7/28 8/12–8/30	8/31–9/15	9/16–10/4	10/5–10/31 11/7–12/10	↓1/6 11/1–11/6 12/11–12/30	1/7–1/25 12/31	1/26–2/11	2/12–3/2 3/16–4/17
1954	4/14–4/30	5/1–5/14	5/15–5/30	5/31–8/7	8/8–8/22	8/23–9/8	9/9–9/29 11/5–11/11	9/30–11/4 11/12–12/4	12/5–12/23	↓1/18 12/24	1/19–2/4	2/5–4/13
1955	4/7–4/22	4/23–5/6	5/7–7/13	7/14–7/30	7/31–8/14	8/15–9/1	9/2–11/8	11/9–11/27	11/28–12/16	↓1/10 12/17	1/11–3/17	3/18–4/6
1956	3/29–4/12	4/13–4/29	4/30–7/6	7/7–7/21	7/22–8/5	8/6–8/26 9/30–10/11	8/27–9/29 10/12–10/31	11/1–11/18	11/19–12/8	↓1/4 2/3–2/15 12/9	1/5–2/2 2/16–3/11	3/12–3/28
1957	3/21–4/4	4/5–6/12	6/13–6/28	6/29–7/12	7/13–7/30	7/31–10/6	10/7–10/23	10/24–11/11	11/12–12/2 12/29	↓2/12 12/3–12/28	2/13–3/4	3/5–3/20
1958	3/13–4/2 4/11–5/17	4/3–4/10 5/18–6/5	6/6–6/20	6/21–7/4	7/5–7/26 8/24–9/11	7/27–8/23 9/12–9/28	9/29–10/16	10/17–11/5	11/6 ↓1/14	1/15–2/6	2/7–2/24	2/25–3/12

107

PLACE OF MERCURY—1959–1969

	ARIES	TAURUS	GEMINI	CANCER	LEO	VIRGO	LIBRA	SCORPIO	SAGITT.	CAPRI.	AQUAR.	PISCES
1959	3/6–5/12	5/13–5/28	5/29–6/11	6/12–6/28	6/29–9/5	9/6–9/21	9/22–10/9	10/10–10/31 11/26–12/13	1/10 11/1–11/25 12/14	1/11–1/30	1/31–2/17	2/18–3/5
1960	4/17–5/4	5/5–5/19	5/20–6/2	6/3–7/1 7/7–8/10	7/2–7/6 8/11–8/27	8/28–9/12	9/13–10/1	10/2–12/7	1/4 12/8–12/27	1/5–1/23 12/28–12/31	1/24–2/9	2/10–4/16
1961	4/10–4/25	4/26–5/9	5/10–5/27	5/28–8/3	8/4–8/17	8/18–9/3	9/4–9/26 10/22–11/9	9/27–10/21 11/10–11/29	11/30–12/19	1/1–1/13 12/20	1/14–1/31 2/24–3/17	2/1–2/23 3/18–4/9
1962	4/3–4/17	4/18–5/2	5/3–7/10	7/11–7/25	7/26–8/9	8/10–8/28	8/29–11/4	11/5–11/22	11/23–12/11	12/12 1/6	1/7–3/14	3/15–4/2
1963	3/26–4/8	4/9–5/2 5/10–6/13	5/3–5/9 6/14–7/3	7/4–7/17	7/18–8/2	8/3–8/25 9/16–10/9	8/26–9/15 10/10–10/27	10/28–11/15	11/16–12/5	1/1 1/20–2/14 12/6	1/2–1/19 2/15–3/8	3/9–3/25
1964	3/16–4/1	4/2–7/8	7/9–7/23	7/24–7/8	7/9–7/26	7/27–10/3	10/4–10/19	10/20–11/7	11/8–11/29 12/16	2/9 11/30–12/15	2/10–2/28	2/29–3/15
1965	3/9–5/14	5/15–6/1	6/2–6/15	6/16–6/30	7/1–7/30 8/3–9/7	7/31–8/2 9/8–9/24	9/25–10/11	10/12–11/1	11/2 1/12	1/13–2/2	2/3–2/20	2/21–3/8
1966	3/3–3/21 4/17–5/8	5/9–5/23	5/24–6/6	6/7–6/25	6/26–8/31	9/1–9/16	9/17–10/4	10/5–10/29 11/13–12/10	1/6 10/30–11/12 12/11–12/31	1/7–1/26	1/27–2/12	2/13–3/2 3/22–4/16
1967	4/14–4/30	5/1–5/15	5/16–5/30	5/31–8/7	8/8–8/23	8/24–9/8	9/9–9/29	9/30–12/4	12/5–12/23	1/1–1/18 12/24	1/19–2/5	2/6–4/13
1968	4/7–4/21	4/22–5/5	5/6–5/28 6/13–7/12	5/29–6/12 7/13–7/30	7/31–8/14	8/15–8/31	9/1–9/27 10/7–11/7	9/28–10/6 11/8–11/26	11/27–12/15	1/1/11 12/16	1/12–1/31 2/11–3/16	2/1–2/10 3/17–4/6
1969	3/30–4/13	4/14–4/29	4/30–7/7	7/8–7/21	7/22–8/6	8/7–8/26 10/7–10/8	8/27–10/6 10/9–10/31	11/1–11/19	11/20–12/8	12/9 1/3	1/4–3/11	3/12–3/29

PLACE OF MERCURY—1970–1980

1970	3/22–4/5	4/6–6/12	6/13–6/29	6/30–7/13	7/14–7/30	7/31–10/6	10/7–10/24	10/25–11/12	11/13–12/2	12/3–12/31 ↑2/12	2/13–3/4	3/5–3/21
1971	3/14–3/31 4/18–5/16	4/1–4/17 5/17–6/6	6/7–6/20	6/21–7/5	7/6–7/25 8/29–9/10	7/26–8/28 9/11–9/29	9/30–10/16	10/17–11/5	1/2–1/13 11/6 ↑	1/1 1/14–2/6	2/7–2/25	2/26–3/13
1972	3/5–5/11	5/12–5/28	5/29–6/11	6/12–6/27	6/28–9/4	9/5–9/20	9/21–10/8	10/9–10/29 11/29–12/11	↑1/10 10/30–11/28 12/12 ↑	1/11–1/30	1/31–2/17	2/18–3/4
1973	4/16–5/5	5/6–5/19	5/20–6/3	6/4–6/26 7/16–8/10	6/27–7/15 8/11–8/27	8/28–9/12	9/13–10/1	10/2–12/7	↑1/3 12/8–12/27	1/4–1/22 12/28 ↑	1/23–2/8	2/9–4/15
1974	4/11–4/27	4/28–5/11	5/12–5/28	5/29–8/4	8/5–8/19	8/20–9/5	9/6–9/27 10/26–11/10	9/28–10/25 11/11–12/1	12/2–12/20	↑1/15 12/21 ↑	1/16–2/1 3/2–3/16	2/2–3/1 3/17–4/10
1975	4/5–4/18	4/19–5/3	5/4–7/11	7/12–7/27	7/28–8/11	8/12–8/29	8/30–11/5	11/6–11/24	11/25–12/13	↑1/7 12/14 ↑	1/8–3/15	3/16–4/3
1976	3/26–4/9	4/10–4/28 5/19–6/12	4/29–5/18 6/13–7/3	7/4–7/17	7/18–8/2	8/3–8/24 9/21–10/9	8/25–9/20 10/10–10/28	10/29–11/15	11/16–12/5	↑1/1 1/25–2/14 12/6 ↑	1/2–1/24 2/15–3/8	3/9–3/25
1977	3/18–4/2	4/3–6/9	6/10–6/25	6/26–7/9	7/10–7/27	7/28–10/3	10/4–10/20	10/21–11/8	11/9–11/30 12/21 ↑	↑2/9 12/1–12/20	2/10–3/1	3/2–3/17
1978	3/10–5/15	5/16–6/2	6/3–6/16	6/17–7/1	7/2–7/26 8/13–9/8	7/27–8/12 9/9–9/25	9/26–10/13	10/14–11/2	11/3 ↑	↑1/12 1/13–2/3	2/4–2/21	2/22–3/9
1979	3/3–3/27 4/17–5/9	5/10–5/25	5/26–6/8	6/9–6/26	6/27–9/1	9/2–9/17	9/18–10/6	10/7–10/29 11/18–12/11	↑1/17 10/30–11/17 12/12 ↑	1/8–1/27	1/28–2/13	2/14–3/2 3/28–4/16
1980	4/14–5/1	5/2–5/15	5/16–5/30	5/31–8/8	8/9–8/23	8/24–9/9	9/10–9/29	9/30–12/4	↑1/1 12/5–12/24	1/2–1/20 12/25–12/31	1/21–2/6	2/7–4/13

PLACE OF MERCURY—1981–1987

	ARIES	TAURUS	GEMINI	CANCER	LEO	VIRGO	LIBRA	SCORPIO	SAGITT.	CAPRI.	AQUAR.	PISCES
1981	4/8–4/23	4/24–5/7	5/8–5/27 6/22–7/11	5/28–6/21 7/12–7/31	8/1–8/15	8/16–9/1	9/2–9/26 10/13–11/8	9/27–10/12 11/9–11/27	11/28–12/16	1/1–1/11 12/17	1/12–1/30 2/16–3/16	1/31–2/15 3/17–4/7
1982	3/31–4/14	4/15–4/30	5/1–7/8	7/9–7/23	7/24–8/7	8/8–8/26	8/27–11/1	11/2–11/20	11/21–12/9	1/4 12/10–12/31	1/5–3/12	3/13–3/30
1983	3/23–4/6	4/7–6/13	6/14–6/30	7/11–7/14	7/15–7/31	8/1–8/28 9/5–10/7	8/29–9/4 10/8–10/25	10/26–11/13	11/14–12/3	1/12–2/13 12/4	1/1–1/11 2/14–3/5	3/6–3/22
1984	3/14–3/30 4/25–5/16	3/31–4/24 5/15–6/6	6/7–6/21	6/22–7/5	7/6–7/25	7/26–9/29	9/30–10/16	10/17–11/5	11/6–11/30 12/7	12/1–12/6	2/8–2/26	2/27–3/13
1985	3/6–5/12	5/13–5/29	5/30–6/12	6/13–6/28	6/29–9/5	9/6–9/21	9/22–10/9	10/10–10/30 12/4–12/11	10/31–12/3 12/12	1/11–1/31	2/1–2/17	2/18–3/5
1986	3/3–3/17 4/17–5/6	5/7–5/21	5/22–6/4	6/5–6/25 7/23–8/10	6/26–7/22 8/11–8/28	8/29–9/13	9/14–10/2	10/13–12/8	1/4 12/9–12/28	1/5–1/23 12/29	1/24–2/10	2/11–3/2 3/11–4/16
1987	4/12–4/28	4/29–5/12	5/13–5/28	5/29–8/5	8/6–8/20	8/21–9/6	9/7–9/27 10/31–11/10	9/28–10/30 11/11–12/2	12/3–12/21	1/16 12/22	1/17–2/2 3/11–3/12	2/3–3/10 3/13–4/11

PLACE OF MERCURY—1988–2000

1988	4/4–4/19	4/20–5/3	5/4–7/11	7/12–7/27	7/28–8/11	8/12–8/29	8/30–11/5	11/6–11/24	11/25–12/13	12/14– 1/9	1/10–3/15	3/16–4/3
1989	3/27–4/10	4/11–4/28 5/28–6/11	4/29–5/27 6/12–7/4	7/5–7/19	7/20–8/3	8/4–8/25 9/26–10/10	8/26–9/25 10/11–10/29	10/30–11/16	11/17–12/6	1/28–2/13 12/7– 1/1	1/2–1/27 2/14–3/9	3/10–3/26
1990	3/19–4/3	4/4–6/10	6/11–6/26	6/27–7/10	7/11–7/28	7/29–10/4	10/5–10/21	10/29–11/9	11/10–11/30 12/25–	12/1–12/24 2/10–	2/11–3/2	3/3–3/18
1991	3/11–4/15	4/16–6/3	6/4–6/18	6/19–7/3	7/4–7/25 8/19–9/9	7/26–8/18 9/10–9/26	9/27–10/14	10/15–11/3	11/4– 1/13	1/14–2/4	2/5–2/22	2/23–3/10
1992	3/3–4/2 4/14–5/9	5/10–5/25	5/26–6/8	6/9–6/26	6/27–9/2	9/3–9/18	9/19–10/6	10/7–10/28 11/21–12/11	10/29–11/20 12/12– 1/8	1/9–1/28	1/29–2/15	2/16–3/2 4/3–4/13
1993	4/15–5/2	5/3–5/17	5/18–5/31	6/1–8/9	8/10–8/25	8/26–9/10	9/11–9/29	9/30–12/5	12/6–12/25 1/2–1/20	12/26– 1/21–2/6	1/21–2/6	2/7–4/14
1994	4/9–4/24	4/25–5/8	5/9–5/27 7/2–7/9	5/28–7/1 7/10–8/2	8/3–8/16	8/17–9/2	9/3–9/26 10/19–11/9	9/27–10/18 11/10–11/28	11/29–12/18	12/19– 1/12	1/13–3/17	3/18–4/8
1995	4/2–4/16	4/17–5/1	5/2–7/9	7/10–7/24	7/25–8/8	8/9–8/27	8/28–11/3	11/14–11/21	11/22–12/10	12/11–12/31 1/5–	1/6–3/13	3/14–4/1
1996	3/24–4/6	4/7–6/12	6/13–7/1	7/2–7/15	7/16–7/31	8/1–8/25 9/12–10/7	8/26–9/11 10/8–10/25	10/26–11/13	11/14–12/3	1/17–2/13 12/4– 2/8	1/11–1/16 2/14–3/6	3/7–3/23
1997	3/15–3/31	4/1–6/7	6/8–6/22	6/23–7/7	7/8–7/25	7/26–10/1	10/2–10/18	10/19–11/6	11/7–11/29 12/13–	11/30–12/12	2/9–2/26	2/27–3/14
1998	3/8–5/13	5/14–5/31	6/1–6/14	6/15–6/29	6/30–9/6	9/7–9/23	9/24–10/10	10/11–10/31	11/1– 1/11	1/12–2/1	2/2–2/19	2/20–3/7
1999	3/2–3/17 4/17–5/7	5/8–5/22	5/23–6/5	6/6–6/25 7/31–8/9	6/26–7/30 8/10–8/30	8/31–9/15	9/16–10/4	10/5–10/29 11/9–12/9	10/30–11/8 12/10–12/30	12/31– 1/5	1/6–1/25 12/31–	1/26–2/11
2000	4/12–4/28	4/29–5/13	5/14–5/28	5/29–8/6	8/7–8/21	8/22–9/6	9/7–9/27 11/7–11/7	9/28–11/6 11/8–12/2	12/3–12/21	12/22–12/31 1/17–	1/18–2/4	2/5–4/11

YOUR MOST FREQUENT FAULT: ARIES—Haste; TAURUS—Stubbornness; GEMINI—Loquaciousness; CANCER—Inattention; LEO—Boastfulness; VIRGO—Timidity; LIBRA—Vanity; SCORPIO—Lack of sympathy; SAGITTARIUS—Sarcasm; CAPRICORN—Curiosity; AQUARIUS—Procrastination; PISCES—Self-immolation.

VENUS: LOVE AND ATTRACTION

Venus indicates how successfully (or perhaps unsuccessfully) your ego, emotions, and intellect are integrated to form your social attitudes and responses to other people, in your public as well as private relationships. Venus indicates what things you are likely to value and what you do not value, what you think is acceptable and adds to the quality of your life as well as what things are not acceptable and are to be avoided. It suggests the potential of your financial status and your luck in general.

Venus in Aries. You have a tendency to embrace enthusiastically relationships of all kinds for the sheer joy of energetic circulation. Unfortunately your penchant for undue haste when dealing with others can sometimes be interpreted as rudeness though you may have meant it as a sign of your passionate interest. You are friendly and, most of the time, attractively uncomplicated. Though you are not always discriminating in your values and relationships, your open eagerness is inspiring and contagious to those with shyer personalities, and even those who like to think they are superior may be attracted in spite of themselves to your guileless pursuit of their attentions. In some instances your lack of discrimination is more a case of not wanting to take the necessary time to make proper evaluations. You're not likely to seek a peaceful or mundane existence, preferring to be active and among people to find inspiration. Social groups you happen to be in are always a little livelier for your presence, and if you do happen to find yourself in a less than stimulating atmosphere and cannot do anything to animate this slow-moving society, you simply lose interest in the company. In more personal relationships your restlessness and impatience must be controlled, and you must learn to allow relationships to grow at their own pace, not at one that you dictate. You are an enthusiastic lover but can be very careless of your partner's feelings. Sometimes it is better to wait and find out what is wanted than to rush ahead and overwhelm others with what you think they need.

Venus in Taurus. You probably aren't the kind of person who rushes around in a social gathering slapping everyone on the back, spouting one-liners or the latest gossip. In fact, you are not likely to be very glib or talkative unless other factors in your natal chart support such behavior. You genuinely enjoy the society of others but most of the time prefer to keep a low but friendly profile. You have a somewhat pragmatic streak when it comes to other people and thus have a tendency consciously or subconsciously to make practical use of your social connections. However, your affections for the most part are deep and sincere. Friendships you establish usually last a lifetime unless a friend demonstrates serious reasons for you to lose trust in the relationship. You are not quick to lose your affection for someone, but once betrayed, you are not likely to forgive or forget. When it comes to forming close relationships, especially romantic partnerships, you don't like rushing into things or going against your instincts, and when you do, you are invariably disappointed at the outcome. You may feel more comfortable and be more successful if you take time and allow the relationship to form a solid base of mutual understanding and care slowly. You have a strong physical identification with life, and it makes you very fond of personal comfort, music, art, food, and fine wine, as well as all the other sensual delights. You not only love beautiful things for their own sake but have an appreciative eye for their monetary value as well.

114 ☉ Cancer JUNE 22–JULY 23

Venus in Gemini. Consciously or subconsciously you are likely to be an accomplished flirt. It would be a mistake to accuse you of being emotionally shallow because other factors in your natal chart account for the depth of your emotional commitment. However, when it comes to purely social relationships, you are remarkably instinctive and adept at small talk and flattery. The influence of Gemini indicates that your physical pleasure in relationships is never as satisfying (at least in the long run) as the intellectual one you experience through interaction with others. Circulating and getting to know everybody and everything that is going on are far more to your liking than becoming too physically or emotionally intense. You derive a great deal of inspiration from having a wide variety of relationships with different kinds of people from vastly different backgrounds and experiences from your own. Anything or anyone new or different immediately gains your interest. You have a wonderful sense of humor and a sharp and ready wit, and you don't mind being teased, a good thing, too, because you're a big tease yourself. If other factors in your chart support it, you are also an excellent ad-libber or extemporaneous speaker. You're apt to have subscriptions to many magazines and more than likely can't pass a bookstore without at least going in to see what's on the sale table. You can develop your skills with people and become a superior organizer or networker for various groups. You are also likely to have talent in writing, teaching, sales, and all areas that involve communication and information.

Venus in Cancer. When it comes to socializing, you are likely to derive the most pleasure from family gatherings, and entertaining other people in your home is high on the list of your favorite ways to socialize. You are almost sure to place great value on and take interest in domestic and family life unless other factors in your natal chart interfere with this proclivity. Even if you prefer to remain unmarried, you will probably keep a cozy, well-managed home and will remain responsive to the needs and welfare of your parents or siblings even if you don't reside with them.

Venus in Cancer in your horoscope indicates good relationships with young children, primarily because you instinctively know how to amuse them and play games with them on their own level rather than as an adult. You are sensitive but not particularly shy in taking the initiative in establishing relationships with those who interest you for either personal or business reasons. And when you do want to connect personally with people, your usual approach is likely to be that of putting them at ease by treating them just like family members. You can sometimes go to extremes in your attitudes, but your normal response to others, especially to those close to you, is usually one of warmth and caring. You can also become too possessive and jealous at times, driving away the very people you care for the most. You like to collect things, especially household items and antiques, and you may have a special interest in history and genealogy.

Venus in Leo. It shouldn't take much to stimulate your interest and participation in being with others and, in the process, gaining many friends and acquaintances. The enthusiastic people-oriented qualities of Venus in Leo contribute some very outgoing, magnanimous elements to your social attitudes and behavior, and unless problems in your background and upbringing have seriously interfered with the development of these positive traits, life can be a grand adventure for you. It must not be forgotten that there is also sure to be a measure of ego involvement in the establishment of your social relationships. You may have a tendency to be overly impressed with status. Consciously or subconsciously you recognize a certain pecking order in social relationships and in social situations (and for the good of everyone concerned you had better not be placed at the bottom of the list). Whatever the social situation happens to be, you like to play a dominant role. However, no matter how gregarious or overdramatic you seem in superficial social situations, when it comes to personal relationships, you place great value on sincerity and loyalty. You have a generous, philanthropic attitude toward society in general and, given the opportunity, will achieve much for charitable and other worthwhile causes. You are likely to show special talent for or at least interest in art or design. You may also have a particular gift for public relations, promotion, fund-raising, and organization. Though you may be a bit of a spendthrift when it comes to personal finances, you may have a flair for economics, speculative ventures, and banking.

Venus in Virgo. You tend to be inhibited in social gatherings, especially when you are unfamiliar with all or most of the people. You are not particularly good at or perhaps even willing to engage in small talk or at spontaneously introducing yourself. However, you are by no means antisocial, and you respond positively to those who go out of their way to put you at ease and to those with similar interests or with whom you can quickly find some kind of personal identification, such as people who may also be shy or possess some other readily observable link to you. If you are unable to make any such personal contacts, you are likely to find yourself cleaning the ashtrays or reading the titles of books on a shelf while trying to think of a way to beat a hasty retreat. When confronted with intensely personal contacts, you're apt to withdraw immediately to a safe distance. Of course, if you are just as interested in connecting with someone as he or she appears to be in connecting with you, you hope the other person will understand that your facade of shyness is merely to gain some time to analyze the situation. When given such time, you are able to feel more comfortable and in control. It is then that matters can proceed to a more personal level. When it comes to friends, you tend to be a loyal and caring partner, but your sympathy leaves you vulnerable to being exploited. Knowing this leaves you little choice but to limit your close relationships to very few.

Venus in Libra. Relationships and interaction with others are important to you, and you tend to approach these matters with a certain intellectual interest and objectivity rather than a spontaneous emotional outpouring. You are not particularly shy, but whether or not you go out of your way to grab the social spotlight depends on the support of other factors in your natal chart. You may have a natural flair for knowing how to treat others and in the process get them to cooperate. However, you can sometimes be quite manipulative in going about selecting those with whom you wish to associate. It doesn't mean that your friendship when offered is insincere or shallow; it just means that you may have more than one motive for establishing associations with others and that you go about it in such a charming manner that other people may not always be aware of the true reason for your interest. The social graces and mannerisms that you develop are not likely to be so flirtatious as to be obvious but are probably flattering enough for you to be eagerly sought after by others. When it comes to close personal relationships, you have a very romantic nature, though you may not be consistently passionate. If you are unable to establish intellectual rapport with someone, you are not even likely to get to the romantic stage. You are very likely to have talent for music or art with natal Venus in Libra. You may also have interest in the law, literature, public relations, or design (particularly in the area of jewelry, home decoration, or flowers).

Venus in Scorpio. Your social attitudes and behavior are influenced primarily by emotional need rather than a sense of practicality or expediency, even though these factors are an important part of why you eventually hold on to or let go of relationships and associations. You are not usually shy and, in fact, may be quite gregarious, but how much public attention you actually seek is determined by other factors in your natal chart. It is likely, however, you'll be interested in controlling social groups and their activities more in a behind-the-scenes manner than by being an obvious leader. You have a strongly passionate nature that you must control if you wish to avoid letting possessiveness, obsessiveness, or jealousy destroy your personal as well as business associations. Even if you are outwardly easygoing, you may consciously or subconsciously try to control relationships. Most of your interactions with others, even fleeting or superficial ones, are tinged with a certain intensity. When people get your attention for any reason, you really tend to focus on them; that can be very disconcerting to some people while very flattering to others. Your social instincts and behavior are remarkably keen, direct, and purposeful. You are usually not one to mince words or engage in idle flattery unless you have some definite purpose. You are intrigued by people who radiate an aura of mystery about themselves, and you may enjoy creating the same type of illusion about your own public image. Secret societies, finance, research and investigation, use of resources, and psychology are areas that attract your interest and participation.

Venus in Sagittarius. Your social attitudes, behavior, and expressions are more than likely to exhibit the essential honesty that is traditionally associated with Sagittarius. However, it is also possible that your sense of social tact and diplomacy is sadly missing at times. When thinking that you're just being truthful, you blurt out statements that could have been softened by a little more discreet phraseology. However, those who know you well will sooner or later accept a certain bluntness as part of your charm and perhaps even come to appreciate the honesty with which your words were intended rather than object to the way they were phrased. Not only are you yourself likely to be very honest, but honesty and sincerity are two traits you value highly in others. You are friendly and outgoing and can easily win many friends and acquaintances. You are idealistic and can be easily hurt by others who fail to respond to a relationship in the same way you do. For this reason, uncomplicated friendships are easier for you to handle than deeply passionate entanglements that, more often than not, leave you feeling hurt and confused. Your idealism makes you passionate to a certain extent, but how much sustained physical action that passion translates into will depend on other factors in your natal chart. You have a good sense of humor and a quick wit. You are apt to be interested in religion, politics, publishing, higher education, and international travel. Some of your best friends as well as your marriage partner may be from a race or culture different from your own.

Venus in Capricorn. You will often encounter the restrictive influence of Venus in Capricorn in dealing with various romantic entanglements. Either you have some inhibition or reservation, or your partner may be afflicted with some impediment, but more often than not, something comes along to restrict the emotional freedom in your romantic relationships. Nor can your social attitudes and behavior be said to be altogether glib or spontaneous, even though you may truly enjoy social gatherings. Perhaps you are shy, or perhaps your cautious nature makes you feel more comfortable in situations and relationships in which social intercourse is rather formal, purposeful, and to some extent, calculated. Whether or not you consciously realize it, this type of restricted societal approach helps remove the possibility of any sort of rejection, which is something you wish to avoid at all cost. No matter how easygoing or strong your outer personality may appear, it is likely that underneath, you harbor a certain amount of personal insecurity when it comes to interacting with others. It is possible that you will marry someone older or more mature than you or that you will marry rather late in life. Whether or not you actually intend this to be so, you nevertheless want to make some practical use of your social connections—that is, to realize some personal advancement. However, you are not totally self-serving in this respect since you may be just as willing to help a friend in the same way. In fact, you can be a reliable source of mutual favors and benefits to your friends.

Venus in Aquarius. You have wide-ranging social attitudes and behavioral patterns. For you, a restricted code of social acceptability does not exist, and you eagerly accept all types of people into your social circle. As a matter of fact, as far as you are concerned, it's a case of the more, the merrier and perhaps the more different, the better, for you have such an eclectic social nature that you truly appreciate and value the uniqueness of those of different cultures or backgrounds. You are a people-oriented individual who would suffer if denied access to a telephone and who has no trouble attracting many friends and acquaintances. Though you tend to have a less than passionate approach to relationships, no one denies your fierce loyalty. As a romantic partner you may not demonstrate sustained passion, but your interest will be steady and faithful. It's difficult to predict whether your attitude toward love and marriage will be traditional or you will rebel against accepted practices. Either attitude would be perfectly within the framework of Venus in Aquarius. You may marry suddenly or unexpectedly, and your choice of marriage partner may be considered (at least by others) somewhat out of the ordinary. It is also possible you will end up marrying a friend. Your passions may be confined to dealing with life on a higher plane. You get very concerned, for example, when aroused by humanitarian principles or spiritual zeal. You are apt to be a good fund-raiser and organizer and excellent at public relations and to have a facility for international finance or diplomacy.

Venus in Pisces. You will interact with others according to your emotional background, and though you can try to overcome any negative influence from childhood, it will be especially difficult to do so if that influence was sustained throughout your developing years. Your social attitudes and behavior are also profoundly influenced by your emotional state at any given time, so that when you are unhappy, you are apt to retreat, while at other times you can be open and gregarious. Though the Piscean influence generally indicates a certain natural shyness, you are apt to love having lots of other people around. However, it must be said that you are vulnerable to those around you and, as a result, need to spend a certain time alone or have a private spot to retreat to in order to restore your equilibrium and sort out the various influences you have encountered each day. You can be severely hurt if a relationship does not go well, and as a result, you may be more than a little timid when it comes to attempting new associations. Discrimination in selecting relationships can be difficult for you because of your compassionate, idealistic nature. You effortlessly seem to attract a lot of people, who then proceed to take advantage of you. You have an active imagination and can become a fantastic storyteller or writer. You are sensitive to (and perhaps talented in) music and art and may be especially fond of dance and theater. It is also possible that your marriage partner may be in one of these fields.

How to Find the Place of Venus in Your Chart

Find your year in the left-hand column and read across the chart until you find your birth date. The top of that column will tell you where Venus lies in your chart.

PLACE OF VENUS—1880–1891

	ARIES	TAURUS	GEMINI	CANCER	LEO	VIRGO	LIBRA	SCORPIO	SAGITT.	CAPRI.	AQUAR.	PISCES
1880	4/14–5/7	5/8–6/1	6/2–6/25	6/26–7/20	7/21–8/13	8/14–9/6	9/7–9/30	1/1–1/4 10/1–10/25	1/5–1/30 10/26–11/18	1/31–2/24 11/19–12/13	2/25–3/19 12/14–12/31	3/20–4/13
1881	2/3–3/3	3/4–7/7	7/8–8/5	8/6–9/1	9/2–9/27	9/28–10/21	10/22–11/14	11/15–12/8	12/9–12/31		1/1–1/7	1/8–2/2
1882	3/15–4/7	4/8–5/2	5/3–5/26	5/27–6/20	6/21–7/15	7/16–8/10	8/11–9/6	9/7–10/6	1/1 10/7–12/31	1/2–1/25	1/26–2/18	2/19–3/14
1883	4/28–5/22	5/23–6/16	6/17–7/11	7/12–8/4	8/5–8/29	8/30–9/22	9/23–10/16	10/17–11/9	1/1–2/4 11/10–12/3	2/5–3/6 12/4–12/27	3/7–4/1 12/28–12/31	4/2–4/27
1884	2/15–3/10	3/11–4/5	4/6–5/4	5/5–9/7	9/8–10/7	10/8–11/3	11/4–11/28	11/29–12/22	12/23–12/31		1/1–1/20	1/21–2/14
1885	3/30–4/22	4/23–5/16	5/17–6/10	6/11–7/4	7/5–7/29	7/30–8/23	8/24–9/16	9/17–10/12	1/1–1/16 10/13–11/6	1/17–2/9 11/7–12/4	2/10–3/5 12/5–12/31	3/6–3/29
1886	5/7–6/3	6/4–6/29	6/30–7/25	7/26–8/19	8/20–9/12	9/13–10/7	10/8–10/31	11/1–11/23	11/24–12/17	12/18–12/31	1/1–1/6 2/19–4/1	1/7–2/18 4/2–5/6
1887	2/28–3/24	3/25–4/17	4/18–5/13	5/14–6/8	6/9–7/6	7/7–8/11 9/19–11/5	8/12–9/18 11/6–12/8	12/9–12/31		1/1–1/10	1/11–2/3	2/4–2/27
1888	4/13–5/7	5/8–5/31	6/1–6/25	6/26–7/19	7/20–8/12	8/13–9/6	9/7–9/30	1/1–1/4 10/1–10/24	1/5–1/29 10/25–11/18	1/30–2/23 11/19–12/12	2/24–3/19 12/13–12/31	3/20–4/12
1889	2/3–3/4	3/5–7/7	7/8–8/5	8/6–9/1	9/2–9/26	9/27–10/21	10/22–11/14	11/15–12/8	12/9–12/31		1/1–1/6	1/7–2/2
1890	3/15–4/7	4/8–5/1	5/2–5/26	5/27–6/20	6/21–7/15	7/16–8/10	8/11–9/6	9/7–10/7	1/1 10/8–12/31	1/2–1/25	1/26–2/18	2/19–3/14
1891	4/27–5/22	5/23–6/16	6/17–7/10	7/11–8/4	8/5–8/28	8/29–9/21	9/22–10/15	10/16–11/8	1/1–2/5 11/9–12/2	2/6–3/5 12/3–12/26	3/6–4/1 12/27–12/31	4/2–4/26

PLACE OF VENUS—1892-1906

1892	2/14-3/9	3/10-4/4	4/5-5/4	5/5-9/7	9/8-10/7	10/8-11/2	11/3-11/27	11/28-12/22	12/23-12/31		1/1-1/20	1/21-2/13
1893	3/29-4/22	4/23-5/16	5/17-6/9	6/10-7/4	7/5-7/28	7/29-8/22	8/23-9/16	9/17-10/11	1/1-1/15 10/12-11/6	1/16-2/8 11/7-12/4	2/9-3/4 12/5-12/31	3/5-3/28
1894	5/5-6/2	6/3-6/29	6/30-7/24	7/25-8/18	8/19-9/12	9/13-10/6	10/7-10/30	10/31-11/23	11/24-12/17	12/18-12/31	1/1-1/8 2/13-4/2	1/9-2/12 4/3-5/4
1895	2/28-3/23	3/24-4/17	4/18-5/12	5/13-6/7	6/8-7/6	7/7-8/13 9/13-11/6	8/14-9/12 11/7-12/8	12/9-12/31		1/1-1/10	1/11-2/3	2/4-2/27
1896	4/13-5/6	5/7-5/31	6/1-6/24	6/25-7/19	7/20-8/12	8/13-9/5	9/6-9/29	1/1-1/3 9/30-10/24	1/4-1/29 10/25-11/17	1/30-2/23 11/18-12/12	2/24-3/18 12/13-12/31	3/19-4/12
1897	2/2-3/4	3/5-7/7	7/8-8/5	8/6-8/31	9/1-9/26	9/27-10/20	10/21-11/13	11/14-12/7	12/8-12/31		1/1-1/6	1/7-2/1
1898	3/14-4/6	4/7-5/1	5/2-5/25	5/26-6/19	6/20-7/14	7/15-8/10	8/11-9/16	9/7-10/7	10/8-12/31	1/1-1/24	1/25-2/17	2/18-3/13
1899	4/27-5/21	5/22-6/15	6/16-7/10	7/11-8/3	8/4-8/28	8/29-9/21	9/22-10/15	10/16-11/8	1/1-2/5 11/9-12/2	2/6-3/5 12/3-12/26	3/6-3/31 12/27-12/31	4/1-4/26
1900	2/14-3/10	3/11-4/5	4/6-5/5	5/6-9/8	9/9-10/8	10/9-11/3	11/4-11/28	11/29-12/22	12/23-12/31		1/1-1/19	1/20-2/13
1901	3/30-4/22	4/23-5/16	5/17-6/10	6/11-7/4	7/5-7/29	7/30-8/23	8/24-9/16	9/17-10/12	1/1-1/15 10/13-11/7	1/16-2/9 11/8-12/5	2/10-3/5 12/6-12/31	3/6-3/29
1902	5/7-6/3	6/4-6/29	6/30-7/25	7/26-8/19	8/20-9/12	9/13-10/7	10/8-10/30	10/31-11/23	11/24-12/17	12/18-12/31	1/1-1/11 2/7-4/4	1/12-2/6 4/5-5/6
1903	2/28-3/23	3/24-4/17	4/18-5/13	5/14-6/8	6/9-7/7	7/8-8/17 9/7-11/8	8/18-9/6 11/19-12/9	12/10-12/31		1/1-1/10	1/11-2/3	2/4-2/27
1904	4/13-5/7	5/8-5/31	6/1-6/25	6/26-7/19	7/20-8/12	8/13-9/6	9/7-9/30	1/1-1/4 10/1-10/24	1/5-1/29 10/25-11/18	1/30-2/23 11/19-12/12	2/24-3/19 12/13-12/31	3/20-4/12
1905	2/3-3/5 5/9-5/27	3/6-5/8 5/28-7/7	7/8-8/5	8/6-9/1	9/2-9/26	9/27-10/21	10/22-11/14	11/15-12/8	12/9-12/31		1/1-1/7	1/8-2/2
1906	3/15-4/7	4/8-5/1	5/2-5/26	5/27-6/20	6/21-7/15	7/16-8/10	8/11-9/7	9/8-10/8 12/16-12/25	1/1 10/9-12/15 12/26-12/31	1/2-1/25	1/26-2/18	2/19-3/14

123

PLACE OF VENUS—1907-1916

	ARIES	TAURUS	GEMINI	CANCER	LEO	VIRGO	LIBRA	SCORPIO	SAGITT.	CAPRI.	AQUAR.	PISCES
1907	4/28-5/22	5/23-6/16	6/17-7/10	7/11-8/3	8/4-8/28	8/29-9/21	9/22-10/15	10/16-11/8	1/1-2/6 11/9-12/2	2/7-3/6 12/3-12/26	3/7-4/1 12/27-12/31	4/2-4/27
1908	2/14-3/9	3/10-4/5	4/6-5/5	5/6-9/8	9/9-10/7	10/8-11/2	11/3-11/27	11/28-12/22	12/23-12/31		1/1-1/20	1/21-2/13
1909	3/29-4/21	4/22-5/16	5/17-6/9	6/10-7/4	7/5-7/28	7/29-8/22	8/23-9/16	9/17-10/11	1/1-1/15 10/12-11/6	1/16-2/8 11/7-12/5	2/9-3/3 12/6-12/31	3/4-3/28
1910	5/7-6/3	6/4-6/29	6/30-7/24	7/25-8/18	8/19-9/12	9/13-10/6	10/7-10/30	10/31-11/23	11/24-12/17	12/18-12/31	1/1-1/15 1/29-4/4	1/16-1/28 4/5-5/6
1911	2/28-3/23	3/24-4/17	4/18-5/12	5/13-6/8	6/9-7/7	7/8-11/8	11/9-12/8	12/9-12/31			1/11-2/2	2/3-2/27
1912	4/13-5/6	5/7-5/31	6/1-6/24	6/25-7/18	7/19-8/12	8/13-9/5	9/6-9/30	1/1-1/4 9/31-10/24	1/5-1/29 10/25-11/17	1/30-2/23 11/18-12/12	2/24-3/18 12/13-12/31	3/19-4/12
1913	2/3-3/6 5/2-5/30	3/7-5/1 5/31-7/7	7/8-8/5	8/6-8/31	9/1-9/26	9/27-10/20	10/21-11/13	11/14-12/7	12/8-12/31		1/1-1/6	1/7-2/2
1914	3/14-4/6	4/7-5/1	5/2-5/25	5/26-6/19	6/20-7/15	7/16-8/10	8/11-9/6	9/7-10/9 12/6-12/30	10/10-12/5 12/31	1/1-1/24	1/25-2/17	2/18-3/13
1915	4/27-5/21	5/22-6/15	6/16-7/10	7/11-8/3	8/4-8/28	8/29-9/21	9/22-10/15	10/16-11/8	1/1-2/6 11/9-12/2	2/7-3/6 12/3-12/26	3/7-4/1 12/27-12/31	4/2-4/26
1916	2/14-3/9	3/10-4/5	4/6-5/5	5/6-9/8	9/9-10/7	10/8-11/2	11/3-11/27	11/28-12/21	12/22-12/31		1/1-1/19	1/20-2/13

PLACE OF VENUS—1917–1931

1917	3/29–4/21	4/22–5/15	5/16–6/9	6/10–7/3	7/4–7/28	7/29–8/21	8/22–9/16	9/17–10/11	1/1–1/14 10/12–11/6	1/15–2/7 11/7–12/5	2/8–3/4 12/6–12/31	3/5–3/28
1918	5/7–6/2	6/3–6/28	6/29–7/24	7/25–8/18	8/19–9/11	10/6–10/29	11/9–12/8	10/30–11/22	11/23–12/16	12/17–12/31	1/1–4/5	4/6–5/6
1919	2/27–3/22	3/23–4/16	4/17–5/12	5/13–6/7	6/8–7/7	7/8–11/8	11/9–12/8	12/9–12/31		1/1–1/9	1/10–2/2	2/3–2/26
1920	4/12–5/6	5/7–5/30	5/31–6/23	6/24–7/18	7/19–8/11	8/12–9/4	9/5–9/30	1/1–1/3 9/31–10/23	1/4–1/28 10/24–11/17	1/29–2/22 11/18–12/11	2/23–3/18 12/12–12/31	3/19–4/11
1921	2/3–3/6 4/26–6/1	3/7–4/25 6/2–7/7	7/8–8/5	8/6–8/31	9/1–9/25	9/26–10/20	10/21–11/13	11/14–12/7	12/8–12/31		1/1–1/6	1/7–2/2
1922	3/13–4/6	4/7–4/30	5/1–5/25	5/26–6/19	6/20–7/14	7/15–8/9	8/10–9/6	9/7–10/10 11/29	10/11–11/28	1/1–1/24	1/25–2/16	2/17–3/12
1923	4/27–5/21	5/22–6/14	6/15–7/9	7/10–8/3	8/4–8/27	8/28–9/20	9/21–10/14	1/1 10/15–11/7	1/2–2/6 11/8–12/1	2/7–3/5 12/2–12/25	3/6–3/31 12/26	4/1–4/26
1924	2/13–3/8	3/9–4/4	4/5–5/5	5/6–9/8	9/9–10/7	10/8–11/2	11/3–11/26	11/27–12/21	12/22		1/19	1/20–2/12
1925	3/28–4/20	4/21–5/15	5/16–6/8	6/9–7/3	7/4–7/27	7/28–8/21	8/22–9/15	9/16–10/11	1/14 10/12–11/6	1/15–2/7 11/7–12/5	2/8–3/3 12/6	3/4–3/27
1926	5/7–6/2	6/3–6/28	6/29–7/23	7/24–8/17	8/18–9/11	9/12–10/5	10/6–10/29	10/30–11/22	11/23–12/16	12/17	4/5	4/6–5/6
1927	2/27–3/22	3/23–4/16	4/17–5/11	5/12–6/7	6/8–7/7	7/8–11/9	11/10–12/8	12/9		1/8	1/9–2/1	2/2–2/26
1928	4/12–5/5	5/6–5/29	5/30–6/23	6/24–7/17	7/18–8/11	8/12–9/4	9/5–9/28	1/3 9/29–10/23	1/4–1/28 10/24–11/16	1/29–2/22 11/17–12/11	2/23–3/17 12/12	3/18–4/11
1929	2/3–3/7 4/20–6/2	3/8–4/19 6/3–7/7	7/8–8/4	8/5–8/30	8/31–9/25	9/26–10/19	10/20–11/12	11/13–12/6	12/7–12/30	12/31		1/6–2/2
1930	3/13–4/5	4/6–4/30	5/1–5/24	5/25–6/18	6/19–7/14	7/15–8/9	8/10–9/6	9/7–10/11 11/22	10/12–11/21		1/23	1/24–2/16	2/17–3/12
1931	4/26–5/20	5/21–6/14	6/15–7/9	7/10–8/2	8/3–8/26	8/27–9/20	9/21–10/14	1/3 10/15–11/7	1/4–2/6 11/8–12/1	2/7–3/5 12/2–12/25	3/6–3/31 12/26	4/1–4/25

125

PLACE OF VENUS—1932–1943

	ARIES	TAURUS	GEMINI	CANCER	LEO	VIRGO	LIBRA	SCORPIO	SAGITT.	CAPRI.	AQUAR.	PISCES
1932	2/13–3/8	3/9–4/4	4/5–5/5, 7/13–7/27	5/6–7/12, 7/28–9/8	9/9–10/6	10/7–11/1	11/2–11/26	11/27–12/20	12/21		1/18	1/19–2/12
1933	3/28–4/20	4/21–5/14	5/15–6/8	6/9–7/2	7/3–7/27	7/28–8/21	8/22–9/15	9/16–10/10	10/11–11/6	1/14–2/6, 11/7–12/5	2/7–3/2, 12/6	3/3–3/27
1934	5/6–6/1	6/2–6/27	6/28–7/23	7/24–8/17	8/18–9/10	9/11–10/4	10/5–10/28	10/29–11/21	11/22–12/15	12/16	4/5	4/6–5/5
1935	2/26–3/21	3/22–4/15	4/16–5/11	5/12–6/7	6/8–7/7	7/8–11/9	11/10–12/8	12/9		1/18	1/9–2/1	2/2–2/25
1936	4/11–5/4	5/5–5/29	5/30–6/22	6/23–7/17	7/18–8/10	8/11–9/3	9/4–9/28	9/29–10/22	1/4–1/28, 10/23–11/16	1/29–2/21, 11/17–12/11	2/22–3/17, 12/12	3/18–4/10
1937	2/2–3/9, 4/14–6/3	3/10–4/13, 6/4–7/7	7/8–8/4	8/5–8/30	8/31–9/24	9/25–10/19	10/20–11/12	11/13–12/6	12/7–12/30	12/31	1/5	1/6–2/1
1938	3/12–4/5	4/6–4/29	4/30–5/24	5/25–6/18	6/19–7/13	7/14–8/9	8/10–9/6	9/7–10/13, 11/16	10/14–11/15	1/22	1/23–2/15	2/16–3/11
1939	4/26–5/20	5/21–6/13	6/14–7/8	7/9–8/2	8/3–8/26	8/27–9/19	9/20–10/13	1/4, 10/14–11/6	1/5–2/5, 11/7–11/30	2/6–3/5, 12/1–12/24	3/6–3/30, 12/25	3/31–4/25
1940	2/12–3/8	3/9–4/4	4/5–5/6, 7/6–7/31	5/7–7/5, 8/1–9/8	9/9–10/6	10/7–11/1	11/2–11/26	11/27–12/20	12/21		1/18	1/19–2/11
1941	3/27–4/19	4/20–5/14	5/15–6/7	6/8–7/2	7/3–7/26	7/27–8/20	8/21–9/14	9/15–10/10	10/11–11/5	1/14–2/6, 11/6–12/5	2/7–3/2, 12/6	3/3–3/26
1942	5/6–6/1	6/2–6/27	6/28–7/22	7/23–8/16	8/17–9/10	9/11–10/4	10/5–10/28	10/29–11/21	11/22–12/15	12/16	4/6	4/7–5/5
1943	2/26–3/21	3/22–4/15	4/16–5/10	5/11–6/7	6/8–7/7	7/8–11/9	11/10–12/17	12/8		1/7	1/8–1/31	2/1–2/25

127

PLACE OF VENUS—1944–1958

1944	4/11–5/4	5/5–5/28	5/29–6/22	6/23–7/16	7/17–8/10	8/11–9/3	9/4–9/27	1/2 9/28–10/22	1/3–1/27 10/23–11/15	1/28–2/21 11/16–12/9	2/22–3/16 12/10	3/17–4/10
1945	2/2–3/10 4/8–6/4	3/11–4/7 6/5–7/7	7/8–8/3	8/4–8/30	8/31–9/24	9/25–10/18	10/19–11/11	11/12–12/5	12/6–12/29	12/30		1/5	1/6–2/1
1946	3/12–4/4	4/5–4/28	4/29–5/23	5/24–6/17	6/18–7/13	7/14–8/8	8/9–9/6	9/7–10/15 11/8	10/16–11/7		1/22	1/23–2/15	2/16–3/11
1947	4/25–5/18	5/19–6/13	6/14–7/8	7/9–7/31	8/1–8/25	8/26–9/18	9/19–10/13	1/5 10/14–11/6	1/6–2/5 11/7–11/30	2/6–3/4 12/1–12/24	3/5–3/30 12/25	3/31–4/24
1948	2/12–3/7	3/8–4/4	4/5–5/6 6/29–8/2	5/7–6/28 8/3–9/8	9/9–10/6	10/7–10/31	11/1–11/25	11/26–12/19	12/20			1/17	1/18–2/11
1949	3/26–4/19	4/20–5/13	5/14–6/6	6/7–7/1	7/2–7/26	7/27–8/20	8/21–9/14	9/15–10/9	1/12 10/10–11/4	1/13–2/5 11/5–12/5	2/6–3/1 12/6	3/2–3/25
1950	5/6–6/1	6/2–6/26	6/27–7/22	7/23–8/16	8/17–9/9	9/10–10/3	10/4–10/27	10/28–11/20	11/21–12/14	12/15–12/31		4/6	4/7–5/5
1951	2/25–3/21	3/22–4/15	4/16–5/11	5/12–6/7	6/8–7/8	7/9–11/9	11/10–12/7	12/8		1/1–1/7	1/8–1/31	2/1–2/24
1952	4/10–5/4	5/5–5/28	5/29–6/22	6/23–7/16	7/17–8/9	8/10–9/3	9/4–9/27	1/2 9/28–10/22	1/3–1/27 10/23–11/15	1/28–2/21 11/16–12/10	2/22–3/16 12/11	3/17–4/9
1953	2/3–2/14 4/1–6/5	2/15–3/31 6/6–7/7	7/8–8/4	8/5–8/30	8/31–9/24	9/25–10/18	10/19–11/11	11/12–12/5	12/6–12/29	12/30		1/5	1/6–2/2
1954	3/12–4/4	4/5–4/28	4/29–5/23	5/24–6/17	6/18–7/13	7/14–8/8	8/9–9/6	9/7–10/23 10/28	10/24–10/27		1/22	1/23–2/15	2/16–3/11
1955	4/25–5/19	5/20–6/13	6/14–7/8	7/9–8/1	8/2–8/25	8/26–9/18	9/19–10/12	1/16 10/13–11/5	1/7–2/6 11/6–11/30	2/7–3/4 12/1–12/24	3/5–3/30 12/25	3/31–4/24
1956	2/12–3/7	3/8–4/4	4/5–5/8 6/24–8/4	5/9–6/23 8/5–9/8	9/9–10/5	10/6–10/31	11/1–11/25	11/26–12/19	12/20			1/17	1/18–2/11
1957	3/26–4/19	4/20–5/13	5/14–6/6	6/7–7/1	7/2–7/26	7/27–8/19	8/20–9/14	9/15–10/9	1/12 10/10–11/4	1/13–2/5 11/5–12/6	2/6–3/1 12/7	3/2–3/25
1958	5/6–6/1	6/2–6/26	6/27–7/22	7/23–8/15	8/16–9/9	9/10–10/3	10/4–10/27	10/28–11/20	11/21–12/14	12/15		4/6	4/7–5/5

PLACE OF VENUS—1959–1969

	ARIES	TAURUS	GEMINI	CANCER	LEO	VIRGO	LIBRA	SCORPIO	SAGITT.	CAPRI.	AQUAR.	PISCES
1959	2/25–3/20	3/21–4/14	4/15–5/10	5/11–6/6	6/7–7/8 9/21–9/24	7/9–9/20 9/25–11/9	11/10–12/7	12/8 ↳		↳ 1/7	1/8–1/31	2/1–2/24
1960	4/10–5/3	5/4–5/28	5/29–6/21	6/22–7/15	7/16–8/9	8/10–9/2	9/3–9/27	9/28–10/21	1/3–1/26 10/22–11/15	1/27–2/20 11/16–12/10	2/21–3/5 12/11–12/31	3/16–4/9
1961	2/2–6/4	6/5–7/6	7/7–8/2	8/3–8/28	8/29–9/22	9/23–10/17	10/18–11/10	11/11–12/4	12/5–12/27	12/28 ↳	1/1–1/4	1/5–2/1
1962	3/10–4/2	4/3–4/27	4/28–5/22	5/23–6/16	6/17–7/11	7/12–8/7	8/8–9/5	9/6 ↳		↳ 1/20	1/21–2/13	2/14–3/9
1963	4/24–5/18	5/19–6/11	6/12–7/6	7/7–7/30	7/31–8/24	8/25–9/17	9/18–10/11	↳1/5 10/12–11/4	1/6–2/4 11/5–11/28	2/5–3/3 11/29–12/22	3/4–3/29 12/23 ↳	3/30–4/23
1964	2/10–3/6	3/7–4/3	4/4–5/8 6/17–8/4	5/9–6/16 8/5–9/7	9/8–10/4	10/5–10/30	10/31–11/24	11/25–12/18	12/19 ↳		↳ 1/16	1/17–2/9
1965	3/25–4/17	4/18–5/11	5/12–6/5	6/6–6/29	6/30–7/24	7/25–8/18	8/19–9/12	9/13–10/8	↳1/11 10/9–11/4	1/12–2/4 11/5–12/6	2/5–2/28 12/7 ↳	3/1–3/24
1966	5/5–5/30	5/31–6/25	6/26–7/20	7/21–8/14	8/15–9/7	9/8–10/2	10/3–10/26	10/27–11/19	11/20–12/12	2/6–2/24 12/13 ↳	↳2/5 2/25–4/5	4/6–5/4
1967	2/23–3/19	3/20–4/13	4/14–5/9	5/10–6/5	6/6–7/7 9/9–9/30	7/8–9/8 10/1–11/8	11/9–12/6	12/7–12/31	1/1–1/25 10/21–11/13	↳1/5	1/6–1/29	1/30–2/22
1968	4/8–5/2	5/3–5/26	5/27–6/20	6/21–7/14	7/15–8/7	8/8–9/1	9/2–9/25	9/26–10/20	1/1–1/25 10/21–11/13	1/26–2/19 11/14–12/8	2/20–3/14 12/9 ↳	3/15–4/7
1969	2/2–6/5	6/6–7/5	7/6–8/2	8/3–8/28	8/29–9/22	9/23–10/16	10/17–11/9	11/10–12/3	12/4–12/27	12/28 ↳	↳1/3	1/4–2/1

128

PLACE OF VENUS—1970–1980

1970	3/10-4/2	4/3-4/26	4/27-5/21	5/22-6/15	6/16-7/11	7/12-8/7	8/8-9/6	9/7-12/31		↙1/20	1/21-2/13	2/14-3/9
1971	4/23-5/17	5/18-6/11	6/12-7/5	7/6-7/31	8/1-8/23	8/24-9/16	9/17-10/10	1/1-1/6 10/11-11/4	1/7-2/4 11/15-11/28	2/5-3/3 11/29-12/22	3/4-3/28 12/23↰	3/29-4/22
1972	2/10-3/7	3/8-4/2	4/3-5/9 6/11-8/5	5/10-6/10 8/6-9/6	9/7-10/4	10/5-10/29	10/30-11/23	11/24-12/17	12/8↰		↙1/15	1/16-2/9
1973	3/24-4/17	4/18-5/11	5/12-6/4	6/5-6/29	6/30-7/24	7/25-8/18	8/19-9/12	9/13-10/8	↙1/10 10/9-11/4	1/11-2/3 11/5-12/16	2/4-2/27 12/7↰	2/28-3/23
1974	5/4-5/30	5/31-6/24	6/25-7/20	7/21-8/13	8/14-9/7	9/8-10/1	10/2-10/25	10/26-11/18	11/19-12/12	1/29-2/27 12/13↰	2/28-4/5	4/6-5/3
1975	2/23-3/18	3/19-4/12	4/13-5/8	5/9-6/5	6/6-7/8 9/2-10/3	7/9-9/1 10/4-11/8	11/9-12/6	12/7-12/31		↙1/5	1/6-1/29	1/30-2/22
1976	4/8-5/1	5/2-5/26	5/27-6/19	6/20-7/13	7/14-8/7	8/8-8/31	9/1-9/25	9/26-10/19	1/11-1/25 10/20-11/13	1/26-2/18 11/14-12/8	2/19-3/14 12/19↰	3/15-4/7
1977	2/2-6/5	6/6-7/5	7/6-8/1	8/2-8/27	8/28-9/21	9/22-10/16	10/17-11/9	11/10-12/3	12/4-12/26	12/27↰	↙1/3	1/4-2/1
1978	3/9-4/1	4/2-4/26	4/27-5/21	5/22-6/15	6/16-7/11	7/12-8/7	8/8-9/6	9/7	↙1/19	↙1/19	1/20-2/12	2/13-3/8
1979	4/23-5/17	5/18-6/10	6/11-7/5	7/6-7/29	7/30-8/23	8/24-9/16	9/17-10/10	1/6 10/11-11/3	1/7-2/4 11/4-11/27	2/5-3/2 11/28-12/21	3/3-3/28 12/22↰	3/29-4/22
1980	2/9-3/5	3/6-4/2	4/3-5/11 6/5-8/5	5/12-6/4 8/6-9/6	9/7-10/3	10/4-10/29	10/30-11/23	11/24-12/17	12/18-12/31		↙1/15	1/16-2/8

129

PLACE OF VENUS—1981–1987

	ARIES	TAURUS	GEMINI	CANCER	LEO	VIRGO	LIBRA	SCORPIO	SAGITT.	CAPRI.	AQUAR.	PISCES
1981	3/24–4/16	4/17–5/10	5/11–6/4	6/5–6/28	6/29–7/23	7/24–8/17	8/18–9/11	9/12–10/7	1/1–1/10 10/8–11/4	1/11–2/3 11/5–12/7	2/4–2/27 12/8–	2/28–3/23
1982	5/4–5/29	5/30–6/24	6/25–7/19	7/20–8/13	8/14–9/6	9/7–9/30	10/1–10/24	10/25–11/17	11/18–12/11	1/22–3/1 12/12–	–1/21 3/2–4/5	4/6–5/3
1983	2/22–3/18	3/19–4/12	4/13–5/8	5/9–6/5	6/6–7/9 8/27–10/4	7/10–8/26 10/5–11/8	11/9–12/5	12/6–12/30	12/31–	–1/4	1/5–1/28	1/29–2/21
1984	4/7–4/30	5/1–5/25	5/26–6/18	6/19–7/13	7/14–8/6	8/7–8/31	9/1–9/24	9/25–10/19	–1/24 10/20–11/12	1/25–2/17 11/13–12/7	2/18–3/13 12/8–	3/14–4/6
1985	2/2–6/5	6/6–7/5	7/6–8/1	8/2–8/26	8/27–9/20	9/21–10/15	10/16–11/8	11/9–12/2	12/3–12/26	12/27–	–1/3	1/4–2/1
1986	3/8–4/1	4/2–4/25	4/26–5/20	5/21–6/14	6/15–7/10	7/11–8/6	8/7–9/6	9/7–	–1/6 10/10–11/2	–1/19 2/4–3/2	1/20–2/11	2/12–3/7
1987	4/22–5/16	5/17–6/10	6/11–7/6	7/5–7/29	7/30–8/22	8/23–9/15	9/16–10/9	10/10–11/2	1/7–2/3 11/3–11/26	2/4–3/2 11/27–12/21	3/3–3/27 12/22–	3/28–4/21

PLACE OF VENUS—1988–2000

1988	2/9–3/5	3/6–4/2	4/3–5/16 5/27–8/5	5/17–5/26 8/6–9/6	9/7–10/3	10/4–10/28	10/29–11/22	11/23–12/16	12/17	1/10–2/2 11/5–12/8	1/14 2/3–2/26 12/9	1/15–2/8 2/27–3/22
1989	3/23–4/15	4/16–5/10	5/11–6/3	6/4–6/28	6/29–7/22	7/23–8/16	8/17–9/11	9/12–10/7	10/8–11/4 1/9	11/5–12/8 1/16–3/2	12/9 1/15 3/3–4/5	4/6–5/2
1990	5/3–5/29	5/30–6/23	6/24–7/18	7/19–8/12	8/13–9/6	9/7–9/30	10/1–10/24	10/25–11/17	11/18–12/11	1/16–3/2 12/12	3/3–4/5 1/4	1/5–1/27
1991	2/22–3/17	3/18–4/11	4/12–5/7	5/8–6/4	6/5–7/10 8/21–10/5	7/11–8/20 10/6–11/8	11/9–12/5	12/6–12/30	12/31 1/24	1/4 1/25–2/17 11/13–12/7	2/18–3/12 12/8 1/2	3/13–4/6
1992	4/7–4/30	5/1–5/24	5/25–6/18	6/19–7/12	7/13–8/6	8/7–8/30	8/31–9/23	9/24–10/18	10/19–11/12	11/13–12/7	12/8 1/2	1/3–2/1
1993	2/2–6/5	6/6–7/4	7/5–7/31	8/1–8/26	8/27–9/20	9/21–10/14	10/15–11/7	11/8–12/1	12/2–12/25	12/26 1/18	1/19–2/11	2/12–3/7
1994	3/8–3/31	4/1–4/25	4/26–5/19	5/20–6/14	6/15–7/10	7/11–8/6	8/7–9/6	9/7 1/6	10/10–11/2	2/4–3/1 11/27–12/20	3/2–3/27 12/21	3/28–4/20
1995	4/21–5/15	5/16–5/9	5/10–7/4	7/5–7/28	7/29–8/21	8/22–9/15	9/16–10/9	10/10–11/2	11/3–11/26	11/27–12/20	12/21 1/13	1/14–2/7
1996	2/8–3/4	3/5–4/2	4/3–8/6	8/7–9/6	9/7–10/2	10/3–10/28	10/29–11/21	11/22–12/16	12/17 1/9	1/10–2/1 11/5–12/10	2/2–2/25 12/11	2/26–3/22
1997	3/23–4/15	4/16–5/9	5/10–6/2	6/3–6/27	6/28–7/22	7/23–8/16	8/17–9/10	9/11–10/7	10/8–11/4	11/5–12/10	12/11 1/8	4/6–5/2
1998	5/3–5/28	5/29–6/23	6/24–7/18	7/19–8/12	8/13–9/5	9/6–9/29	9/30–10/23	10/24–11/16	11/17–12/10	1/9–3/3 12/11	3/4–4/5	4/6–5/2
1999	2/21–3/17	3/18–4/11	4/12–5/7	5/8–6/4	6/5–7/11 8/15–10/6	7/12–8/14 10/7–11/7	11/8–12/4	12/5–12/29	12/30 1/23	1/3 1/24–2/16 11/12–12/7	1/4–1/27	1/28–2/20
2000	4/6–4/29	4/30–5/24	5/25–6/17	6/18–7/12	7/13–8/5	8/6–8/29	8/30–9/23	9/24–10/18	10/19–11/11	1/24–2/16 11/12–12/7	2/17–3/12 12/8–12/30	3/13–4/5

YOUR MOST CONSPICUOUS TRAIT: ARIES—Courage; TAURUS—Fortitude; GEMINI—Alertness; CANCER—Loyalty: LEO-Magnanimity; VIRGO—Efficiency; LIBRA-Friendliness; SCORPIO—Determination; SAGITTARIUS-Fidelity; CAPRICORN-Sincerity; AQUARIUS-Cooperation; PISCES-Compassion.

MARS: THE SPARK OF LIFE

Mars is that spark of desire, of passion, the impetus to action that puts us out there in life, doing, acting, being ourselves, putting ourselves forward. It is that first impulse we have—acted upon or not—to connect deeply with another person, to make a move in a situation, or to change a circumstance we are in by taking steps to move out of what is and create what we want things to be.

The placement of Mars in our charts lets us know just how our sexuality is experienced and expressed, the way in which we take action, and what our motivation is in doing what we do. It points to where the life-force is most evident in our lives and where we need to take action to feel alive, vital, and connected with our inner source of being.

Passion and our individual manner of expressing it in our lives—not just sexually but in all that we do—are the domain of Mars. Its symbol is the same as the one for masculine energy, for it represents acting upon, initiating, and overtly expressing our human need to put ourselves forward in ways that let our individuality emerge, come alive, and make an impact on others. Here we are the selves that connect to others in a forceful, overt, physical, assertive, and sometimes leadership way. It is with this energy that we move ahead, make new beginnings, and express that spontaneous inner self that makes for joyful excitement in life and a sense of being separate, unique— a distinct self forging an individual impact on the world and others.

Mars in Aries makes for a dynamic and forceful manner of going after what we want. With the planet in its own sign, action is the place where this individual feels most comfortable. Taking the lead and moving forward in a direct, decisive, and exciting way are part of what attracts others to him or her.

Aries Mars individuals often stimulate others to action as well, inspiring them by example to express whatever their unique individualities may be. Sexually these are passionate and impulsive lovers, likely to move forward aggressively and competently in any situation that involves conflict, competition, or conquest.

Mars in Taurus produces a determined, thorough individual, one who cannot be deterred once forward motion toward a goal has commenced. Satisfaction in completion is one of the themes of this person's life. The identity may also be wrapped up in attachment to material or sensual rewards, desires that can be made manifest in tangible ways.

This person may not seem instantly propelled toward fulfilling a desire but is steadfast and unstoppable in continuing the pursuit until acquisition is assured. Sexually as well, there is a stability and loyalty that come with a Taurus Mars, along with a particularly highly developed sensuality.

Mars in Gemini makes for a variable energy in the individual. This is someone who does innumerable things at once, perhaps not completing any of them but certainly making many connections simultaneously. The desires here are most often expressed verbally, perhaps even to the exclusion of any action at all.

Sexually this is an exciting, entertaining, and charming lover, with a propensity toward ambivalence. Multiple relationships may be looked upon as preferable, or any union may be stimulating only if made up of a great many connections on all levels. This is a Renaissance person, performing a little bit of this and a dash of that, with a marvelous versatility of experiences in a great many fields.

Mars in Cancer impacts upon the emotionality of expression, which makes up a significant part of any action this person takes. Intuitions are particularly strong here, and this is a person who readily senses change in a situation or mood and accordingly alters his or her way of approaching a situation.

Loving is as important as sexual conquest or fulfillment for the Cancer Mars person, whose sexuality is wrapped up with being taken care of and/or nurturing another, marked by a great sensitivity to emotional fluctuations. The sense of self often changes at a moment's notice, as do the emotional whims and reactions of this reactive, passionate, and responsive human being.

Mars in Leo produces a rather overpowering personality, with a glow that sometimes can be blinding but also with a light that can lead the way for others out of the darkness. This indefatigable leader thrives on appreciation and admiration. Action almost doesn't count to this individual unless there's an audience and some form of adulation.

Romance and fun, creativity and excitement are some of the ways in which this person's passion gets expressed. Sex, as part of the Leo Mars person's well-being, is considered of great significance, though overinvolvement with the self sometimes makes passion a one-way affair. With deep creative fulfillment, however, an instinctively loving and generous self emerges.

Mars in Virgo denotes an individual who takes great pains to see that everything is cared for or healed no matter how great the effort it requires. This person takes great pride, too, in figuring out the solutions to all levels and kinds of problems—from those of a practical or medical nature to more complex emotional ones.

The sexuality of this person is subdued and delicate, responsive to subtlety. This individual's great sensuality and emotional sensitivity know no bounds once stimulated, but getting there may be quite some challenge. Mars Virgo's manner of approaching others is likewise an indirect and subtle form of engagement.

Mars in Libra can be quite the flirt, ever alert to the possibility of making new connections with romantic potential. This general sociability could mask an indecisiveness about commitment as well as speak to the truly friendly nature of someone desiring contact and enjoying making others feel good about themselves.

Creating harmony and taking actions that make for peaceful results are how this identity gets expressed. The sexual nature is usually indirect because attracting others is easier for this person than going after whatever or whoever is truly desired. Libra Mars individuals take pleasure in interactions at all levels, especially those with open-minded possibilities.

Mars in Scorpio intensifies the feelings of desire in an individual and simultaneously makes them less easy to be expressed directly. Desire itself is involved with much more here than pure physical responsiveness to beauty or a yearning for connection, fulfillment, or satisfaction. It also connects to deeper, sometimes negative emotional dispositions that speak of the secret, the forbidden, and the unknown in one's psyche and history.

Sexually voracious once repression has lifted, this kind of person may tend to self-destructiveness in relationships. Learning to transform and redirect these tendencies helps the Scorpio Mars personality attain a happier and more fulfilling identity.

Mars in Sagittarius is suggestive of the happy wanderer, an exciting, enthusiastic adventurer whose passionate pursuits inspire some great stories later on. This person finds ease and satisfaction among people, even in completely new social situations, wherever laughter, lightness, and jovial exchanges abound. A desire to expand the horizons leads to emotional, physical, sexual, and spiritual exploration.

Sexually this can be a very generous lover—with an equal likelihood that this generosity is shared by more than one recipient. Having a good time is part of the motto here, though once committed, Sagittarius Mars people live up to their social roles quite nobly.

Mars in Capricorn intensifies the focus on attaining one's object of desire, along with the seriousness and determination with which this is accomplished. There is usually a struggle this person goes through before coming fully to terms with his or her desiring nature. Perhaps a strict or religious upbringing or the absence of one or both parents makes moving optimistically toward what he or she wants a difficult task.

Sexually this is an accomplished lover, though perhaps conventional or formal. Marriage may create a safer environment for Capricorn Mars individuals to explore fully their own depths of sexual and sensual satisfaction.

Mars in Aquarius makes for an unusual energy with surprises and excitement galore. The identity of this individual is complex and unpredictable, with a certain edge of detachment as well. The lack of judgments about or interference with the lives of others makes this person an ideal friend.

Sexually these can be either highly sublimated individuals or people with erratic desire natures that seem to blow hot one day—or year or relationship—and cold the next. But whatever is to be said, they are individuals with flashes of brilliance and intuition that can inspire, shock, excite, and entertain but never bore you.

Mars in Pisces lends a kind of magical undertone to the desire nature, so that sex is often expressed as some unearthly kind of transcendence. It may be difficult for this individual to know just what that real, comfortable inner self wants to pursue. More often, taking life as it comes, the Pisces Mars person bravely confronts and endures whatever befalls.

A free-flowing sensuality is present in all interactions, with private fulfillments remaining much of a mystery to all but the participants. The Pisces Mars person is ever alert to the spiritual and emotional significance of sexual encounters, and his or her mission seems something a bit deeper, farther out than the norm, and more mystical.

How to Find the Place of Mars in Your Chart

Find your birth year in the left-hand column and read across the chart until you find your birth date. The top of that column will tell you where Mars lies in your chart.

PLACE OF MARS—1880–1891

	♈ ARIES	♉ TAURUS	♊ GEMINI	♋ CANCER	♌ LEO	♍ VIRGO	♎ LIBRA	♏ SCORP.	♐ SAGITT.	♑ CAPRI.	♒ AQUAR.	♓ PISCES
1880		2/13	2/14–4/11	4/12–6/1	6/2–7/20	7/21–9/5	9/6–10/21	10/22–12/3	12/4			
1881	5/13–6/21	6/22–8/3	8/4–9/23	9/24					↳1/13	1/14–2/22	2/23–4/2	4/3–5/12
1882			1/12–2/25	↳1/11 2/26–5/7	5/8–6/30	7/1–8/18	8/19–10/2	10/3–11/14	11/15–12/25	12/26		
1883	4/21–5/29	5/30–7/10	7/11–8/23	8/24–10/14	10/15					↳2/2	2/3–3/12	3/13–4/20
1884					↳6/4	6/5–7/27	7/28–9/12	9/13–10/25	10/26–12/5	12/6		
1885	3/31–5/8	5/9–6/18	6/19–7/31	8/1–9/16	9/17–11/8	11/9				↳1/12	1/13–2/19	2/20–3/30
1886						↳7/1	7/2–8/21	8/22–10/5	10/6–11/14	11/15–12/23	12/24	
1887	3/11–4/18	4/19–5/29	5/30–7/11	7/12–8/26	8/27–10/13	10/14–12/5	12/6				↳1/30	1/31–3/10
1888							↳2/26 3/10–7/21	2/27–3/9 7/22–9/10	9/11–10/22	10/23–12/1	12/2	
1889	2/17–3/28	3/29–5/9	5/10–6/22	6/23–8/6	8/7–9/22	9/23–11/10	11/11–12/31				↳1/9	1/10–2/16
1890								1/1–2/28 6/17–7/21	3/1–6/16 7/22–9/23	9/24–11/5	11/6–12/16	12/17
1891	1/26–3/7	3/8–4/19	4/20–6/3	6/4–7/19	7/20–9/4	9/5–10/21	10/22–12/7	12/8				↳1/25

PLACE OF MARS—1892–1906

Year											
1892	12/28 ↓										
1893	↓ 2/10	2/11–3/28	3/29–5/13	5/14–6/29	6/30–8/15	8/16–10/1	10/2–11/16	11/17–12/31			
1894	6/23–8/18 10/13–12/30	8/19–10/12 12/31 ↓						↓ 1/24 1/1–2/13	1/25–3/13	3/14–5/6	5/7–11/8	11/9–12/27
1895		↓ 3/1	3/2–4/21	4/22–6/10	6/11–7/28	7/29–9/13	9/14–10/29	10/30–12/11	12/12 ↓	2/14–3/27	3/28–5/9	5/10–6/22
1896	5/22–7/1	7/2–8/15	8/16–12/31						↓ 1/22	1/23–3/2	3/3–4/11	4/12–5/21
1897		1/1–3/21	3/22–5/17	5/18–7/8	7/9–8/25	8/26–10/9	10/10–11/21	11/22 ↓	1/1	1/2–2/10	2/11–3/20	3/21–4/28
1898	4/29–6/6	6/7–7/18	7/19–9/2	9/3–10/30	10/31 ↓							
1899				1/16–4/14	↓ 1/15 4/15–6/15	6/16–8/5	8/6–9/20	9/21–11/2	11/3–12/13	12/14 ↓		
1900	4/8–5/16	5/17–6/26	6/27–8/9	8/10–9/26	9/27–11/22	11/23 ↓				↓ 1/21	1/22–2/28	3/1–4/7
1901					3/2–5/10	↓ 3/1 5/11–7/13	7/14–8/31	9/1–10/14	10/15–11/23	11/24 ↓		
1902	3/19–4/26	4/27–6/6	6/7–7/20	7/21–9/4	9/5–10/23	10/24–12/19	12/20 ↓				↓ 1/1	1/2–2/8	2/9–3/18
1903						4/20–5/30	↓ 4/19 5/31–8/6	8/7–9/22	9/23–11/2	11/3–12/11	12/12 ↓	
1904	2/27–4/6	4/7–5/17	5/18–6/30	7/1–8/14	8/15–10/1	10/2–11/19	11/20 ↓				↓ 1/19	1/20–2/26
1905							↓ 1/13	1/14–8/21	8/22–10/7	10/8–11/17	11/18–12/27	12/28 ↓
1906	2/5–3/16	3/17–4/28	4/29–6/11	6/12–7/27	7/28–9/12	9/13–10/29	10/30–12/16	12/17 ↓				↓ 2/4

139

PLACE OF MARS—1907–1923

	♈ ARIES	♉ TAURUS	♊ GEMINI	♋ CANCER	♌ LEO	♍ VIRGO	♎ LIBRA	♏ SCORP.	♐ SAGITT.	♑ CAPRI.	♒ AQUAR.	♓ PISCES
1907								↳2/4	2/5–4/1	4/2–10/13	10/14–11/28	11/29↳
1908	1/11–2/22	2/23–4/6	4/7–5/22	5/23–7/7	7/8–8/23	8/24–10/9	10/10–11/25	11/26↳				↳1/10
1909	7/21–9/26 11/21↳								1/10–2/23	2/24–4/9	4/10–5/25	9/27–11/20 5/26–7/20
1910	↳1/22	1/23–3/13	3/14–5/1	5/2–6/18	6/19–8/5	8/6–9/21	9/22–11/6	11/7–12/19	12/20↳			
1911	6/3–7/15	7/16–9/5 11/30↳	9/6–11/29						↳1/31	2/1–3/13	3/14–4/22	4/23–6/2
1912		↳1/30	1/31–4/4	4/5–5/27	5/28–7/16	7/17–9/2	9/3–10/17	10/18–11/29	11/30↳			
1913	5/8–6/16	6/17–7/28	7/29–9/15	9/16↳					↳1/10	1/11–2/18	2/19–3/29	3/30–5/7
1914				↳5/1	5/2–6/25	6/26–8/14	8/15–9/28	9/29–11/10	11/11–12/21	12/22↳		
1915	4/17–5/25	5/26–7/5	7/6–8/18	8/19–10/7	10/8↳					↳1/29	1/30–3/9	3/10–4/16
1916					↳5/28	5/29–7/22	7/23–9/8	9/9–10/21	10/22–12/1	12/2↳		
1917	3/27–5/4	5/5–6/14	6/15–7/27	7/28–9/11	9/12–11/1	11/2↳				↳1/9	1/10–2/16	2/17–3/26
1918						↳1/10 2/26–6/23	1/11–2/25 6/24–8/16	8/17–9/30	10/1–11/10	11/11–12/19	12/20↳	
1919	3/7–4/14	4/15–5/25	5/26–7/8	7/9–8/22	8/23–10/9	10/10–11/29	11/30↳				↳1/26	1/27–3/6
1920							↳1/31 4/24–7/10	2/1–4/23 7/11–9/4	9/5–10/18	10/19–11/27	11/28	
1921	2/13–3/24	3/25–5/5	5/6–6/18	6/19–8/2	8/3–9/18	9/19–11/6	11/7–12/25	12/16↳			↳1/4	1/5–2/12
1922								↳2/18	2/19–9/13	9/14–10/30	10/31–12/11	12/12↳
1923	1/21–3/3	3/4–4/15	4/16–5/30	5/31–7/15	7/16–8/31	9/1–10/17	10/18–12/3	12/4–12/31				↳1/20

PLACE OF MARS—1924–1933

	♈ ARIES	♉ TAURUS	♊ GEMINI	♋ CANCER	♌ LEO	♍ VIRGO	♎ LIBRA	♏ SCORP.	♐ SAGITT.	♑ CAPRI.	♒ AQUAR.	♓ PISCES	♂ Retrograde R D
1924	12/19 ↝							1/1–1/19	1/20–3/6	3/7–4/24	4/25–6/24 8/25–10/19*	6/25–8/24* 10/20–12/18	5♊7/24–25♋9/22
1925	↝2/4	2/5–3/23	3/24–5/9	5/10–6/25	6/26–8/12	8/13–9/28	9/29–11/13	11/14–12/27	12/28 ↝				
1926	6/15–7/31	8/1 ↝						10/26–12/7	12/8 ↝	2/9–3/22	3/23–5/3	5/4–6/14	19♉9/29–4♉12/7
1927		↝2/21	2/22–4/16	4/17–6/5	6/6–7/24	7/25–9/10	9/11–10/25		↝1/18	1/19–2/27	2/28–4/7	4/8–5/16	
1928	5/17–6/25	6/26–8/8	8/9–10/2 12/20* ↝	10/3–12/19*	5/13–7/3	7/4–8/21	8/22–10/5	10/6–11/18	11/19–12/28	12/29			9♋11/12
1929			↝3/10	3/11–5/12	10/21* ↝ 3/30–6/10					↝2/6	2/7–3/16	3/17–4/24	20♊1/27
1930	4/25–6/2	6/3–7/14	7/15–8/27	8/28–10/20	10/1–11/13	6/11–8/1	8/2–9/16	9/17–10/30	10/31–1/29	12/10 ↝			17♌12/19
1931				2/17–3/29*		↝7/6 11/14 ↝				↝1/17	1/18–2/24	2/25–4/2	27♌3/9
1932	4/3–5/11	5/12–6/21	6/22–8/4	8/5–9/30		↝7/6 7/7–8/25		8/26–10/8	10/9–11/18	11/19–12/27	12/28 ↝		
1933													20♍1/21–1♍4/13

141

PLACE OF MARS—1934–1944

	♈ ARIES	♉ TAURUS	♊ GEMINI	♋ CANCER	♌ LEO	♍ VIRGO	♎ LIBRA	♏ SCORP.	♐ SAGITT.	♑ CAPRI.	♒ AQUAR.	♓ PISCES	Retrograde R ☌ D
1934	3/14–4/22	4/23–6/2	6/3–7/15	7/16–8/30	8/31–10/17	10/18–12/10	12/11↳					2/4–3/13	
1935							↳7/29	7/30–9/16	9/17–10/29	10/30–12/7	12/8↳		2♎–2/28–6☌–5/18
1936	2/23–4/2	4/3–5/13	5/14–6/26	6/27–8/10	8/11–9/27	9/28–11/15	11/16↳				↳1/15	1/16–2/22	
1937							↳1/6	1/7–3/13 5/16–9/9*	3/14–5/15* 8/10–9/30	10/1–11/12	11/13–12/22	12/23↳	6♐*4/15–19/9♏6/28
1938	2/1–3/13	3/14–4/24	4/25–6/8	6/9–7/23	7/24–9/8	9/9–10/26	10/27–12/12	12/13↳				↳1/31	
1939								↳1/30	1/31–3/22	3/23–5/25 7/23–9/25*	5/26–7/22* 9/26–11/20	11/21↳	5♑7/23–2♐8/24
1940	1/5–2/18	2/19–4/2	4/3–5/18	5/19–7/4	7/5–8/20	8/21–10/6	10/7–11/21	11/22↳					
1941	7/4↳							↳1/5	1/6–2/18	2/19–4/3	4/4–5/17	5/18–7/3	↳9/4
1942	↳1/12	1/13–3/8	3/9–4/27	4/28–6/15	6/16–8/2	8/3–9/18	9/19–11/2	11/3–12/16	12/17↳				24♈9/7–11♈11/11
1943	5/29–7/8	7/9–8/24	8/25↳						↳1/27	1/28–3/9	3/10–4/18	4/19–5/28	22♊10/28
1944			↳3/29*	3/30–5/23	5/24–7/13	7/14–8/30	8/31–10/14	10/15–11/26	11/27↳				5♏11/11

PLACE OF MARS—1945-1960

1945	5/4-6/12	6/13-7/24	7/25-9/8	9/9-11/12 12/28↘	11/13-12/27*			
1946				↙4/23*	4/24-6/21	6/22-8/10	8/11-9/25	9/26-11/7	11/8-12/18	↙1/6
1947	4/13-5/22	5/23-7/2	7/3-8/14	8/15-10/2	10/3-12/2	12/3↘		10/19-11/27	11/28	12/19	↙1/26	3/6-4/12	↙14♋5/22
1948				2/14-5/19*	↙2/13* 5/20-7/18	7/19-9/4	9/5-10/18		1/27-3/5	8m̃1/9-18♌3/30
1949	3/23-5/1	5/2-6/11	6/12-7/24	7/25-9/8	9/9-10/28	10/29-12/27	12/28↘			1/6-2/12	2/13-3/22
1950						↙3/29* 3/30-6/12*	6/13-8/11	8/12-9/26	9/27-11/7	11/8-12/16	12/17-12/31	11≏2/13-22m̃5/5
1951	3/2-4/10	4/11-5/21	5/22-7/3	7/4-8/18	8/19-10/4	10/5-11/24	11/25↘		8/28-10/12	10/13-11/21	1/11-1/22	13≏1/2
1952							↙1/20	1/21-8/27	12/21↘		11/22-12/30	12/31↘	11♏3/25-1m̃6/11
1953	2/9-3/20	3/21-5/1	5/2-6/14	6/15-7/29	7/30-9/14	9/15-11/1	11/2-12/20		8/25-10/21	10/22-12/4	12/5↘	↙2/8	8♈5/23-25♐7/30
1954								↙2/9	2/10-4/12 2/4-8/24*	4/13-7/3*			
1955	1/16-2/26	2/27-4/10	4/11-5/26	5/27-7/11	7/12-8/27	8/28-10/13	10/14-11/29	11/30↘	1/15-2/28	2/29-4/14	4/15-6/3	6/4-12/6*	23π8/11-13♐10/11
1956	12/7↘							↙1/14	12/24↘			↙1/15	
1957	↙1/28	1/29-3/17	3/18-5/4	5/5-6/21	6/22-8/8	8/9-9/24	9/25-11/8	11/9-12/23					
1958	6/8-7/21	7/22-9/21 10/30*	9/22-10/29*		6/2-7/20		7/21-9/5	9/6-10/21	10/22-12/3	↙2/3	2/4-3/17	3/18-4/27	4/28-6/7	2π10/11-6♉12/21
1959		↙2/10	2/11-4/10	4/11-6/1					↙12/4				
1960	5/12-6/20	6/21-8/2	8/3-9/21	9/22-12/31*					↙1/14	1/15-2/23	2/24-4/2	4/3-5/11	18≈11/21

143

PLACE OF MARS—1961–1971

	♈ ARIES	♉ TAURUS	♊ GEMINI	♋ CANCER	♌ LEO	♍ VIRGO	♎ LIBRA	♏ SCORP.	♐ SAGITT.	♑ CAPRI.	♒ AQUAR.	♓ PISCES	☌ Retrograde R D
1961	4/19–5/27	5/28–7/8	7/9–8/21	1/1–5/5*	5/6–6/27	6/28–8/16	8/17–9/30	10/1–11/12	11/13–12/23	12/24 ↘	2/1–3/11	3/12–4/18	0♎27
1962				8/22–10/10	10/11 ↘	6/3–7/26	7/27–9/11	9/12–10/24	10/25–12/4	↙1/31 12/5 ↘	1/13–2/19	2/20–3/28	24♌12/26
1963		5/7–6/16	6/17–7/29	7/30–9/14	↙6/2 9/15–11/15	11/6 ↘				↙1/12	12/23		5♊3/17
1964	3/29–5/6						6/29–8/19	8/20–10/3	10/4–11/13	11/14–12/22		1/30–3/8	
1965		4/17–5/27	5/28–7/10	7/11–8/24	8/25–10/11	↙6/28* 10/12–12/3	12/4				↙1/29 12/1 ↘		28♍1/28 8♍4/20
1966	3/9–4/16							2/12–9/9*	9/10–10/22	10/23–11/30		1/9–2/16	
1967		3/27–5/7	5/8–6/20	6/21–8/4	8/5–9/20	9/21–11/8	11/9–12/28	12/29			↙1/8		3♏3/9 15≏5/26
1968	2/17–3/26							↙2/24	2/25–9/20*	9/21–11/3	11/4–12/14	12/15	
1969	1/24–3/6	3/7–4/17	4/18–6/1	6/2–7/17	7/18–9/2	9/3–10/19	10/20–12/5	12/6–12/31				↙1/23	16♐4/27 1♐7/8
1970								1/1–1/22	1/23–3/11	3/12–5/2	5/3–11/5*	11/6–12/25	
1971	12/26 ↘												21♒7/10℞ 11♒9/80

PLACE OF MARS—1972–1980

1972	↳2/9	2/10–3/26	3/27–5/11	5/12–6/27	6/28–8/14	8/15–9/29	9/30–11/14	11/15–12/29	12/30↴				
1973	6/20–8/11 10/29–12/23*	8/12–10/28* 12/24↴							↳2/11	2/12–3/25	3/26–5/7	5/8–6/19	9♉9/19℞ 25♈11/25D
1974		↳2/26	2/27–4/19	4/20–6/8	6/9–7/26	7/27–9/11	9/12–10/27	10/28–12/9	12/10↴				
1975	5/21–6/30	7/1–8/13	8/14–10/16 11/25↴	10/17–11/24*					↳1/20	1/21–3/2	3/3–4/10	4/11–5/20	2♋11/6℞
1976			↳3/17*	3/18–5/15	5/16–7/5	7/6–8/23	8/24–10/7	10/8–11/19	11/20–12/31				14♊1/20D
1977	4/27–6/5	6/6–7/16	7/17–8/31	9/1–10/25	10/26↴					1/1–2/8	2/9–3/19	3/20–4/26	11♌12/12℞
1978				1/26–4/9*	↳1/25* 4/10–6/13	6/14–8/3	8/4–9/18	9/19–11/1	11/2–12/11	12/12↴			22♋3/1D
1979	4/7–5/15	5/16–6/25	6/26–8/7	8/8–9/23	9/24–11/18	11/19↴				↳1/19	1/20–2/26	2/27–4/6	
1980					3/11–5/3*	↳3/10* 5/4–7/9	7/10–8/28	8/29–10/11	10/12–11/21	11/22–12/29	12/30–12/31		15♍1/16℞ 25♌4/6D

*In these periods, Mars (♂) is Retrograde during some or all of the time. See right-hand column.

PLACE OF MARS—1981–1987

	♈ ARIES	♉ TAURUS	♊ GEMINI	♋ CANCER	♌ LEO	♍ VIRGO	♎ LIBRA	♏ SCORP.	♐ SAGITT.	♑ CAPRI.	♒ AQUAR.	♓ PISCES
1981	3/16–4/24	4/25–6/4	6/5–7/17	7/18–8/31	9/1–10/19	10/20–12/14	12/15 ↗				1/1–2/5	2/6–3/15
1982							↙ 8/2	8/3–9/18	9/19–10/30	10/31–12/9	12/10 ↗	
1983	2/24–4/4	4/5–5/15	5/16–6/28	6/29–8/12	8/13–9/28	9/29–11/17	11/18 ↗				↙ 1/16	1/17–2/23
1984								↙ 1/9	1/10–8/16		11/15–12/24	12/25 ↗
1985	2/2–3/14	3/15–4/25	4/26–6/8	6/9–7/23	7/24–9/8	9/9–10/26	10/27–12/13	12/14 ↗		10/5–11/14		↙ 2/1
1986							10/8–11/22	11/23 ↗	2/2–3/26	3/27–10/7	10/8–11/24	11/25 ↗
1987	1/8–2/19	2/20–4/4	4/5–5/19	5/20–7/5	7/6–8/21	8/22–10/7						↙ 1/7

PLACE OF MARS—1988–2000

Year												
1988	7/13–10/22 11/1↱						↳1/7	1/8–2/21	2/22–4/5	4/6–5/21	5/22–7/12 10/23–10/31
1989	↳1/18	1/19–3/9	3/10–4/27	4/28–6/15	6/16–8/2	8/3–9/18	9/19–11/3	11/4–12/16	12/17↱		
1990	5/31–7/11	7/12–8/30 12/14↱						↳1/28	1/29–3/10	3/11–4/19	4/20–5/30
1991		↳1/20	1/21–4/1	4/2–5/25	5/26–7/14	7/15–8/31	9/1–10/15	10/16–11/27	11/28↱			
1992	5/5–6/13	6/14–7/25	7/26–9/11	9/12↱		6/23–8/10	8/11–9/25	9/26–11/7	↳1/8	1/9–2/16	2/17–3/26	3/27–5/4
1993				↳4/26	4/27–6/22				11/8–12/18	12/19↱		
1994	4/14–5/22	5/23–7/2	7/3–8/15	8/16–10/3	10/4–12/11	12/12↱				↳1/26	1/27–3/6	3/7–4/13
1995						1/22–5/23 5/24–7/20 ↳1/21	7/21–9/6	9/7–10/19	10/20–11/29	11/30↱		
1996	3/24–5/1	5/2–6/11	6/12–7/24	7/25–9/8	9/9–10/29	10/30↱ 3/8–6/18 ↳1/2	1/3–3/7 6/19–8/13	8/14–9/27		↳1/7	1/8–2/14	2/15–3/23
1997									9/28–11/8	11/9–12/17	12/18↱	
1998	3/4–4/11	4/12–5/22	5/23–7/5	7/6–8/19	8/20–10/6	10/7–11/26 11/27↱					↳1/24	1/25–3/3
1999						5/5–7/3 ↳1/25	1/26–5/4 7/4–9/1	9/2–10/15	10/16–11/25	11/26↱		
2000	2/11–3/21	3/22–5/2	5/3–6/15	6/16–7/30	7/31–9/15	9/16–11/1	11/13–12/22	12/23–12/31			↳1/2	1/3–2/10

YOUR RULING PLANET: ARIES—Mars; TAURUS—Venus; GEMINI—Mercury; CANCER—The Moon; LEO—The Sun; VIRGO—Mercury; LIBRA—Venus; SCORPIO—Mars; SAGITTARIUS—Jupiter; CAPRICORN—Saturn; AQUARIUS—Uranus; PISCES—Neptune.

147

JUPITER: FORTUNE AND BOUNTY

Jupiter represents the potential for your growth and expansion on many levels—physical, mental, and spiritual—as well as the accumulation of such things as material assets, power, and status. Jupiter represents honors, recognition, and personal advancement that come to you. It is also indicative of your father and your father's family and position. It represents higher education—that is, the degrees you obtain or the subjects you pursue on your own after you have reached adulthood. Your religious attitude and training are represented by Jupiter as well as your interest and participation in cultural pursuits. Jupiter represents good fortune in the sense of giving you capacity to enjoy life to the fullest regardless of whether or not you are wealthy.

Jupiter in Aries. The areas in which you experience growth and expansion will have a tendency to get out of control. How inclined or efficient you are at regaining control when it has been lost is indicated by other factors in your natal chart and, of course, is determined by your particular background and the maturity you have developed. For example, you may earn or attract wealth and other assets, but it is likely you also have an equal generosity of spirit when it comes to spending money. If you have not learned efficient methods of handling your income or assets, then you never quite get ahead financially. Another highly possible situation with Jupiter in Aries is your having the good fortune to make a lot of money so fast that you aren't prepared to handle it properly or that you become so busy acquiring money you don't have time to enjoy it. When it comes to expanding your intellectual horizons, Jupiter in Aries is an indication that you may eagerly seek information and education but that in your haste you may easily miss the facts or fail to pay attention to them. You may rush into situations even though you may not have all the knowledge or information required. You want to know everything at once and become impatient with the more plodding, patient approach to learning. You can become passionate concerning the subjects and issues that interest you, and they include religious zeal. Your passion serves as inspiration to others and makes you an effective teacher. You do not pay much attention to limitations, and in your enthusiasm you can easily lose sight of practicality or reality. You are apt to be fond of sports and risk-taking pursuits for both business and pleasure.

Jupiter in Taurus. You are concerned with expanding your physical world, its pleasures and its traditional structures. However, when you gain monetary or other advantages, you may be so worried about hanging on to them that you lose the opportunity to enjoy them or to use them as a step to further progress; much will depend on your individual background and the values you have learned. You are nevertheless comfortable with wealth and status, and it is likely you'll use whatever advantages you gain not only to promote your personal growth and progress but also to improve the quality of life for others. In addition to gaining material wealth, you want your growth in any area to be tangible. In other words, you want physical signs of progress. In the area of education, for example, even if you are a dedicated scholar, you'll want to use your knowledge to earn more money or gain prestige in the community. You have an appreciation for music and art, and if Jupiter is well placed in your natal chart, it can indicate talent in these areas and the opportunity to develop such talent. You may have interest in banking and finance, building and real estate, food and fashion. You may have a green thumb and, if not, certainly an appreciation for plants and flowers even if you don't grow them yourself. Jupiter in Taurus gives the capacity to enjoy physical pleasures and personal comfort. However, when emotionally insecure or upset, you may go to one extreme or the other, either wasting assets you would not normally risk and becoming involved with physical pleasure to the exclusion of more important matters or, on the other hand, becoming very miserly and rejecting personal pleasures and comfort altogether.

Jupiter in Gemini. Jupiter in Gemini indicates that your areas of personal growth and expansion involve your intellect—that is, what you know (or can learn) and your continuing involvement with ideas, information, and communication. It is also an indication that you will broaden your intellectual horizons through marriage or partnership. No matter what you do for a living, your growth as an individual is directly tied to developing a network of connections that continually provides you with information and mental stimulation. Whether this type of personal expansion also happens to make you a wealthy person or advances your standard of living in other ways is coincidental, not an inevitable result. Jupiter in Gemini is also an indication of how well you circulate in your immediate community and of your interest and participation in community activities. While part of your vital learning process is destined to occur in your own neighborhood, travel, whether for business or pleasure, is an important part of your overall education. You will always be able to pick up valuable information and make important connections when you travel. Though Jupiter in Gemini indicates intellectual curiosity that can lead to important discoveries, it unfortunately also includes a tendency for you to become too scattered or overly concerned with trivial matters or gossip. Being able to organize material is just as important as collecting it, and inundating yourself with too much information can be a stumbling block to actually making use of it. Publishing, advertising, engineering, design, teaching, writing, and communications are some particular areas that will attract your interest and participation. Computers, electronic equipment, and transportation are other fields in which you may become involved. You may also have clever mechanical skills and some artistic talent.

Jupiter in Cancer. The strongest area of your personal growth and expansion is connected with your emotional development, which in turn is directly related to the influence of your family background, your family connections and resources, and the state of your domestic environment as a child and as an adult. Whatever you do in life, you need to establish a strong emotional support system for yourself, and perhaps just as important, you must be willing to be part of such a system for others. If your background has unfortunately provided a negative influence, it may be doubly difficult to turn your emotional behavior and attitudes in a positive direction, but the more successfully you manage to do this, the more correspondingly successful you will be as an individual and in many other areas. Another factor is family resources and connections and your ability to make use of them. If you are fortunate enough to have important family connections that help advance your career or you have material wealth through inheritance, there is a lesson to be learned in using them wisely but not automatically depending on them to provide a life-style and advantages without your efforts to do something productively on your own. On the other hand, you have the responsibility of providing and preserving resources and connections for your family. The concept of nurturing is a strong element in this Jupiter sign position, and you are likely to be a talented cook, caterer, psychological counselor, or educator. You may also have a flair for art and design. You may think, learn, and generally do better in an environment near the ocean or other body of water or may receive your higher education in such an environment.

Jupiter in Leo. This sign position indicates that your growth as an individual is directly connected with your spiritual development, expansion of your intellect through higher education or advanced training, and interest and participation in cultural pursuits. Any of these concerns may or may not actually involve your profession or be the means of economic advancement; however, achieving personal growth is often the key to being successful in other areas of life. Your creative instincts are likely to be enhanced with this Jupiter position. Of course, it doesn't guarantee you will have artistic talent, but it does mean that developing the use of whatever creativity and imagination you do possess is an important step in being successful in many other areas. Whatever direction your efforts take, they are liable to be somewhat overdone or exaggerated, as is the usual case with Leo's influence, but that doesn't have to be a negative factor in what you do, unless you lose sight of the fact that things are out of proportion. Generosity as well as maintaining high principles and loyalty are a big part of your growth. The pomp and pageantry of traditional rituals attract your imagination and inspire your enthusiastic participation. Advertising, direct mail, publishing, broadcasting, politics, and foreign trade may be other areas of particular interest for you. In addition to the areas already mentioned, your higher education is apt to involve sociology, philosophy, theology, or anthropology. Working with children or to advance the cause of philanthropic groups is an excellent way to expand your own growth. You are likely to have great interest in sports and risk-taking ventures for both business and pleasure. Long-distance travel is an important stimulating factor in your overall development, and opportunities to travel should not be missed.

Jupiter in Virgo. Jupiter in Virgo signifies important managerial and executive abilities. Even if you yourself don't happen to possess such qualities, you are likely to recognize these talents in others. Part of your personal growth and advancement may be directly connected to your efforts to place qualified people (yourself included) in the positions where they can do the most good. Your efficient organization of material, labor, and other types of systems is another key to success. You want tangible proof of your own growth and progress—that is, some sort of physical evidence or at least irrefutable proof of what your influence and efforts have accomplished. You want to use in some meaningful, even public manner the knowledge and skills that have contributed to your growth as an individual. You want to know that you have made a difference, and unless other factors in your natal chart indicate a more inhibited nature, you want others to be aware of it as well. As suggested above, you are also very often to be found just as seriously involved with the progress, growth, and ultimate effectiveness of others as you are with your own. The idealism associated with Jupiter and the perfection-oriented nature of Virgo can sometimes become a severe limitation for you. When nothing and no one seem good enough or perfect enough, you may tend to use this as an excuse for your own idleness, and on a more personal level, you may give up relationships that might have eventually become valuable emotional contacts if you had managed to overlook certain shortcomings. Your education, religion, and cultural pursuits (including artistic talent) will tend toward your embracing traditional thoughts and expressions. If you are not careful, you can become overly concerned with unimportant details.

Jupiter in Libra. Your personal growth is, to a large extent, likely to be dependent on associations or partnerships you establish with others. Your understanding of (or willingness to understand) human relationships and interactions is somehow going to play an important role in making you a successful person, in your personal relationships as well as in your job or career. Jupiter's influence in Libra indicates an increased capacity to get along with and (if this planet is well placed in your natal chart) to favorably influence others. If you fail to develop this potential, then it is quite possible you will correspondingly fail in other areas of personal growth. Another important part of your growth potential involves developing, increasing, and, above all, using your intellectual abilities. Part of the intellectual understanding you are expected to gain includes being able to equalize Jupiter's tendency for overabundance and the Libran requirement for balance between excess and austerity. You are likely to encounter many inequitable situations in life, and rather than look around for others to do something about them, it will be up to you to tip the scales to achieve a better equilibrium. Such out-of-balance circumstances will be personal and include your habits or life-style, but they will also include efforts you make in your immediate society because Jupiter in Libra suggests you have an inspired sense of justice. For instance, you may work (professionally or as a volunteer) in such areas as civil rights, housing for the homeless, or improved housing in disadvantaged areas or in the cause of other community issues. Your higher education is likely to be in law, psychology and counseling, or literature. There is also the indication that you have certain aesthetic tastes, an appreciation (and perhaps talent) for art and music.

Jupiter in Scorpio. Jupiter in Scorpio indicates that your intellectual interests are likely to be dictated by intense emotional desires or that your intellectual understanding is accompanied by a good deal of emotional enthusiasm. Your personal growth is connected with emotional development. Destructive emotions like possessiveness, obsessiveness, and jealousy correspondingly limit your growth as an individual. There may also be an unfortunate tendency for manipulation, and you may engage in this practice without fully realizing its destructive potential. If zeal overwhelms reasonableness and moderation, there is danger you may lapse into fanaticism. Your challenge in life is dealing with resources, your own as well as others, material as well as nonmaterial. By making the most of your assets, monetary assets and personal talents and abilities, you will grow as an individual and gain success in other areas as well. This means conservation, as opposed to waste, and careful development and investment. Failing to develop or use resources properly is as bad as wasting them. Other people, their monetary and personal assets, are important human resources. You can become successful through teaching, training, or doing other types of work that help others to be more productive and develop their own potentials. You may be remarkable in your ability to understand nature and its elementary forces and thus may have a flair for science, research, and development. Food is an elementary resource, and in this respect you are apt to be a gourmet as well as gourmand. Conservation means preserving to a certain extent, but it also includes finding ways to turn old and useless items and material into something new. Renovation of buildings and homes, land reclamation, waste recycling all are areas that fall into this category and in which you might be involved.

Jupiter in Sagittarius. Your growth and success as an individual involve developing an effective, dynamic personality. Though others may succeed by other means, a vital factor in your achievements is going to be your ability to influence people and the outcome of circumstances through the force of your physical presence. You must leave others with a strong impression, stamp your efforts with the indelible mark of your personality. This may seem very self-centered, perhaps even shallow, but it doesn't have to be if in addition to developing a forceful, effective personality, you give yourself a depth of knowledge, sincerity, and spiritual awareness. Being known as a seeker of truth, having a real message to give to others, and inspiring others with enthusiasm and energy are the keys to greatness for you. You will benefit greatly from travel. Opportunities to be with and understand people of different cultures should not be missed. Politics, philosophy, languages, and education are particular areas of study or participation. Your work or study may also be in advertising and sales, broadcasting, and theater. You may be interested in banking or finance, and a certain risk-taking spirit may lead you into speculation. There may be a tendency for you to be pompous or overly impressed with wealth and status, or you may have to deal with these traits in other people. If Jupiter is especially well placed in your natal chart, you may experience the type of good fortune that places you in just the right place at the right time. It may not be the kind of luck that enables you to win the lottery (although that possibility can't be ruled out), but it brings you favorable circumstances and more than an average share of advantages in life.

Jupiter in Capricorn. Jupiter in Capricorn signifies that you are not likely to be given the advantages of inspirational factors to guide your thoughts and behavior in life. Trying to achieve personal growth, you will be limited to gaining understanding through experience and maturity rather than being inspired by such things as religion or philosophy. Whether self-taught or formally educated, you will want to turn your knowledge into more earning power or increased status or both. It isn't that you cannot be personally of a more spiritual or esoteric nature or even have a career in one of those areas, for that is indicated by other factors in your natal chart. It is just that most circumstances life presents will come down to matters that require a more worldly approach. You are going to be primarily concerned with the material world since that is where you will be able to achieve the most. In addition, your growth and success will rarely be a matter of whimsy or a lucky break. Luck for you will always be accompanied by responsibility. You either want to or are forced to keep track of where you have been, where you are at present, and where you are going. Jupiter in Capricorn means it will be your responsibility to separate form from substance to get at the heart of matters. There is executive and managerial ability with Jupiter in Capricorn, and you must not only develop your own skills in this area but also help others who have such valuable traits to attain positions of authority and in the process affect your own advancement. Politics, city planning, engineering, design, building, real estate development, law, law enforcement, and education are some particular areas that may interest you.

Jupiter in Aquarius. You will experience your greatest personal growth on an intellectual level. Expanding your intellectual horizons may or may not bring economic suc-

Jupiter: Fortune and Bounty 157

cess or have anything directly to do with your job or career, but it is likely to have a significant influence on these matters. Success as an individual is one of the surest keys to success in many other areas of life. Jupiter in Aquarius indicates you are likely to have the capacity for operating efficiently with established ideas and institutions while at the same time being receptive to and participating in ideas and activities which appear out of the ordinary, fantastic, or bizarre to other people. The ability to go between the traditional and the nontraditional can make you a valuable member of society. How deeply you are concerned with yourself as an individual is indicated by other factors in your natal chart, but Jupiter in Aquarius signifies that whatever your point of reference, an important part of personal growth involves being an effective member of society. Unless there are negative factors in your natal chart to counteract it, you are likely to have broad-minded social attitudes and can be an effective catalyst within various organizations and groups. Communication is the most important mechanism at your disposal. It won't be enough for you to expand your intellect without your also being able to communicate your knowledge and understanding to others. Nor is it enough for you to develop and use your own skills and methods of communicating; you must also be willing to help others communicate. Jupiter in Aquarius suggests the possibility that you have clever mechanical or artistic skills. You may have interest and may work in the field of computers, engineering, technology, music, finance, or community housing development.

Jupiter in Pisces. Your personal growth is directly connected to emotional development. Understanding your emotions and acquiring the maturity that accompanies personal growth may depend on your ability to make prudent choices that place you in positions of emotional strength. Establishing stable relationships and strong values will help mitigate impediments to proper emotional development. You may have a tendency to take what you consciously or subconsciously perceive as vulnerability and turn it into a risk-taking attitude that can take a wide variety of forms, from foolhardy behavior that others interpret as a death wish to developing the instincts and capabilities of a successful commodities trader. Much will depend on your particular emotional background. The more negative your childhood or circumstances, the more likely you are to develop correspondingly negative risk-taking behavior. Overcoming such a situation may be your biggest struggle, which, of course, will have a significant influence on your success in other areas of life. If Jupiter in your natal chart is particularly well placed, it is an indication that your home and family will prove an encouraging environment for learning. Enhanced emotional capacity demonstrates that you may have artistic talent, psychic abilities, and a particular facility for mathematics and understanding abstract concepts. There can be an unfortunate tendency for a certain emotional dependency, which includes a good deal of overindulgence and even a destructive dependency on addictive substances. Religion, art, and philosophy can supply inspiration that helps you attain growth as an individual, and you should not miss the opportunities to explore these areas. You may find you are more intellectually stimulated and creative near the ocean or other watery environment, and there is the possibility that education or training you receive as an adult will take place in such an environment.

SATURN: THE TEACHER

Saturn, known as the taskmaster of the zodiac, indicates by sign and house placement where an individual needs to take responsibility for his or her own obstacles to satisfaction and success. Connections between Saturn and other planets or luminaries (Sun or Moon) in your own chart note how and which aspects of your personality suffer from a sense of personal limitation. This limitation is often sensed as being the fault of another person or situation that holds you back from getting what you want, expressing what you want to say, or being what you want to be. Looking for clarification to the placement of your Saturn by sign and by house as well (that is, the first-house position of Saturn has certain similarities to the Saturn in Aries reading, etc.) can help you understand just how you feel oppressed, unappreciated, or generally unfulfilled in an area of your life. Along with understanding comes the need for a certain amount of applied discipline toward achieving satisfaction there and in restructuring your thoughts and behavior in such a way that you are able to see yourself overcoming the fear and distrust that impede the joyful reaching of your goals.

As we look directly at the areas in which we find ourselves feeling dissatisfied and perhaps inadequate, we can understand and accept the way we need to take responsibility for a level of strength in decision making that allows us to act to restructure the situation that exists. Once this shift has been made, our perspective is readily translated into a new way of behaving, altering the effect we have on others as well as the kinds of circumstances we create in our lives. Taking responsibility for ourselves is that crucial first step that Saturn focuses upon in order to enable us to reap the rewards in life that we deserve.

Saturn in Aries presents difficulties in spontaneously asserting oneself, along with making it hard for an individual to feel at home with his or her own instincts for leadership and competition. Moving toward success may always be a struggle for this person. Though the talents, resources, and abilities are present, an Aries Saturn tends to undermine his or her best efforts with either a negative attitude or the inner sense of not really deserving the rewards forthcoming.

Becoming aware of how one's own sense of self determines the outcome of a situation is the first step. Once this knowledge and experience of one's own power grow clearer, he or she can then take responsibility for clearing up the mess made of situations that held great promise but were not followed through because of feared inadequacies.

This person tends to doubt the very instincts that can lead to satisfaction, fulfillment, and ultimate success. Instead of moving forward when action is warranted, the Saturn in Aries person needs to overcome the hesitancy that causes him or her to hold back and delay what would have been an instinctively correct move ahead.

Saturn in Taurus indicates difficulties in one's ability to achieve satisfaction and to experience pleasure. A sense of lack—no matter what or how much a person possesses, earns, or owns—or, in extreme cases, the issue of poverty or survival is at the forefront of this person's mind.

Doubting his or her own creative gifts as well, this person may fail to develop what are magnificent talents and end up doing something less than is fulfilling to earn money, forever pursuing the elusive goal of "having enough."

Learning to acknowledge and appreciate the simple gifts and pleasures of life can help the Saturn in Taurus person begin to overcome attitudes that thwart an experience of satisfaction in life. Concentrating on the lack of something tends to perpetuate the sense of poverty, whereas dwelling on the result of efforts one has made successfully can lead directly to greater success.

Saturn in Gemini indicates one who is continually frustrated by a felt inability to express himself or herself. A sense of being either overwhelmed or ignored by others or of never having the right words to say in a given situation can lead to an alienated and isolated state of being.

The Gemini Saturn person is constantly censoring the very thoughts that need to be expressed or so harshly judging any ideas that come to mind that they are never presented, no matter what their actual value. This person may turn out to be his or her own most severe critic, bringing censure in situations where greater acceptance and encouragement are needed.

Habit patterns of this self-censoring attitude are the biggest obstacle and the hardest thing to turn around. The person may be so convinced of the lack of value of his or her own ideas that thinking of them as potentially powerful and transforming could be a concept quite difficult to accept and act upon. In actuality the Saturn in Gemini's thoughtful consideration of all matters leads to exceptionally well-conceived ideas that are evidence of constructive and valuable applications of serious thinking.

Saturn in Cancer could make for difficulty in human relationships because it indicates a way in which a person feels cut off from the deep feeling and nurturing parts of the self. Barriers to knowing what one's most basic emotional needs are make connections of any depth, tenderness, and compassion hard to initiate, let alone to maintain.

Strong defenses are common in people with this planetary setup, for they are often victims of severe emotional deprivation as children, lacking quality parenting as well as examples of good loving. Looking to their personal histories in a truth-seeking, defense-free way (usually with the help of a counselor of some sort) can lead to a clearer understanding of their individual obstacles to creating closeness and cultivating trust with others.

162 ☾ Cancer JUNE 22–JULY 23

Rather deep-seated defenses need to be confronted to turn around lifelong habits and even to begin to imagine the possibility of letting in the emotionally nourishing relationships too often substituted for by monetary or other obsessions with love substitutes.

Saturn in Leo impedes a sense of fun in life and may also lead to involvement with addictive substances—anything from alcohol or drugs to food—that represent the person's struggle to derive some sensations of pleasure. As the light inside a person dims, a sense of pessimism and even cynicism about life evolves.

Most often this individual has a very dour attitude toward others, distorted expectations about almost every situation that arises, and a less obvious sense of doubt about himself or herself. This negativity about life could produce a person who works extra hard at having fun or totally withdraws from loving connections with others.

Chronic low self-esteem—the sense that he or she hasn't whatever it takes to get to the place most desired or to achieve whatever is most coveted or doesn't deserve to enjoy whatever good comes to pass—plagues the Saturn in Leo person. Once this individual has come to terms with, acknowledged, and released the inner barriers to pleasure and satisfaction, he or she can then joyfully and successfully get involved with what once seemed like a big, bad world out there.

Saturn in Virgo denotes a great strain in an individual's ability to bring joy and ease to everyday life, a sense of serving others, or the enjoyment of good health and well-being. Rigidity about these things could make for the adherence to an unsatisfying routine or getting stuck in an attitude that everything needs to be done in a certain way to be correct but that nothing is ever good enough anyway.

This person may be a chronic complainer or may just feel silently embittered about how everything is so difficult in life. Escape from even the effort of enjoying life could result in one's working so hard to take care of others that the desires and needs of the self are obscured or totally forgotten. Everyday life may be so overscheduled that there is little time for enjoying it.

One of the ways of convincing the Saturn in Virgo person to try to look at life with a renewed sense of satisfaction and constructive purpose is to emphasize how everything gets done so much more easily and successfully with an attitude of joyfulness. This can help turn barriers into bridges toward a positive state of well-being and service.

Saturn in Libra can contribute to a difficulty in giving, sharing, and making the level of connections that foster relationships in our lives. Such challenges relate to a sense of lack in terms of feelings we don't have enough of in our lives: love, affection, loyalty, acknowledgment, and appreciation. We may then tend to withhold those very things from loved ones—especially partners—and thereby perpetuate the situation.

This frustration in connecting with others usually stems from our inability to nurture relationships with a knowledge and assertion of what we ourselves need. In order to improve this situation, we need to become aware of the ways in which we prevent the good feelings from passing between us and others, denying the harmony that we can open up to in relationships.

We also need to face the ways in which we deny ourselves the acceptance we need and instead constantly seek it from others. Once strengthened, our sense of increased self-esteem will allow us to give in relationships what before we expected and demanded that others give to us.

Saturn in Scorpio has a very powerful effect that is usually unconscious and often not readily obvious even to the beholder of such a placement. Scorpio fuels our sense of power and ability to transform the difficult inner workings of our lives into something constructive, enduring, and beautiful. That process is here made doubly difficult because Saturn's presence tends to hold us in a place of negativity so that we either doubt our power or turn it over to others, seeing others as our oppressors, as able to frustrate us from what we desire most, to deny us our deepest fulfillments.

Overcoming the effects of Saturn in Scorpio calls for some in-depth psychological work to overcome the emotional blocks that may have crystallized inside us. It is not unlikely that our sexual sense of self has become frozen into a numbness that needs gentle but continual stimulation on the physical level, as in some kind of bodywork, to reawaken.

The benefit, however, of overcoming these deeply instilled barriers and fears is an awareness of our power to create what we want in our lives, demonstrating it to others as well.

Saturn in Sagittarius tends to foreshorten our perspective, put obstacles in the way of a joyful view of life and the future. We then need to expand our consciousness and work to our full intellectual capacity to improve our lives, to broaden our horizons, overcoming our areas of greatest difficulty.

Facing the fact that we create our own mental limitations—seeing perhaps only our losses and failures to achieve in the material world around us—almost forces us, for the sake of our own well-being, to explore other levels of endeavor and achievement.

Indulging in sports—noncompetitively—or in academic explorations and even involvement with religious pursuits can lead us to the peacefulness that comes from our inner measures of success.

We must allow ourselves to find areas in which we can learn to enjoy the process of what we are doing, letting that be our guide to a life that unfolds from our inner purpose. Joy is our guide here if we will but listen to it and abide.

Saturn in Capricorn signifies a hard worker, but depending upon how that energy is applied in life, it can make either for success and satisfaction or for continual self-denial and frustration. Saturn in its own sign heightens the emphasis on career and a sense of professional purpose in the world. One's public identity becomes the key to challenges to his or her reputation as well as to how his or her works are received.

An overemphasis on public self, however, could lead the individual to cultivating a hollow shell of a self that feels no true inner satisfaction at all. On the other hand, as one learns to look inward for the strength and inner purpose on one's path, great works of value can be achieved, to the benefit of others as well as the self—and to society. The key is to take one's cues from the instinctive sense of what one can do to protect and ensure the safety and success of the lives of those around us and then, surely, successfully, to act from that intuitive knowledge.

Saturn in Aquarius can represent a lack of appreciation and acknowledgment of one's uniqueness and, consequently, a lack of recognition in the world. This may be a person who, always striving to conform to the status quo, may not realize the great worth of living his or her inner values, unique sense of purpose, and individual perspective on the world. In denying the self full expression in this way, he or she is holding back from others the true sharing that makes for a sense of union in relationships as well.

Friendships, too, are hard when one is unable to recognize and share parts of oneself that are difficult to deal with alone. A lack of true companionship can lead to isolation and even a sense of alienation from others.

The Saturn in Aquarius individual first needs to take responsibility for the ways in which the self is not acknowledged and expressed so that others don't become the focus of misdirected anger and frustration. Working to feel and free that self one hides from others—and even from himself or herself—can then liberate an enormous innovative energy with which he or she can make a positive impact on the world.

Saturn in Pisces tends to impede the sense of connection to others in a very basic way. A resulting sense of isolation may then make it hard for us to discover what we want to put forth to others, how to foster deep connections, or even how to relate because we lack the compassion that is necessary for us to connect meaningfully and find satisfaction in our emotional lives. A sense of profound pessimism about the world, stemming from this aloneness, may serve only to reinforce our negativity and keep us bound by our own worst fears.

In order not to drive ourselves to destructive escapism to avoid the world as we see it, we need to turn all that negativity around and with it construct a worldview that acknowledges the great link we all have to one another. This can revitalize our faith in ourselves as well as strengthen our intuitive ways of tapping into the artistic and magical forces that help us bring ourselves out of the darkness and shine light, too, on the paths of others to guide their ways to satisfaction, fulfillment, and joy.

192 ♈ Aries MARCH 21–APRIL 20

Moon in Pisces (♓): Overcome limitations and problems; express charitable and sympathetic leanings; pursue peaceful and spiritual interests; boost self-confidence; find the causes for fears, worries, doubts; take care of confidential matters; visit those who are ill, convalescing, or confined.

URANUS: THE UNEXPECTED VISITOR

Uranus has to do with the cosmic power of intuitive knowledge, marked by flashes of genius in some, and with the milder forms of intuition that we all possess from time to time to varying degrees in our own unique ways. Heeding our own inner wisdom is the lesson Uranus teaches us all. When we ignore the inner voice that speaks to us of the need for change, accidents may befall us, startling us into paying attention to what we really need to do in order to develop and evolve in consciousness. Uranus is, therefore, also known as the great awakener.

Uranus in Aries (or the first house) produces an uncanny awareness in the individual of what is needed in any situation—one who responds intuitively and quickly as needed. Trust that first reaction, and act on it. This person needs to act out a very individualistic and assertive self.

Uranus in Taurus (or the second house) indicates a certain genius for material affairs. A financial wizard of sorts, this extraordinary innovator is able to create resources needed for survival. Startling revelations help this person attract and dispense material resources for the good of all.

Uranus in Gemini (or the third house) sparks the intellectual acuity of the individual. This person's heightened mental awareness makes for stimulating and inspiring conversation filled with intuitive knowledge and verging on brilliance. Inadvertent truths are revealed in even the most everyday interactions.

Uranus in Cancer (or the fourth house) denotes an emotional depth as well as an impatience with the less conscious members of one's family. The revelation of emotional truths clarifies and enhances others' relationships. If inner needs and feelings aren't fully expressed, erratic emotional outbursts are likely.

Uranus in Leo (or the fifth house) denotes a certain unique playfulness and particular gifts in dealing with children, releasing an awareness of the loving, creative inner child. Creativity needs appreciation as well as expression to blossom into a constructive force here.

Uranus in Virgo (or the sixth house) represents the flair for enhancing the mundane aspects of life with an appreciation of the uniqueness of each moment and every task. This inventor of some efficiency-increasing technique also inspires appreciation of the everyday in others.

Uranus in Libra (or the seventh house) brings to relationships unsettling conditions that are sudden, stimulating, and growth-inducing. This individual brings change into others' lives and forces awareness of a self that would otherwise have remained hidden and unconscious to both parties.

Uranus in Scorpio (or the eighth house) makes for an erratic intensity: first apparent detachment and then sudden eruptions of deep feelings that urgently need expression. A valuable confidant, the individual possesses fantastic objective insights on situations in which there is no personal involvement.

Uranus in Sagittarius (or the ninth house) imparts an unpredictably venturesome nature to one whose greatest source of self-discovery is in academia, on the road, or in exploring higher consciousness. Intellectual genius alternates with apathy; friendships are many, but superficial.

Uranus in Capricorn (or the tenth house) marks the professional pioneer, one whose inventions or innovative works affect the lives of a great many others. This person is, however, definitely a misfit in terms of regular employment, unless his or her uniqueness has been utilized.

Uranus in Aquarius (or the eleventh house) emphasizes the uniqueness of the individual, at home with genius, unpredictability, and sudden change. This person suddenly sparks a friendship of seeming depth and importance and just as suddenly disappears, having enlightened both himself or herself and the other person in some special way.

Uranus in Pisces (or the twelfth house) produces an amazingly intuitive person, sometimes psychic, for whom feelings are mysterious, unpredictable, and uncontrollable. This person needs to channel great energies so that they don't become destructive and can then use that power to great advantage for all.

NEPTUNE: THE DREAMER

Neptune is the outer planet that links us with an inner source of peace, comfort, and unity with all humankind. Where it is placed by sign and house in our charts indicates a place of renewal for us, where we can nurture our souls and find refuge from the wear and tear of our daily lives, the demands or our relationships, and the struggle for survival that our lives may comprise.

Finding that center of inspiration and faith, of replenishment and inner peace enables us to move forward with hope, encouraging others and being assured that we are on the right path for ourselves.

Neptune in Aries (or the first house). Taking action is the way to find a sense of renewal and hope. Trust your instincts; moving ahead with your first impulse helps reinforce your trust in yourself.

Neptune in Taurus (or the second house). Creativity and letting your dreams take tangible form enable you to connect with an inner strength and satisfaction about life. Let your senses guide you, too, to the refreshing respite that nourishes your soul.

Neptune in Gemini (or the third house). Writing, speaking, dialoguing with yourself are all ways of channeling that inner voice that enables you to move forward confidently, at ease with your own decisions. Heed the voice beyond the chatter.

Neptune in Cancer (or the fourth house). Respond affirmatively to the intuitions that guide you in just the right ways to care for yourself emotionally. The compassion emanating from within helps you cultivate an abundance of givingness in dealing with others.

Neptune in Leo (or the fifth house). Total involvement in a hobby, activity, or even free play centers you, bringing back that creative, loving inner self. Dramatizing situations that are difficult for you helps you to generate innovative solutions.

Neptune in Virgo (or the sixth house). Intricate forms of creative involvement—crafts, weaving—help you turn heavily analytical energies into patterns of beauty, easing your burden and bringing inner calm. Create for yourself an oasis of order and perfection.

Neptune in Libra (or the seventh house). Places of great beauty can soothe your soul, as mind and senses glory in their aesthetically pleasing ambience. Moments of sacred communion in relationships also renew your faith in yourself and the kind of life you live.

Neptune in Scorpio (or the eighth house). Stay with difficult feelings, allowing them to expand till they fill you; they then change into something else, yielding the sense of renewal you crave. This is transformation, your path to peace.

Neptune in Sagittarius (or the ninth house). Often an idea or philosophy inspires you to ponder and generate connections and solutions that free you from mental burdens. Meeting others for a sharing of perspectives inspires a sense of hope as well.

Neptune in Capricorn (or the tenth house). Straightening out some mess, solving another's problems, making order out of chaos in a satisfying and visible way help you clear out barriers to an inner sense of strength and purpose. Lists help, too.

Neptune in Aquarius (or the eleventh house). You need to discover your own unique way of renewing hope, to go about your work of inspiring others. Sharing time with a friend also brings you back in touch with the sacred space of your inner being.

Neptune in Pisces (or the twelfth house). You are well acquainted with the source of your own inner refreshment and harmony—in music, poetry, art, the sounds of the ocean, or reciting a childhood prayer. The tools are familiar; sharing them is enhancing.

PLUTO: THE POWER PLANET

The farthest of all the planets in our solar system, Pluto symbolically rules that which is deepest within us, most powerful, yet often hardest to grab hold of and focus on in our daily lives. Connected with the concept of transformation, Pluto points in our charts to where conscious change needs to take place. This process involves becoming aware of, acting to own and acknowledge, and then letting go of whatever destructive life patterns we have evolved over time. This is transformation, the most difficult and the most powerful tool we have available to us in changing not only our lives but our inner selves.

Taking negative energy and turning it into a constructive force for good in our personal lives and in our society is a critical, life-preserving task. The work we do—as noted by Pluto's placement in our charts by sign and house position—recreates ourselves and makes our world a healthy place in which we can live and raise future generations.

Pluto in Aries (or the first house). We need to make sure that the impulses we follow are not just our destructive ones. The power we possess must be recognized and directed with consciousness so that its impact on others is positive and inspiring.

Pluto in Taurus (or the second house). Our deep knowledge of pleasure can bring hedonism to the depths of decadence. Instead, we can learn to appreciate and channel our life-force joyfully with whoever we are and in all that we create and enjoy.

Pluto in Gemini (or the third house). The magnificent and magical power of language needs to be recognized so that its destructive potential is not unleashed on the world in our interactions with others. Silence is sacred; it can be a tool for great change.

Pluto in Cancer (or the fourth house). Being faithful to our moods and the shifting tides of our feelings can bring us to a place of truth within ourselves. Knowing when the compassionate, loving emotions are called for comes from this process.

Pluto in Leo (or the fifth house). The place of most challenge and greatest potential is in allowing the inner child to play and be attended. Herein lies the precious gift of abandoning ourselves to joy, too often forgotten on our way to becoming adults.

Pluto in Virgo (or the sixth house). In our illnesses and daily woes comes the stuff of which our healing powers are made. Recognizing our diseases and finding our own cures enable us to extend that gift to others.

Pluto in Libra (or the seventh house). In the disharmony of our relationships are the seeds of answers to what we lack within us. Understanding this brings completeness, the strengthening of ourselves, and our union with others.

Pluto in Scorpio (or the eighth house). Our wishes for self-destruction point the way to which parts of us we need to release in order for our new selves to be born. Letting go of and forgiving who we were pave the way to our own rebirth.

Pluto in Sagittarius (or the ninth house). Beyond competition and intellectual strivings is a power much greater than anything we can aim for or name. Tapping into and channeling it for the good of all require a new understanding and a widened perspective.

Pluto in Capricorn (or the tenth house). Once we have done our best to achieve our goals, it is time to let go. At this point we will realize the truth and power of where we are and be brought to our next best place of success and fulfillment.

Pluto in Aquarius (or the eleventh house). Recognizing the importance of being part of something greater than our individual selves can guide us to taking personal risks that enlarge us at all levels. We then form a new kind of human being, creating an evolved society of humanity.

Pluto in Pisces (or the twelfth house). At one with the suffering of others, we are aware of the deepest, most personal level of being human. Faith then heals all those parts of us and our world—in pain, in lack, or in inability to change.

How to Find the Place of Jupiter, Saturn, Uranus, Neptune, and Pluto in Your Chart

Find your birth year in the left-hand column and read across the chart until you find your birth date. The top of that column will tell you where Jupiter, Saturn, Uranus, Neptune, and Pluto lie in your chart.

Key: ♈ ARIES | ♉ TAURUS | ♊ GEMINI | ♋ CANCER | ♌ LEO | ♍ VIRGO | ♎ LIBRA | ♏ SCORPIO | ♐ SAGITT. | ♑ CAPRI. | ♒ AQUAR. | ♓ PISCES | ℞ Retrograde

PLACE OF JUPITER, SATURN, URANUS, NEPTUNE, AND PLUTO—1880–1885

FIND YOUR BIRTH YEAR HERE	TABLE I-♃-Find Period including birthday. Your Jupiter is in — Sign	TABLE II-♄-Find Period including birthday. Your Saturn is in — Sign	TABLE III-♅ Your Uranus is in — Sign	TABLE IV-♆ Your Neptune is in — Sign	TABLE V-♇ Your Pluto is in — Sign
1880	1/1–4/2 ♓ 4/3–12/31 ♈	All Yr. ♈	All Yr. ♍	All Yr. ♉	All Yr. ♉
1881	1/1–4/11 ♈ 4/12–12/31 ♉	1/1–4/5 ♈ 4/6–12/31 ♉	All Yr. ♍	All Yr. ♉	All Yr. ♉
1882	1/1–4/21 ♉ 4/22–9/19 ♊ 9/20–11/17 ♋ 11/18–12/31 ♊	All Yr. ♉	All Yr. ♍	All Yr. ♉	All Yr. ♉
1883	1/1–5/4 ♊ 5/5–9/26 ♋ 9/27–12/31 ♌	1/1–5/23 ♉ 5/24–12/31 ♊	All Yr. ♍	All Yr. ♉	All Yr. ♉
1884	1/1–1/16 ♌ 1/17–5/21 ♋ 5/22–10/17 ♌ 10/18–12/31 ♍	All Yr. ♊	1/1–10/13 ♍ 10/14–12/31 ♍ ♎	All Yr. ♉	All Yr. ♉
1885	1/1–2/25 ♍ 2/26–6/14 ♌ 6/15–11/15 ♍ 11/16–12/31 ♎	1/1–7/5 ♊ 7/6–12/31 ♋	1/1–4/11 ♎ 4/12–7/28 ♍ 7/29–12/31 ♍ ♎	All Yr. ♉	All Yr. ♊

PLACE OF JUPITER, SATURN, URANUS, NEPTUNE, AND PLUTO—1886–1893

Year							
1886	1/1–3/29 3/30–7/15 7/16–12/16 12/17–12/31	♓ ♈ ♓ ♈	All Yr.	♋	All Yr.	♌	All Yr.	♊
1887	1/1–4/28 4/29–8/15 8/16–12/31	♈ ♉ ♈	1/1–8/18 8/19–12/31	♋ ♌	All Yr.	♌	1/1–8/15 8/16–9/21 9/22–12/31	♌ ♋ ♌	All Yr.	♊
1888	1/1–1/14 1/15–6/2 6/3–9/10 9/11–12/31	♉ ♈ ♉ ♈	1/1–3/9 3/10–4/20 4/21–12/31	♌ ♋ ♌	All Yr.	♌	1/1–5/25 5/26–12/31	♌ ♋	All Yr.	♊
1889	1/1–2/5 2/6–7/23 7/24–9/25 9/26–12/31	♈ ♉ ♉ ♉	1/1–10/6 10/7–12/31	♌ ♍	All Yr.	♌	1/1–3/20 3/21–12/31	♌ ♋	All Yr.	♊
1890	1/1–2/22 2/23–12/31	♊ ♋	1/1–2/24 2/25–6/27 6/28–12/31	♍ ♌ ♍	1/1–12/9 12/10–12/31	♌ ♍	All Yr.	♋	All Yr.	♊
1891	1/1–3/7 3/8–12/31	♋ ♓	1/1–12/26 12/27–12/31	♍ ♎	1/1–4/4 4/5–9/25 9/26–12/31	♍ ♌ ♍	All Yr.	♋	All Yr.	♊
1892	1/1–3/16 3/17–12/31	♓ ♈	1/1–1/22 1/23–8/29 8/30–12/31	♎ ♍ ♎	All Yr.	♍	All Yr.	♋	All Yr.	♊
1893	1/1–2/24 3/25–8/20 8/21–10/19 10/20–12/31	♈ ♉ ♈ ♉	All Yr.	♎	All Yr.	♍	All Yr.	♋	All Yr.	♊

177

PLACE OF JUPITER, SATURN, URANUS, NEPTUNE, AND PLUTO—1894–1900

FIND YOUR BIRTH YEAR HERE	TABLE I- ♃ -Find Period including birthday. Your Jupiter is in	Sign	TABLE II- ♄ -Find Period including birthday. Your Saturn is in	Sign	TABLE III- ♅ Your Uranus is in	Sign	TABLE IV- ♆ Your Neptune is in	Sign	TABLE V- ♇ Your Pluto is in	Sign
1894	1/1–4/1 4/2–8/13 8/14–12/31	♉ ♊ ♋	1/1–11/6 11/7–12/31	♎ ♏	All Yr.	♏	All Yr.	♊	All Yr.	♊
1895	1/1–4/10 4/11–9/4 9/5–12/31	♊ ♋ ♌	All Yr.	♏	All Yr.	♏	All Yr.	♊	All Yr.	♊
1896	1/1–2/29 3/1–4/17 4/18–9/27 9/28–12/31	♌ ♋ ♌ ♍	All Yr.	♏	All Yr.	♏	All Yr.	♊	All Yr.	♊
1897	1/1–10/27 10/28–12/31	♍ ♎	1/1–2/16 2/7–4/9 4/10–10/26 10/27–12/31	♏ ♐ ♏ ♐	1/1–12/1 12/2–12/31	♏ ♐	All Yr.	♊	All Yr.	♊
1898	1/1–11/26 11/27–12/31	♎ ♏	All Yr.	♐	1/1–7/3 7/4–9/10 9/11–12/31	♏ ♏ ♐	All Yr.	♊	All Yr.	♊
1899	1/1–12/25 12/26–12/31	♏ ♐	All Yr.	♐	All Yr.	♐	All Yr.	♊	All Yr.	♊
1900	All Yr.	♐	1/1–1/20 1/21–7/18 7/19–10/16 10/17–12/31	♐ ♑ ♐ ♑	All Yr.	♐	All Yr.	♊	All Yr.	♊

PLACE OF JUPITER, SATURN, URANUS, NEPTUNE, AND PLUTO—1901–1911

1901	1/1–1/18 1/19–12/31	♐ ♑	All Yr.	♑	1/1–7/19 7/20–12/25 12/26–12/31	♊ ♋ ♊	All Yr.	♇
1902	1/1–2/6 2/7–12/31	♑ ♒	All Yr.	♑	1/1–5/20 5/21–12/31	♊ ♋	All Yr.	♇
1903	1/1–2/19 2/20–12/31	♒ ♓	1/1–1/19 1/20–12/31	♑ ♒	All Yr.	♋	All Yr.	♇
1904	1/1–2/29 3/1–8/6 8/9–8/31 9/1–12/31	♓ ♈ ♓ ♈	All Yr.	♒	1/1–12/19 12/20–12/31	♋ ♌	All Yr.	♇
1905	1/1–3/7 3/8–7/20 7/21–12/4 12/5–12/31	♈ ♉ ♈ ♉	1/1–4/12 4/13–8/16 8/17–12/31	♒ ♓ ♒	All Yr.	♌	All Yr.	♇
1906	1/1–3/9 3/10–7/30 7/31–12/31	♉ ♊ ♋	1/1–1/7 1/8–12/31	♒ ♓	All Yr.	♌	All Yr.	♇
1907	1/1–8/18 8/9–12/31	♋ ♌	All Yr.	♓	All Yr.	♌	All Yr.	♇
1908	1/1–9/11 9/12–12/31	♌ ♍	1/1–3/18 8/19–12/31	♓ ♈	All Yr.	♌	All Yr.	♇
1909	1/1–10/11 10/12–12/31	♍ ♎	All Yr.	♈	All Yr.	♌	All Yr.	♇
1910	1/1–11/11 11/12–12/31	♎ ♏	1/1–5/16 5/17–12/14 12/15–12/31	♈ ♉ ♈	All Yr.	♌	All Yr.	♇
1911	1/1–1/29 12/10–12/31	♏ ♐	1/1–1/19 1/20–12/31	♈ ♉	All Yr.	♌	All Yr.	♇

179

PLACE OF JUPITER, SATURN, URANUS, NEPTUNE, AND PLUTO—1912–1920

FIND YOUR BIRTH YEAR HERE	TABLE I-♃-Find Period including birthday. Your Jupiter is in	Sign	TABLE II-♄-Find Period including birthday. Your Saturn is in	Sign	TABLE III-♅ Your Uranus is in	Sign	TABLE IV-♆ Your Neptune is in	Sign	TABLE V-♇ Your Pluto is in	Sign
1912	All Yr.	♐	1/1–7/6 7/17–11/30 12/1–12/31	♉ ♊ ♉	1/1–1/30 1/31–9/4 9/5–11/11 11/12–12/31	♑ ♒ ♑ ♒	All Yr.	♋	All Yr.	♊
1913	1/1 + 2 1/3–12/31	♐ ♑	1/1–3/25 3/26–12/31	♉ ♊	All Yr.	♒	All Yr.	♋	All Yr.	♊
1914	1/1–1/21 1/22–12/31	♑ ♒	1/1–8/24 8/25–12/6 12/7–12/31	♊ ♋ ♊	All Yr.	♒	1/1–9/22 9/22–12/14 12/15–12/31	♋ ♌ ♋		♊ ♋
1915	1/1–2/3 2/4–12/31	♒ ♓	1/1–5/11 5/12–12/31	♊ ♋	All Yr.	♒	1/1–7/18 7/19–12/31	♋ ♌	All Yr.	♋
1916	1/1–2/11 2/12–6/25 6/26–10/26 10/27–12/31	♓ ♈ ♉ ♈	1/1–10/16 10/17–12/7 12/8–12/31	♋ ♌ ♋	All Yr.	♒	1/1–3/19 3/20–5/1 5/2–12/31	♌ ♋ ♌	All Yr.	♋
1917	1/1–2/12 2/13–6/29 6/30–12/31	♈ ♉ ♊	1/1–7/23 7/24–12/31	♋ ♌	All Yr.	♒	All Yr.	♌	All Yr.	♋
1918	1/1–6/12 6/13–12/31	♊ ♋	All Yr.	♌	All Yr.	♒	All Yr.	♌	All Yr.	♋
1919	1/1–8/1 8/2–12/31	♋ ♌	1/1–8/11 8/12–12/31	♌ ♍	1/1–3/31 4/1–8/16 8/17–12/31	♒ ♓ ♒	All Yr.	♌	All Yr.	♋
1920	1/1–8/26 8/27–12/31	♌ ♍	All Yr.	♍	1/1–1/21 1/22–12/31	♒ ♓	All Yr.	♌	All Yr.	♋

PLACE OF JUPITER, SATURN, URANUS, NEPTUNE, AND PLUTO—1921–1931

1921	1/1–9/25 9/26–12/31	♍ ♎	1/1–10/7 10/8–12/31	♍ ♎	All Yr.	♓	All Yr.	♌	All Yr.	♋
1922	1/1–10/26 10/27–12/31	♎ ♏	All Yr.	♎	All Yr.	♓	All Yr.	♌	All Yr.	♋
1923	1/1–11/24 11/25–12/31	♏ ♐	1/1–12/19 12/20–12/31	♎ ♏	All Yr.	♓	All Yr.	♌	All Yr.	♋
1924	1/1–12/17 12/18–12/31	♐ ♑	1/1–4/5 4/6–9/13 9/14–12/31	♏ ♎ ♏	All Yr.	♓	All Yr.	♌	All Yr.	♋
1925	All Yr.	♑	All Yr.	♏	All Yr.	♓	All Yr.	♌	All Yr.	♋
1926	1/1–1/5 1/6–12/31	♑ ♒	1/1–1/22 12/3–12/31	♏ ♐	All Yr.	♓	All Yr.	♌	All Yr.	♋
1927	1/1–1/17 1/18–6/5 6/6–9/10 9/11–12/31	♒ ♓ ♈ ♓	All Yr.	♐	1/1–3/30 3/31–11/4 11/5–12/31	♓ ♈ ♓	All Yr.	♌	All Yr.	♋
1928	1/1–1/22 1/23–6/3 6/4–12/31	♓ ♈ ♉	All Yr.	♐	1/1–1/12 1/13–12/31	♓ ♈	All Yr.	♌	All Yr.	♋
1929	1/1–6/11 6/12–12/31	♉ ♊	1/1–3/14 3/15–5/4 5/5–11/29 11/30–12/31	♐ ♑ ♐ ♑	All Yr.	♈	1/1–9/20 9/21–12/31	♌ ♍	1/1–2/19 2/20–7/23 7/24–12/31	♍ ♌ ♍
1930	1/1–6/26 6/27–12/31	♊ ♋	All Yr.	♑	All Yr.	♈	All Yr.	♍	All Yr.	♋
1931	1/1–7/17 7/18–12/31	♋ ♌	All Yr.	♑	All Yr.	♈	All Yr.	♍	All Yr.	♋

PLACE OF JUPITER, SATURN, URANUS, NEPTUNE, AND PLUTO—1932–1939

FIND YOUR BIRTH YEAR HERE	TABLE I-♃-Find Period including birthday. Your Jupiter is in	Sign	TABLE II-♄-Find Period including birthday. Your Saturn is in	Sign	TABLE III-♅ Your Uranus is in	Sign	TABLE IV-♆ Your Neptune is in	Sign	TABLE V-♇ Your Pluto is in	Sign
1932	1/1–8/11 8/12–12/31	♌ ♍	1/1–2/23 2/24–8/13 8/14–11/19 11/20–12/31	♑ ♒ ♑ ♒	All Yr.	♈	All Yr.	♍	All Yr.	♋
1933	1/1–9/10 9/11–12/31	♍ ♎	All Yr.	♒	All Yr.	♈	All Yr.	♍	All Yr.	♋
1934	1/1–10/11 10/12–12/31	♎ ♏	All Yr.	♒	1/1–6/6 6/7–10/10 10/11–12/31	♈ ♉ ♈	All Yr.	♍	All Yr.	♋
1935	1/1–11/9 11/10–12/31	♏ ♐	1/1–2/14 2/15–12/31	♒ ♓	1/1–3/28 3/29–12/31	♈ ♉	All Yr.	♍	All Yr.	♋
1936	1/1–12/2 12/3–12/31	♐ ♑	All Yr.	♓	All Yr.	♉	All Yr.	♍	All Yr.	♋
1937	1/1–12/20 12/21–12/31	♑ ♒	1/1–4/25 4/26–10/18 10/19–12/31	♓ ♈ ♓	All Yr.	♉	All Yr.	♍	10/7–11/26 11/27–12/31	♋ ♌
1938	1/1–5/14 5/15–7/30 7/31–12/29 12/30–12/31	♒ ♓ ♒ ♓	1/1–1/14 1/15–12/31	♓ ♈	All Yr.	♉	All Yr.	♍	1/1–8/3 8/4–12/31	♌ ♋
1939	1/1–5/11 5/12–10/30 10/31–12/20 12/21–12/31	♓ ♈ ♓ ♈	All Yr.	♈	All Yr.	♉	All Yr.	♍	1/1–2/7 2/8–6/13 6/14–12/1	♌ ♋ ♌

PLACE OF JUPITER, SATURN, URANUS, NEPTUNE, AND PLUTO—1940–1949

1940	1/1–5/16 5/17–12/31	♈ ♉	1/1–3/20 3/21–12/31	♈ ♉	All Yr.	♉	All Yr.	♍	♌
1941	1/1–5/26 5/27–12/31	♉ ♊	All Yr.	♉	1/1–8/7 8/8–10/5 10/6–12/31	♉ ♊ ♉	All Yr.	♍	♌
1942	1/1–6/10 6/11–12/31	♊ ♋	1/1–5/8 5/9–12/31	♉ ♊	1/1–5/14 5/15–12/31	♉ ♊	1/1–10/3 10/4–12/31	♍ ♎	♌
1943	1/1–6/30 7/1–12/31	♋ ♌	All Yr.	♊	All Yr.	♊	1/1–4/18 4/19–8/2 8/3–12/31	♎ ♍ ♎	♌
1944	1/1–7/26 7/27–12/31	♌ ♍	1/1–6/20 6/21–12/31	♊ ♋	All Yr.	♊	All Yr.	♎	♌
1945	1/1–8/25 8/26–12/31	♍ ♎	All Yr.	♋	All Yr.	♊	All Yr.	♎	♌
1946	1/1–9/25 9/26–12/31	♎ ♏	1/1–8/2 8/3–12/31	♋ ♌	All Yr.	♊	All Yr.	♎	♌
1947	1/1–10/24 10/25–12/31	♏ ♐	All Yr.	♌	All Yr.	♊	All Yr.	♎	♌
1948	1/1–11/15 11/16–12/31	♐ ♑	1/1–9/19 9/20–12/31	♌ ♍	1/1–8/30 8/31–11/12 11/13–12/31	♊ ♋ ♊	All Yr.	♎	♌
1949	1/1–4/12 4/13–6/27 6/28–11/30 12/1–12/31	♑ ♒ ♑ ♒	1/1–4/3 4/4–5/29 5/30–12/31	♍ ♌ ♍	1/1–6/10 6/11–12/31	♊ ♋	All Yr.	♎	♌

PLACE OF JUPITER, SATURN, URANUS, NEPTUNE, AND PLUTO—1950–1957

FIND YOUR BIRTH YEAR HERE	TABLE I-♃-Find Period including birthday. Your Jupiter is in	Sign	TABLE II-♄-Find Period including birthday. Your Saturn is in	Sign	TABLE III-♅ Your Uranus is in	Sign	TABLE IV-♆ Your Neptune is in	Sign	TABLE V-♇ Your Pluto is in	Sign
1950	1/1–4/14 4/15–9/13 9/14–11/30 12/1–12/31	♒ ♓ ♒ ♓	1/1–11/20 11/21–12/31	♍ ♎	All Yr.	♋	All Yr.	♎	All Yr.	♌
1951	1/1–4/21 4/22–12/31	♓ ♈	1/1–3/7 3/8–8/13 8/14–12/31	♎ ♍ ♎	All Yr.	♋	All Yr.	♎	All Yr.	♌
1952	1/1–4/28 4/29–12/31	♈ ♉	All Yr.	♎	All Yr.	♋	All Yr.	♎	All Yr.	♌
1953	1/1–5/9 5/10–12/31	♉ ♊	1/1–10/22 10/23–12/31	♎ ♏	All Yr.	♋	All Yr.	♎	All Yr.	♌
1954	1/1–5/24 5/25–12/31	♊ ♋	All Yr.	♏	All Yr.	♋	All Yr.	♎	All Yr.	♌
1955	1/1–6/12 6/13–11/17 11/18–12/31	♋ ♌ ♍	All Yr.	♏	1/1–8/24 8/25–12/31	♋ ♌	1/1–12/23 12/24–12/31	♎ ♏	1/1–10/19	♌
1956	1/1–1/18 1/19–7/7 7/8–12/12 12/13–12/31	♍ ♌ ♍ ♎	1/1–1/12 1/13–5/14 5/15–10/10 10/11–12/31	♏ ♐ ♏ ♐	1/1–1/28 1/29–6/9 6/10–12/31	♌ ♋ ♌	1/1–3/11 3/12–10/18 10/19–12/31	♏ ♎ ♏	10/20–12/31	♍
1957	1/1–2/19 2/20–8/6 8/7–12/31	♎ ♏ ♎	All Yr.	♐	All Yr.	♌	1/1–6/16 6/17–8/4 8/5–12/31	♏ ♎ ♏	1/1–1/15 1/16–8/18 8/19–12/31	♍ ♌ ♍

PLACE OF JUPITER, SATURN, URANUS, NEPTUNE, AND PLUTO—1958–1965

1958	1/1–1/13 1/14–3/20 3/21–9/7 9/8–12/31	♎ ♏ ♎ ♎ ♏	All Yr.	♐	All Yr.	♏	1/1–4/12 4/13–6/10 6/11–12/31	♍ ♌ ♍
1959	1/1–2/10 2/11–4/24 4/25–10/5 10/6–12/31	♏ ♏ ♐ ♏ ♐	1/1–1/5 1/6–12/31	♐ ♑	All Yr.	♌	All Yr.	♍
1960	1/1–3/1 3/2–6/10 6/11–10/25 10/26–12/31	♐ ♑ ♐ ♑	All Yr.	♑	All Yr.	♌	All Yr.	♍
1961	1/1–3/14 3/15–8/11 8/12–11/3 11/4–12/31	♑ ♑ ♒ ♑ ♒	All Yr.	♑	1/1–10/31 11/1–12/31	♌ ♍	All Yr.	♏	All Yr.	♍
1962	1/1–3/24 3/25–12/31	♒ ♓	1/1–1/2 1/3–12/31	♑ ♒ ♒	1/1–1/9 1/10–8/8 8/9–12/31	♍ ♌ ♍ ♍	All Yr.	♏	All Yr.	♍
1963	1/1–4/3 4/4–12/31	♓ ♈	All Yr.	♒	All Yr.	♍	All Yr.	♏	All Yr.	♍
1964	1/1–4/11 4/12–12/31	♈ ♉	1/1–3/23 3/24–9/16 9/17–12/15 12/16–12/31	♒ ♒ ♓ ♒ ♓	All Yr.	♍	All Yr.	♏	All Yr.	♍
1965	1/1–4/21 4/22–9/20 9/21–11/16 11/17–12/31	♉ ♓ ♈ ♋ ♊	All Yr.	♓	All Yr.	♍	All Yr.	♏	All Yr.	♍

PLACE OF JUPITER, SATURN, URANUS, NEPTUNE, AND PLUTO—1966–1971

FIND YOUR BIRTH YEAR HERE	TABLE I-♃-Find Period including birthday. Your Jupiter is in	Sign	TABLE II-♄-Find Period including birthday. Your Saturn is in	Sign	TABLE III-♅ Your Uranus is in	Sign	TABLE IV-♆ Your Neptune is in	Sign	TABLE V-♇ Your Pluto is in	Sign
1966	1/1–5/4 5/5–9/26 9/27–12/31	♊ ♋ ♌	All Yr.	♓	All Yr.	♍	All Yr.	♏	All Yr.	♍
1967	1/1–1/15 1/16–5/22 5/23–10/18 10/19–10/31	♌ ♋ ♌ ♍	1/1–3/2 3/3–12/31	♓ ♈	All Yr.	♍	All Yr.	♏	All Yr.	♍
1968	1/1–2/26 2/27–6/14 6/15–11/14 11/15–12/31	♍ ♌ ♍ ♎	All Yr.	♈	1/1–9/27 9/28–12/31	♍ ♎	All Yr.	♏	All Yr.	♍
1969	1/1–3/29 3/30–7/14 7/15–12/15 12/16–12/31	♎ ♍ ♎ ♏	1/1–4/28 4/29–12/31	♈ ♉	1/1–5/20 5/21–6/23 6/24–12/31	♎ ♍ ♎	All Yr.	♏	All Yr.	♍
1970	1/1–4/30 5/1–8/14 8/15–12/31	♏ ♎ ♏	All Yr.	♉	All Yr.	♎	1/1–1/3 1/4–5/2 5/3–11/5 11/6–12/31	♏ ♐ ♏ ♐	1/1–12/31	♍
1971	1/1–1/13 1/14–6/4 6/5–9/10 9/11–12/31	♏ ♐ ♏ ♐	1/16–6/17 6/18–12/31	♉ ♊	All Yr.	♎	All Yr.	♐	1/1–10/5 10/6–12/31	♍ ♎

PLACE OF JUPITER, SATURN, URANUS, NEPTUNE, AND PLUTO—1972–1980

Year	Jupiter	Saturn	Uranus	Neptune	Pluto
1972	1/1–2/5 ♐ 2/6–7/23 ♑ 7/24–9/24 ♑ 9/25–12/31 ♑	1/1–1/9 ♊ 1/10–2/20 ♊ ᴙ ♊ 2/21–12/31 .	All Yr. ♎	All Yr. ♐	1/1–4/17 ♎ 4/18–6/30 ♍ ♎ 6/31–12/31
1973	1/1–2/22 ♑ 2/23–12/31 ♒	1/1–7/31 ♊ 8/1–12/31 ♋	All Yr. ♎	All Yr. ♐	All Yr. ♎
1974	1/1–3/7 ♒ ♒ 3/8–12/31 ♓	1/1–1/6 ♋ 1/7–4/17 ♊ ♋ 4/18–12/31 ♋	1/1–11/20 ♎ 11/21–12/31 ♎ ♏	All Yr. ♐	All Yr. ♎
1975	1/1–3/17 ♓ 3/18–12/31 ♈	1/1–9/16 ♋ 9/17–12/31 ♌	1/1–4/30 ♏ ♎ 5/1–9/7 ♏ 9/8–12/31 ♏	All Yr. ♐	All Yr. ♎
1976	1/1–3/25 ♈ 3/26–8/22 ♉ 8/23–10/15 ♊ 10/16–12/31 ♊	1/1–1/13 ♌ 1/14–6/4 ♋ ♌ 6/5–12/31 ♌	All Yr. ♏	All Yr. ♐	All Yr. ♎
1977	1/1–4/2 ♊ 4/3–8/19 ♊ 8/20–12/31 ♋	1/1–11/15 ♌ 11/16–12/31 ♌ ♍	All Yr. ♏	All Yr. ♐	All Yr. ♎
1978	1/1–4/10 ♊ 4/11–9/4 ♋ 9/5–12/31 ♌	1/1–1/4 ♍ 1/5–7/25 ♌ ♍ 7/26–12/31 ♍	All Yr. ♏	All Yr. ♐	All Yr. ♎
1979	1/1–2/28 ♌ 3/1–4/19 ♋ 4/20–9/28 ♌ 9/29–12/31 ♍	All Yr. ♍	All Yr. ♏	All Yr. ♐	All Yr. ♎
1980	1/1–10/26 ♍ 10/27–12/31 ♎	1/1–9/20 ♍ 9/21–12/31 ♍ ♎	All Yr. ♏	All Yr. ♐	All Yr. ♎

PLACE OF JUPITER, SATURN, URANUS, NEPTUNE, AND PLUTO—1981–1989

FIND YOUR BIRTH YEAR HERE	TABLE I- ♃ -Find Period including birthday. Your Jupiter is in	Sign	TABLE II- ♄ -Find Period including birthday. Your Saturn is in	Sign	TABLE III- ♅ Your Uranus is in	Sign	TABLE IV- ♆ Your Neptune is in	Sign	TABLE V- ♇ Your Pluto is in	Sign
1981	1/1–11/25 11/26–12/31	♎ ♏	All Yr.	♎	1/1–2/16 2/17–3/19 3/20–11/15 11/16–12/31	♏ ♐ ♏ ♐	All Yr.	♐	All Yr.	♎
1982	1/1–12/24 12/25–12/31	♏ ♐	1/1–11/28 11/29–12/31	♎ ♏	All Yr.	♐	All Yr.	♐	All Yr.	♎
1983	All Yr.	♐	1/1–5/5 5/6–8/23 8/24–12/31	♏ ♎ ♏	All Yr.	♐	All Yr.	♐	1/1–11/5 11/6–12/31	♎ ♏
1984	1/1–1/18 1/19–12/31	♐ ♑	All Yr.	♏	All Yr.	♐	1/1–1/17 1/18–6/21 6/22–11/20 11/21–12/31	♐ ♑ ♐ ♑	1/1–5/19 5/20–8/27 8/28–12/31	♏ ♎ ♏
1985	1/1–2/5 2/6–12/31	♑ ♒	1/1–11/15 11/16–12/31	♏ ♐	All Yr.	♐	All Yr.	♑	All Yr.	♏
1986	1/1–2/19 2/20–12/31	♒ ♓	All Yr.	♐	All Yr.	♐	All Yr.	♑	All Yr.	♏
1987	1/1–3/1 3/2–12/31	♓ ♈	All Yr.	♐	All Yr.	♐	All Yr.	♑	All Yr.	♏
1988	1/1–3/7 3/8–7/20 7/21–11/29 11/30–12/31	♈ ♉ ♊ ♉	1/1–2/12 2/13–6/9 6/10–11/11 11/12–12/31	♐ ♑ ♐ ♑	1/1–2/13 2/14–5/25 5/26–12/2 12/2–12/31	♐ ♑ ♐ ♑	All Yr.	♑	All Yr.	♏
1989	1/1–3/9 3/10–7/29 7/30–12/31	♉ ♊ ♋	All Yr.	♑	All Yr.	♑	All Yr.	♑	All Yr.	♏

189

PLACE OF JUPITER, SATURN, URANUS, NEPTUNE, AND PLUTO—1990–2000

1990	1/1–8/17 8/18–12/31	♋ ♌	All Yr.	♑	All Yr.	♑	All Yr.	♏
1991	1/1–9/11 9/12–12/31	♌ ♍	1/1–2/5 2/6–12/31	♑ ♒	All Yr.	♑	All Yr.	♏
1992	1/1–10/9 10/10–12/31	♍ ♎	All Yr.	♒	All Yr.	♑	All Yr.	♏
1993	1/1–11/9 11/10–12/31	♎ ♏	1/1–5/20 5/21–6/29 6/30–12/31	♒ ♓ ♒	All Yr.	♑	All Yr.	♏
1994	1/1–12/8 12/9–12/31	♏ ♐	1/1–1/27 1/28–12/31	♒ ♓	All Yr.	♑	All Yr.	♏
1995	1/1–12/31	♐	All Yr.	♓	1/1–3/31 4/1–6/7 6/8–12/31	♑ ♒ ♑	All Yr.	1/1–1/16 1/17–4/21 4/22–11/8 11/9–12/31	♏ ♐ ♏ ♐
1996	1/1–1/2 1/3–12/31	♐ ♑	1/1–4/6 4/7–12/31	♓ ♈	1/1–1/11 1/12–12/31	♑ ♒	All Yr.	♐
1997	1/1–1/20 1/21–12/31	♑ ♒	All Yr.	♈	All Yr.	♒	All Yr.	♐
1998	1/1–2/3 2/4–12/31	♒ ♓	1/1–6/8 6/9–10/24 10/25–12/31	♈ ♉ ♈	All Yr.	♒	1/1–1/27 1/28–8/21 8/22–11/26 11/27–12/31	♑ ♒ ♑ ♒	♐
1999	1/1–2/11 2/12–6/27 6/28–10/22 10/23–12/31	♓ ♈ ♉ ♈	1/1–2/27 2/28–12/31	♈ ♉	All Yr.	♒	All Yr.	♐
2000	1/1–2/13 2/14–6/29 6/30–12/31	♈ ♉ ♊	1/1–8/8 8/9–10/14 10/15–12/31	♉ ♊ ♉	All Yr.	♒	All Yr.	♐

SUCCESSFUL PLANNING WITH THE MOON SIGN GUIDE

"Where is the Moon?" is a question enlightened thinkers of all ages, irrespective of Sun Sign, have asked before coming to a decision or beginning a venture. You, too, should have the benefit of using the wisdom of ancient lunar science. The paragraphs that follow reveal the activities that can be pursued when the Moon occupies a certain sign and is favorably aspected.

Moon in Aries (♈): Begin new enterprises or ventures; make job applications; hire employees; bargain; pioneer some new idea or article; purchase objects made of metal; participate in sports; inspire others with your enthusiasm.

Moon in Taurus (♉): Begin things you desire to be permanent or want to last a long time; buy durable clothing; boost personal income; add to possessions; deal with bankers; open accounts.

Moon in Gemini (♊): Take short journeys; write letters; prepare articles for publication; advertise; give public speeches; make changes that are not apt to be permanent; interview employees; make contacts.

Moon in Cancer (♋): Deal with family matters or women in business or in the home, especially in connection with commodities, food, furniture; plan ocean trips; take care of domestic and property needs; purchase antiques.

Moon in Leo (♌): Contact persons in authority; ask for favors; buy and sell, especially jewelry, gold ornaments, quality clothes and articles; pursue love, social life, entertainment; attend the theater; display executive ability.

Moon in Virgo (♍): Pursue studies that will enhance your skills; seek employment; find improvements in health, hygiene; study statistics; stress the quality of services rendered to others; tend to the needs of pets or dependents.

Moon in Libra (♎): Strengthen marital ties; pursue partnership and cooperative affairs; purchase perfumes, jewelry, home decorations, beauty items, art objects; attend cultural events.

Moon in Scorpio (♏): Take care of tax and estate matters; boost joint resources; exploit hidden talents; make decisions, especially when shrewdness is required; rejuvenate valuable possessions; pursue confidential transactions.

Moon in Sagittarius (♐): Engage in outdoor activities, such as horse racing, hiking, sports, exercise in general; make realistic plans for the future; deal with lawyers, physicians, religious leaders, professional people; plan long journeys or academic goals.

Moon in Capricorn (♑): Be attentive to duties and responsibilities; engage in business related to management or organization, government interests, parental concerns; see influential people; undertake business and career pursuits.

Moon in Aquarius (♒): Pursue hopes and wishes, friendships, social contacts; enjoy clubs or fraternal societies, or seek membership in them; boost revenues from business, occupation; stress humanitarianism; engage in politics.

Cancer JUNE 22–JULY 23

Moon in Pisces (♓): Overcome limitations and problems; express charitable and sympathetic leanings; pursue peaceful and spiritual interests; boost self-confidence; find the causes for fears, worries, doubts; take care of confidential matters; visit those who are ill, convalescing, or confined.

DAILY PREDICTIONS

(All times listed in the following sections are EST.)

October 1990

Monday, October 1 (Moon in Aquarius to Pisces 8:43 A.M.). There's much to learn today if you are willing to take extra time and perhaps travel a short distance to check out details. Gains through property negotiations or maybe via a family member are also possible. Evening hours support domestic pleasures, entertaining friends.

Tuesday, October 2 (Moon in Pisces). Once in a while, an ESP experience or a dream you have will be right on target—and this could be one of those times. Although a health or job matter may be worrying in the A.M., later the sun will shine on a romance, or a marital antagonism will magically resolve itself.

Wednesday, October 3 (Moon in Pisces to Aries 12:43 P.M.). The day may begin with a verbal battle with a family member and close with another domestic encounter. In between, stay away from hassles in your career environment and forgo the urge to tell a higher-up just what you think about a current situation. Get enough rest!

194 ♋ Daily Predictions

Thursday, October 4 (FULL MOON in Aries). Talking at cross-purposes will hinder an early-morning conference, but you have ample support from an influential type who prefers to remain anonymous for now. Emotional fallout from the Full Moon spills over into a marital or partnership conflict in the P.M.

Friday, October 5 (Moon in Aries to Taurus 2:07 P.M.). A basic misconception in an agreement with a partner or collaborator could cause a setback in mutual plans. Potential for this to be cleared up quickly includes a radically changed outlook of all concerned. The evening yields innovative ideas for weekend activity.

Saturday, October 6 (Moon in Taurus). Mixed trends today favor marital or partnership harmony, domestic pleasures, and rewarding creative expression. At risk could be your financial security (if you follow that urge to speculate) and/or the state of your emotions (if you pursue a romantic dream that's really a mirage).

Sunday, October 7 (Moon in Taurus to Gemini 2:48 P.M.). You can be a welcome source of encouragement to a friend who badly needs to have his or her self-confidence built up. No one does this sort of thing better than you. Someone who visits you this evening may have interesting (and helpful) news to impart.

Monday, October 8 (Moon in Gemini). You may launch this week with a well-planned business agenda, which includes pursuing the approval of key people as well as the support of an offstage—and influential—booster. Avoid any accidents in the P.M. as well as friction at home. Romance is alive and doing nicely.

Tuesday, October 9 (Moon in Gemini to Cancer 4:30 P.M.). You can spend this day profitably by putting finishing touches on special plans and projects. You may also want to galvanize your forces for a soon-to-be-presented personal plan. Enhancing talents, skills, and personal appearance may be part of your program.

Wednesday, October 10 (Moon in Cancer). With the best of intentions, you may step on some toes or say the wrong words to the wrong people today. Usually the soul of tact, stellar patterns may prompt you to misdirect the day's energies (except for a pleasant romantic interlude this evening). Better news tomorrow.

Thursday, October 11 (Moon in Cancer to Leo 8:17 P.M.). Postmidnight hours may spell friction with a partner, but this should be merely a brief spat. Everyone's mood seems to brighten as the day wears on and you can accomplish business objectives without interference. Plans for a shared financial venture proliferate.

Friday, October 12 (Moon in Leo). The day begins on a note of frustration as a household upset seems to knock out favorite weekend plans. However, by midafternoon the picture brightens, and between that and an exciting romantic development, you'll feel as though you are sailing smoothly through the galaxy.

Saturday, October 13 (Moon in Leo). Someone you talk with today is likely to give you pertinent facts about a subject of vital interest to you. By keeping this to yourself, you'll be a step ahead of the competition. Enjoyable socializing may include a touch of business, as well, perhaps through a new contact.

Sunday, October 14 (Moon in Leo to Virgo 2:21 A.M.). Big ideas forming in your mind today may include a forthcoming trip, a new theme for a social or community event, or a study program geared toward enhancing one of your most promising talents. Ask your spouse or partner for input; you could be surprised at the results.

Monday, October 15 (Moon in Virgo). Local errands or a routine communication with a cohort may bring forth a treasure trove of new ideas and plans. Your gift for latching on to an opportunity is in top form, so when you see a chance to profitably promote a new angle of a favorite goal, you'll be quick to "go for it."

Tuesday, October 16 (Moon in Virgo to Libra 10:27 A.M.). Delightful news you receive early in the day might be somewhat offset later, as a domestic or family situation seems about to interfere with one of your plans, perhaps a travel itinerary. Your innovative solution to this dilemma may be destined for failure in the P.M.

Wednesday, October 17 (Moon in Libra). Today the outlook is a bit brighter, though there still may be a major obstacle to overcome before you can proceed with your agenda. Possibly the behind-the-scenes help of a friend or relative may work a small miracle. Or you may think of an almost-as-good alternative plan.

Thursday, October 18 (NEW MOON in Libra to Scorpio 8:25 P.M.). This will be a much better day than you have experienced recently, when your dreams have a reasonable chance of coming true—especially the romantic ones. A new domestic influence is making everyone happier, and you can reap the benefits this weekend.

Friday, October 19 (Moon in Scorpio). Once you can manage to get your personal finances in order and allocate funds for the weekend's expenses, you will be practically on your way. Your spouse or partner may be unexpectedly cooperative, or your romantic ideal could be coming closer to realization this evening.

Saturday, October 20 (Moon in Scorpio). If you are emotionally involved, this can be a good time to enchance the relationship. You could be at your best in the company of an admirer. Social pleasures may also be part of the day's plan, with a congenial group of friends providing the background for a happy occasion.

Sunday, October 21 (Moon in Scorpio to Sagittarius 8:10 A.M.). You may be feeling competitive and in the mood for outdoor exercise via a favorite sport—weather permitting. Some of you may be inspired by an idealistic speaker to pursue a humanitarian goal of some sort. Late P.M. brings exciting family news.

Monday, October 22 (Moon in Sagittarius). Following a tried-and-true method may actually prove to be the most direct route to success today. But try to sidestep a squabble with a co-worker, and do your best not to reveal a colleague's confidence. Evening hours bring both creative inspiration and a romantic call.

Tuesday, October 23 (Moon in Sagittarius to Capricorn 9:04 P.M.). Following through on a boring job today could bring a nice payoff. An agreement between you and a partner this evening could be the start of a promising new venture and can double your power for achieving a monetary goal. Good rapport is due to last.

Wednesday, October 24 (Moon in Capricorn). Follow your intuition today and work together with your spouse or a partner. A spirit of cooperation can bring you both to new achievements and right up the ladder to success. Creative and flexible ideas will work better than rigid adherence to traditional methods.

Thursday, October 25 (Moon in Capricorn). If you are unattached, today's theme of love-and-marriage could be of interest to you. Consider ways of encouraging an admirer or of meeting new ones. If you are already married, this is when your relationship can deepen as you work together toward shared goals.

Friday, October 26 (Moon in Capricorn to Aquarius 9:15 A.M.). This might be when you and a financial associate may decide to call a halt to escalating expenses. You may also have a serious discussion about which form of investment or other security measure will be most promising for your combined requirements.

Saturday, October 27 (Moon in Aquarius). An entertainment plan might turn out to be more expensive than you realized. Talk over probable costs with others involved in the affair. A matter concerning a child or a creative project might need extra attention or careful planning this evening.

Sunday, October 28 (Moon in Aquarius to Pisces 6:23 P.M.). You may emerge as the leader in a social setting, perhaps because you are so much at home with the topics of conversation. At the same time, you can learn from a new acquaintance, whose financial expertise may be very helpful to you at this time.

Monday, October 29 (Moon in Pisces). Just about all the signals will be "go" if you are planning a trip today. (There may be a small problem concerning a replacement at work while you're away.) It looks as though an academic goal or a family interest is at the heart of your travel plans (or, perhaps, romance?).

Tuesday, October 30 (Moon in Pisces to Aries 11:15 P.M.). This would be a good day for discussing investments with an expert, or for consulting a lawyer with a view to making up an ironclad contract. Also favored now are travel, contacting distant friends, and a love relationship. (But drive carefully in the P.M.)

Wednesday, October 31 (Moon in Aries). Don't look for any cooperation from a colleague today if you are promoting you own unique agenda in business-financial matters. The competitive spirit burns brightly in his or her heart! Evening hours are relaxing, as those around you fall in with your plans and enjoy your company.

November 1990

Thursday, November 1 (Moon in Aries). A morning conflict with a higher-up can be favorably resolved through a stroke of luck later in the day. Also on the positive side, an investment may prove to be profitable at this time. On a personal note, your love life can reflect the day's upsurge of good fortune.

Friday, November 2 (Moon in Aries to Taurus 12:32 A.M. FULL MOON in Taurus). You can spin through a busy morning, touching all important bases and achieving a special objective by midafternoon. Unfortunately, mixed trends in the P.M. may generate a falling-out with a friend or lover, or a financial disagreement.

Saturday, November 3 (Moon in Taurus). Basic problems or a mix-up in communications might interfere with your getting an early start on today's agenda. As time goes on, prospects brighten for a lively social evening, which may include meeting a new admirer and exchanging views on certain esoteric subjects.

Sunday, November 4 (Moon in Taurus to Gemini 12:07 A.M.). Breaking with the past in order to move ahead may be one way of getting the most out of this promising day. The break may concern a negative habit or relationship. Glamorous romance and a chance to build up an influential alliance can keep you happily on your toes.

Monday, November 5 (Moon in Gemini). Fairly cautious and self-protective by nature, you sometimes tend to do an about-face and rush into adventurous situations. This is what could happen during postmidnight hours of today, so watch your step! Later, an intriguing money opportunity may follow a circuitous route.

Tuesday, November 6 (Moon in Gemini to Cancer 12:08 A.M.). With burgeoning self-confidence and positive magnetism opening many a door for you today, you'll be surprised when someone close to you rejects a perfectly reasonable request. However, this may reflect his or her own problem of stress, simply projected onto you.

Wednesday, November 7 (Moon in Cancer). Your personal powers are intensified today and can help you to attain one or more of your high-priority desires. Except,

200 ☾ Daily Predictions

that is, for a late-morning setback when you march confidently into a VIP's office only to have a request turned down. Evening compensates romantically.

Thursday, November 8 (Moon in Cancer to Leo 12:52 A.M.). Although this can be an excellent day for financial matters and for getting your personal money interests lined up securely, the number-one theme of the day is L-O-V-E! Whether an ongoing romance, a marriage, or a new amour, this can easily become a day to remember.

Friday, November 9 (Moon in Leo). Postmidnight hours can be extremely fortunate, as Lady Luck seems to attend all money-producing or romantic events. The same cannot be said about speculation later in the day. Creativity, romance, and social plans may also be temporarily blocked. Forcing issues won't help—be patient!

Saturday, November 10 (Moon in Leo to Virgo 7:49 A.M.). It may seem almost magical, the way certain events develop today. A matter concerning a child, a lover, a relative, or a creative project could suddenly become firmly in place, pointing in the direction you've envisioned. Open communications contribute, too.

Sunday, November 11 (Moon in Virgo). Somewhere in the background, some confidential matter seems to need attention. But otherwise, this is a great day for travel, community involvement, family harmony, and educational activities. Marital or other partnership interests receive a needed boost as well this evening.

Monday, November 12 (Moon in Virgo to Libra 4:09 P.M.). Mentally, you're quick, alert, and perceptive as you evaluate a business transaction or a personal project. Family and property matters are emphasized this evening. You may be planning some home improvement or renovation, or welcome news about a family member could be heard.

Tuesday, November 13 (Moon in Libra). Though there is fundamental agreement in your household concerning general principles, all may not be peaceful there today, as personalities vie and compete. Your mate or partner may be especially unyielding to attempts made to lighten up the ambience—but keep trying!

Wednesday, November 14 (Moon in Libra). Can you handle a challenge to your self-assurance, vitality, and optimism? You may have to, as someone who has a certain amount of control over your agenda decides to exercise it. But be alert, patient, and tolerant, and you will have a valuable learning experience from it.

Thursday, November 15 (Moon in Libra to Scorpio 2:40 A.M.). A desire to play when you should be working ought to be postponed until the evening hours, when congenial cohorts will appreciate your lively spirits. A cultural activity could provide just the right environment to nurture one of your creative spurts.

Friday, November 16 (Moon in Scorpio). You might just miss a financial opportunity this morning. Timing will be essential. You develop stronger confidence in a creative idea or method this afternoon and should be able to persuade a key person of its value. Avoid verbal warfare with a colleague or partner in the late P.M.

Saturday, November 17 (NEW MOON in Scorpio to Sagittarius 2:40 P.M.). Something dear to your heart will get a new lease on life today, whether this is a romance, a matter pertaining to a child, or a special and original project you've been dallying with lately. Service to others could bring rewards this evening.

Sunday, November 18 (Moon in Sagittarius). A fitness class could transform you today—or you could transform *it*, with your current supercharged vitality. Convivial time spent with favorite cohorts is just the prescription for evening hours, giving you the chance to celebrate a currently burgeoning business deal.

Monday, November 19 (Moon in Sagittarius). Discuss serious plans with co-workers and try to match up talents with assignments if possible. Something you hear today,

202 ☏ Daily Predictions

or someone you meet, can be the link to a fortunate financial development. There is also the possibility that a confidential tip can be worth gold.

Tuesday, November 20 (Moon in Sagittarius to Capricorn 3:32 A.M.). Today you may discover that you and an associate work well together as a team. This might double the success potential of a shared project now in the talking stage. You are in the mood for new and different cuisine, entertainment, or conversation tonight.

Wednesday, November 21 (Moon in Capricorn). Your own enthusiasm and optimism can persuade others to cooperate in one of your current pet projects. You are smart to arrange for rewards all around as the frosting on the cake for your helpers. Your spouse or partner may be in the mood to celebrate a business triumph.

Thursday, November 22 (Moon in Capricorn to Aquarius 4:08 P.M.). A new and untried method for handling a certain work assignment or a personal obligation is now developing. Be on the alert for progressive methods and contemporary tools. A joint financial project could get off to a good start today. Stay with it.

Friday, November 23 (Moon in Aquarius). All that glitters today may not be exactly gold, especially toward the end of the workday when an offer you receive might be misrepresented. Also, be careful about any romantic encounter this evening; an element of secrecy in this case could be a warning signal.

Saturday, November 24 (Moon in Aquarius). Today's agenda could include a cultural or entertainment project. Another person's creative (and financial) input can assure its success. Sharing ideas for an upcoming travel itinerary will be helpful, too. It's always helpful to check with someone who knows the ropes.

Sunday, November 25 (Moon in Aquarius to Pisces 2:33 A.M.). You may be planning to indulge a longing for travel with a short trip to visit relatives or friends, but things may not go as smoothly as you'd like. In fact, the less you expect in the way of promptness, ease of travel, and other people's dispositions, the better.

Monday, November 26 (Moon in Pisces). Get an early start on presenting an unusual or creative idea to the proper parties. Having lunch with an influential person can be another plus for the success of this proposition. Later, consult an expert in a legal or academic matter. Avoid friction at home in the P.M.

Tuesday, November 27 (Moon in Pisces to Aries 9:07 A.M.). Don't make waves in your job environment today, as tempers may be high or someone with an uncertain temperament may overreact. Evening hours are more peaceful, though an unexpected response from your mate or partner may surprise you. Guard your health, too.

Wednesday, November 28 (Moon in Aries). A money-making opportunity could be waiting for you in the early morning, so turn up your alarm. You might be asked to take charge of a project or a committee, through which your prestige can be enhanced. Another late-P.M. challenge by a partner may concern joint funds.

Thursday, November 29 (Moon in Aries to Taurus 11:38 A.M.). Postmidnight hours are rife with upbeat romance and a general theme of good fortune. Later, job news is rewarding, or a colleague may confide interesting information. Today's social trend brings a festive note, perhaps a birthday or anniversary bash?

Friday, November 30 (Moon in Taurus). This is not the day for speculation or overspending your hard-earned cash, even though that's just what you may feel like doing. Keep romance on a light, carefree note. Heavy emotional scenes clash with the day's overall theme of lightheartedness. Late P.M. generates security.

December 1990

Saturday, December 1 (Moon in Taurus to Gemini 11:23 A.M.). Whether by choice or necessity, you may be inclined toward solitary pursuits today, or perhaps need to catch up on certain personal matters that can no longer be postponed. In any case, your energetic approach will soon make a big dent in the work load.

Sunday, December 2 (FULL MOON in Gemini). Good news or an opportunity concerning an educational program may represent the culmination of great effort. There may still be loose ends to be tied up which could be financial. Take extra care of your health today, especially your nerves, digestion, and emotions.

Monday, December 3 (Moon in Gemini to Cancer 10:28 A.M.). You are in good spirits and loaded with the self-assurance that enables you to cope gracefully with some of the opposition you're due to encounter from a colleague. Brace yourself for criticism on the home front, too, as late P.M. brings unanticipated challenge.

Tuesday, December 4 (Moon in Cancer). An up-and-down sort of day begins with some mild confusion at home or a need for you to revise plans to accommodate some responsibility. Your creativity and charisma blossom in the afternoon and can be definite career assets. Late evening presents you with a problem to work out.

Wednesday, December 5 (Moon in Cancer to Leo 11:01 A.M.). This should be an exceptionally fine day for job advancement and financial gain. A confidential matter might get a welcome boost, as there seems to be some help available from an influential person. Evening finds you in a festive mood, enjoying friends.

Thursday, December 6 (Moon in Leo). Money is again highlighted and quick thinking in the A.M. could spark a profitable line of action. But stay with proven financial moves, as this is not the time to gamble with adventurous experiments. Evening may produce a romantic puzzle, or a youngster's challenging behavior.

Friday, December 7 (Moon in Leo to Virgo 2:40 P.M.). Restoring harmony in a relationship recently rather difficult makes you both feel good. On the other hand, a neighbor or relative may be really asking for trouble this evening by bringing up some old grievance; it probably will be up to you to keep the peace.

Saturday, December 8 (Moon in Virgo). Out-of-town scenery looks awfully good to you today. An impromptu trip could be refreshing and stimulate your fertile mind and creative powers. Communications are important now, especially with a family member or a key community figure. Guard health and diet in the late evening.

Sunday, December 9 (Moon in Virgo to Libra 10:01 P.M.). You may be getting an early start on holiday plans, or maybe you are part of a community program now being assembled. A domestic issue may benefit from the input of all the family, or scheduling the household routine to accommodate houseguests could require cooperation.

Monday, December 10 (Moon in Libra). Your mate or a family member will have a lot to say about one of your proposed purchases or entertainment plans. This may develop into a very touchy topic, so try to tone down resentments on all sides. By day's end your agenda will be back on track and ruffled feelings smoothed.

Tuesday, December 11 (Moon in Libra). Property matters, leases, rentals, and so on can be remunerative now. You may also become involved in a glamorous home-decor project as you ready your home for holiday entertaining. Disappointing news or a negative response to a request may dim the evening's activities, but this can change.

Wednesday, December 12 (Moon in Libra to Scorpio 8:28 A.M.). A softening influence on a partnership might mean your mate or colleague is now happier because of a financial or health upswing. In any case, joint ventures and shared interests become more rewarding. Romance and children's interests also flourish.

Thursday, December 13 (Moon in Scorpio). A creative project started today could be headed for success if you approach it with zest and optimism. But in the realm of finances, bypass the urge to overspend or to speculate. A meaningful development in the P.M. almost surely relates to your emotional feelings.

Friday, December 14 (Moon in Scorpio to Sagittarius 8:45 P.M.). From here on your social life is due to become increasingly busy and you are likely to encounter several old friends or former romance partners in your crowded calendar. Crossed signals this evening may result in wrong directions or misunderstood timing.

Saturday, December 15 (Moon in Sagittarius). If you are a snow bunny and live in a cold-weather region, you might be on your way to the slopes this weekend. On the other hand, attractions closer to home may include a chance to advance a promising business deal or an equally promising romance. Late P.M. news is good.

Sunday, December 16 (NEW MOON in Sagittarius). Healthy exercise and wholesome activity continue to attract you. This evening, you may settle in for additional work on a special project that has a peripheral connection with your job. In some ways, you may feel that a new cycle is beginning, and you could be right.

Monday, December 17 (Moon in Sagittarius to Capricorn 9:36 A.M.). A relationship could be enriched today, whether this means more closeness in a business alliance, more harmony in a friendship, or more dynamism in a love affair or marriage. You may be reviewing the course of a business transaction to improve it.

Tuesday, December 18 (Moon in Capricorn). This is another day when close associations improve and become very rewarding. You and your mate or lover could realize that you are actually two sides of the same coin—or deeper knowledge of a business partner's motivation enhances your ability to work well together.

Wednesday, December 19 (Moon in Capricorn to Aquarius 10:00 P.M.). A sudden development in a love relationship can either make or break it. If built on a sound basis, today can bring a positive turning point. If the alliance is forged by weak links, today could signal a quick finale. Family and business interests flourish.

Thursday, December 20 (Moon in Aquarius). Joint resources may come under consideration as you and your spouse or partner sit down and review holiday expenses already committed. The sum total may run off the sides of the sheet, but you'll manage! Lavish entertainment is scheduled, whether you are a host or a guest today.

Friday, December 21 (Moon in Aquarius). You'll be thinking of the pleasure ahead of you today as you rush to get caught up on the day's chores. You may be leaving shortly on an out-of-town trip, and at this point you're cramming all the essentials into a busy entertainment schedule. Avoid money risks.

Saturday, December 22 (Moon in Aquarius to Pisces 8:49 A.M.). Hectic activity in the early A.M. could accompany your departure on a trip or preparations for the weekend's domestic agenda. Contact with distant friends is due anyway, whether in person or via phone. Wherever you are, romance smiles on you.

Sunday, December 23 (Moon in Pisces). Postmidnight hours intensify that romantic urge, and it won't be at all surprising if many an unattached Cancerian gets engaged or married before the year's end. Today could be quite thrilling in that regard, but is also favorable for regular social events or patching up old feuds.

Monday, December 24 (Moon in Pisces to Aries 4:46 P.M.). The early part of the day can be immensely promising, as you are likely to get some good news concerning career-financial advancement, and a strong alliance becomes even stronger. However, evening hours may find you and yours tense, overtired—in the mood to be pampered.

Tuesday, December 25 (Moon in Aries). Mixed trends support business-financial interests, but on the personal side, there still seems to be tension in your environment. Avoid overindulgence, being critical of loved ones, and anything else that might exacerbate the situation. Seek the company of a serene person.

Wednesday, December 26 (Moon in Aries to Taurus 9:10 P.M.). Communications will be important today. There isn't much that can't be talked out and into a peaceful settlement. Involvement in a community project for the holiday season may still be part of your schedule; this is often soothing to the harried nerves!

Thursday, December 27 (Moon in Taurus). You have your vim, vigor, and vitality back in full force after a somewhat hectic festive period. Though there's some temptation toward extravagance today, in general you are holding to moderation in re expenditures. Social pleasures and romantic delights due in the P.M.

Friday, December 28 (Moon in Taurus to Gemini 10:27 P.M.). Have confidence in a hunch you get today and follow through on it when the time is right. This may refer to business, but could have romantic overtones. End-of-year tasks may be keeping you busy at work or at home today, with exciting social plans for tonight.

Saturday, December 29 (Moon in Gemini). Whether you are cooking up a surprise party for a friend or a clever and clandestine business-financial maneuver, you'll enjoy today's behind-the-scenes cloak-and-dagger activities. You might receive unexpected funds by mail—a gift or someone paying off an old debt.

Sunday, December 30 (Moon in Gemini to Cancer 10:03 P.M.). Be very careful about such things as communications, reservations, travel itineraries, and party instructions (and addresses), as snafus are more than likely today. Late-evening hours find you at your best.

Monday, December 31 (FULL MOON in Cancer). You may have to try a bit harder to remain serene and in control today, as those around you tend to be high-strung and unpredictable. Opt for a quiet New Year's Eve with a few good friends, rather than a wild night out. Stellar patterns urge that you be self-protective.

January 1991

Tuesday, January 1 (Moon in Cancer to Leo 9:55 P.M.). Aside from the usual New Year's Day significance, this first day of 1991 brings an important trend in a close relationship. Some confrontation or differences of opinions might be disturbing, but it looks as though all's well in the final outcome.

Wednesday, January 2 (Moon in Leo). This could be a good-news day, indeed, as a business project or a bit of sheer luck could enable you to pursue one of your favorite over-the-rainbow schemes. An innovative idea could be translated into a winning formula—perhaps in the framework of partnership interests.

Thursday, January 3 (Moon in Leo to Virgo 11:58 P.M.). A dominant theme in today's agenda, romance makes its presence strongly felt very early in the A.M. Even though evening hours may produce a slight disagreement on the subject of money, open discussion will be the most rewarding way out of the dilemma.

Friday, January 4 (Moon in Virgo). An impromptu travel plan may emerge from delightfully shared views with your spouse or favorite romance companion. Whatever impediment may have been delaying your joint decision to take off on a pleasurable trek to a not-too-distant destination now seems to evaporate.

Saturday, January 5 (Moon in Virgo). Except for an early-evening conflict with a companion (or perhaps a health problem) today appears to be studded with green lights and other "go" signals. Community interests, local trips, academic and family matters are all favored. A financial upswing is also due.

Sunday, January 6 (Moon in Virgo to Libra 5:34 A.M.). Social and domestic interests are paramount in today's prospects. You may be celebrating someone's birthday, or perhaps you'll host a community or organizational event in your home. For unattached Cancerians, this could be a subtly romantic day.

Monday, January 7 (Moon in Libra). A turnabout in trends makes today one of possible conflict and, at the very least, a time to reassess your views on a special partnership or collaboration. Possibly there were hidden factors in an original agreement, or misunderstandings may have arisen recently. Delay making a firm commitment.

Tuesday, January 8 (Moon in Libra to Scorpio 3:00 P.M.). Although this is definitely not the day for speculation or other financial risk, on the romance scene things may be picking up nicely. There's a hint, however, that you should be guided today by an experience of the past; search your memory and watch your step.

Wednesday, January 9 (Moon in Scorpio). Mixed trends support creative expression, as well as partnership of a creative nature. On the down side, all finances (personal and shared) should be dealt with carefully; no matter how enticing the speculative proposition offered to you, be alert to risks and pitfalls.

Thursday, January 10 (Moon in Scorpio). An intriguing prospect today for some unattached Cancerians is that you may meet your future mate, perhaps at a social or community affair. Also favored are matters concerning children and plans for recreational pleasures. But in the P.M. be cautious in travel and transportation.

Friday, January 11 (Moon in Scorpio to Sagittarius 3:07 A.M.). An interesting opportunity could materialize today, perhaps leading to a higher notch on the job ladder. Evening hours support romance, a brisk exercise workout, and/or a social recreational program. Significant progress can be made on a creative project.

Saturday, January 12 (Moon in Sagittarius). You begin the day with vim and vigor, which carry you through a superactive day's agenda. However, any late evening plans may find you yawning and not your usual lively self. This will be a good time to catch up on rest and relaxation and maybe a few phone calls.

Sunday, January 13 (Moon in Sagittarius to Capricorn 4:01 P.M.). Sometime during the early part of the day you and a close associate will have opposing views on a financial matter; to spend or not to spend may be the question. You're due to reach an accord by early evening, when common sense triumphs for one of you.

Monday, January 14 (Moon in Capricorn). Joint interests progress smoothly today, though it does look as though you will be the one to make whatever compromise may be necessary. You and a favorite companion may decide to move rather quickly on one of your plans, perhaps concerning a creative or travel itinerary.

Tuesday, January 15 (Moon in Capricorn—NEW MOON Solar Eclipse at 6:51 P.M.). This day could be notable for the progress of a shared enterprise, as you and your mate

212 ☊ Daily Predictions

or partner join forces in a most positive manner. You have numerous options for resolving a long-drawn-out problem or redefining a responsibility.

Wednesday, January 16 (Moon in Capricorn to Aquarius 4:05 A.M.). Plans to ensure the security of joint resources could benefit from the advice of an expert. Don't overlook seemingly unimportant details in any financial or other material considerations. Keep primary goals in mind and resist distractions.

Thursday, January 17 (Moon in Aquarius). You may decide to follow a business trend today that includes an element of risk, or the possibility of too high an outlay of cash on your part. Think again before pursuing this particular pot-of-gold enticement. Resist the urge to overspend or speculate in the P.M.

Friday, January 18 (Moon in Aquarius to Pisces 2:24 P.M.). Postmidnight hours could bring a serious commitment (marital or business) between you and a close associate. Later, social expenses may mount rapidly, so be on the alert for sensible curtailments. P.M. features a distant contact or travel discussions.

Saturday, January 19 (Moon in Pisces). News from a distance brightens the A.M. hours, and you may even embark on an impromptu local trip around midday. Discussions and decisions involving legal, academic, or family interests should progress well at this time, but remember to be realistic about long-term costs.

Sunday, January 20 (Moon in Pisces to Aries 10:28 P.M.). This can be an exciting day in terms of marital or other partnership developments, an intriguing social trend, and clues concerning near-future career or business activities. Previously murky pictures are being clarified and your own intuition is intensifying.

Monday, January 21 (Moon in Aries). Postmidnight hours do not support speculation or other risks (with either love or money). Later, challenges from a colleague blend with

January 1991 213

a great financial opportunity; you'll know just how to deal with this situation to extract the benefits and downplay the adverse potentials.

Tuesday, January 22 (Moon in Aries). If you can sidestep a misunderstanding with a higher-up or colleague in the A.M., by afternoon hours you should be more or less in the driver's seat with a promising monetary prospect in view. If you are unattached, you may wish to further a budding romantic attraction now.

Wednesday, January 23 (Moon in Aries to Taurus 4:02 A.M.). The wee small hours could bring the revival of an old anxiety—or an associate may heap responsibility upon you. Later, exhilarating social-romantic plans are sure to be more costly than you expect, but you may feel they are well worth the added expense.

Thursday, January 24 (Moon in Taurus). Mixed trends support creative work (and creative problem-solving) as well as open channels of communication with those around you. However, speculation and other money risks are definite no-no's, and you might also make a note to be meticulous in your handling of joint funds. *Day One*

Friday, January 25 (Moon in Taurus to Gemini 7:07 A.M.). You've earned this nice easy end-of-workweek day, when job chores proceed smoothly and associates are cooperative. This is a good time to prepare for upcoming projects, to line up behind-the-scenes support for special plans, and utilize influential contacts. *Two*

Saturday, January 26 (Moon in Gemini). Be open to inspiration today, whether in a creative context or via a practical way to solve a stubborn problem—perhaps related to a health matter (your health or that of someone close to you). Look to your own prior experience in seeking a way to defuse an antagonism. *Three*

Sunday, January 27 (Moon in Gemini to Cancer 8:24 A.M.). The good news today could concern a joint money investment or arrangement. The so-so news seems to be *Four* centered on your own personal plans, social or romantic expectations, or a domestic issue that keeps resurfacing from time to time. Patience will pay off.

Monday, January 28 (Moon in Cancer). It's fortunate that you'll be self-confident and optimistic today, because you'll need these attributes in order to cope with a series of challenges and criticisms from those around you. However, a small extravagance and exciting romantic or travel prospects brighten the P.M.

Tuesday, January 29 (Moon in Cancer to Leo 9:04 A.M.). A close associate may be difficult in the morning hours, but the picture brightens as the day wears on. Money might be at the root of the problem and could also be the subject of a welcome late-night communication or other development that's ringed with dollar signs.

Wednesday, January 30 (Moon in Leo—FULL MOON Lunar Eclipse at 1:11 A.M.). Your mate, partner, or other stalwart companion can be your tower of strength today, when a few upsets (in plans or in people's attitudes) might make you feel a bit shaky. These days, it does seem to be money that's the root of problems.

Thursday, January 31 (Moon in Leo to Virgo 10:45 A.M.). If you are out in postmidnight hours, be extra careful in travel and transportation; don't take any risks with a solid romance, either. Later in the day, you may find that communications are either disappointing or subject to delays or mechanical snafus.

February 1991

Friday, February 1 (Moon in Virgo). Get your weekend plans in good order early in the day and take advantage of stellar patterns that support a joint venture, local travel, or domestic projects. Late this evening, romance flourishes and you could also find that your creative urges are clamoring for self-expression.

Saturday, February 2 (Moon in Virgo to Libra 3:03 P.M.). Communications with relatives, neighbors and/or long-time friends today can lead to a nice array of social dates in the weeks ahead. If you have scheduled a dinner or party in your home this evening, it should be a great success (with perhaps a surprise guest).

Sunday, February 3 (Moon in Libra). If you are the type of person who successfully mixes business with pleasure (as so many Cancerians are) a social event today could prove to be most productive for you, businesswise. But on the debit side, your mate or partner might not be in a cooperative mood, so be tactful.

Monday, February 4 (Moon in Libra to Scorpio 11:02 P.M.). You may be busily restructuring one of your important plans or projects today, in order to make it more workable and more successful (or profitable). Don't look for domestic or marital harmony in the P.M.; in fact, stay away from any controversial issues.

Tuesday, February 5 (Moon in Scorpio). Postmidnight hours may bring you a temptation to take financial risks (or to overspend wildly), so be on guard. Later, heed the words of wisdom of an expert in business-financial matters. P.M. features romance, pleasant contact with a distant friend, perhaps an impromptu travel plan.

Wednesday, February 6 (Moon in Scorpio). Your business-financial judgment in the morning hours is not to be trusted! You'll be more realistic (and more intuitive) later in the day. Interests concerning children, creative projects, and an important romance are supported in the evening hours.

Thursday, February 7 (Moon in Scorpio to Sagittarius 10:24 A.M.). An extra rush of activity at work or in your everyday routine can keep you hopping and can also bring

216 ♋ Daily Predictions

unexpectedly good results in terms of a new assignment (a creative collaboration, perhaps). Resist the urge to overdo or overindulge in the P.M.

Friday, February 8 (Moon in Sagittarius). Mixed trends today may find you easily distracted from your pursuit of an attainable goal by your fascination with an unrealistic one. Sort out your priorities as well as your qualifications before making firm decisions in either business or personal activities.

Saturday, February 9 (Moon in Sagittarius to Capricorn 11:17 P.M.). If you can keep in mind the fact that almost any risk you take today with your own or joint funds might lead to disaster, then you can enjoy a reasonably upbeat agenda. Late evening could bring a communication from a past friend or lover.

Sunday, February 10 (Moon in Capricorn). Early in the day you might have to make a financial decision involving marital or partnership resources; remember to be a self-protective, cautious Cancerian! Later, social and romantic interests proceed delightfully and an unexpected late-night call brings joy.

Monday, February 11 (Moon in Capricorn). You will derive extra pleasure and satisfaction today through shared ventures, work assignments, and personal plans. Those around you will tend to cooperate, and your love life soars along at a new height. If you are involved in creative work, this can be a productive day.

Tuesday, February 12 (Moon in Capricorn to Aquarius 11:17 A.M.). Postmidnight hours could bring you a bit of financial news or an investment tip that can prove to be profitable for you. Later in the day the unsolicited advice of a knowledgeable person can be just what's needed for you to resolve a problem.

Wednesday, February 13 (Moon in Aquarius). This is not the time to make a major move that could affect your security or life-style. Such a change may happen soon, but

February 1991 ✡ **217**

at this point you are not thinking realistically or considering all the various possibilities. News from a distance is encouraging today and may signal travel.

Thursday, February 14 (Moon in Aquarius—NEW MOON at 12:33 P.M.—to Pisces 9:00 P.M.). This day can be significant because of a shift in your mental attitude, basic values, or deep convictions (there is also an indication that love is a powerful influence). All of this may be beneath the surface for the time being.

Friday, February 15 (Moon in Pisces). Don't allow a prior worry, anxiety, or fear to dim your confidence and enthusiasm of the present time. What's past is past. Seek the company of cheerful, upbeat friends and you'll find you have much to contribute to the social rewards of the upcoming weekend.

Saturday, February 16 (Moon in Pisces). You could find that someone you least suspected shares your personal ideals and values. You may also discover that you and another creative person could be just the right combination to produce a marketable new idea or product. Various avenues are open to you now.

Sunday, February 17 (Moon in Pisces to Aries 4:12 A.M.). This day could be notable for the dynamic new possibilities opening to you in business-career related matters. Perhaps through a social contact or a long-time friend, you are making valuable new acquaintances, who—in time—can be important to you.

Monday, February 18 (Moon in Aries). It would be a good idea to have your day's agenda firmly in place and your own game plan in shipshape order, as today can produce a number of challenges. You can handle these if you are certain of your capabilities and self-assured in your approach to key people.

Tuesday, February 19 (Moon in Aries to Taurus 9:25 A.M.). An early-morning swirl of social activity via phone calls, invitations, chats, etc., may meet with a wet blanket in the form of a boss or other authority figure, who feels you should be spending time on other matters! You might face a minor financial dilemma, too.

Wednesday, February 20 (Moon in Taurus). The social theme (however much disapproved of) continues to dominate your thoughts. You may be planning a surprise birthday party for someone, or becoming involved in a community project. Evening hours might produce a temporary misunderstanding with a loved one.

Thursday, February 21 (Moon in Taurus to Gemini 1:11 P.M.). Today you may have ambivalent feelings about several matters: a job assignment, a proposed trip, a romance that blows hot and cold, and a financial problem (perhaps a joint-funds dilemma). In any case, by day's end you'll sort out the answers.

Friday, February 22 (Moon in Gemini). You could be in line for a favor or some preferred treatment from a higher-up, so be prepared to make the most of it in terms of money and status. You might have mixed emotions concerning weekend plans, perhaps indecisive until late this evening about the itinerary.

Saturday, February 23 (Moon in Gemini to Cancer 3:57 P.M.). Your self-confidence and charisma are heightened today and even a slight—and temporary—setback in romance this evening doesn't dim your enthusiasm and expectations. If you have links with someone at a distance, these could intensify now.

Sunday, February 24 (Moon in Cancer). This day seems to be divided between your inner progress and confidence (excellent, and increasing) and your outer reactions to another's opposition to your plans (you might be at a loss for words, or otherwise uncertain). This will all work out satisfactorily, so don't be discouraged.

Monday, February 25 (Moon in Cancer to Leo 6:13 P.M.). The postmidnight hours could bring you a romantic message that makes up for prior disappointments. Later in the day, interesting new moneymaking possibilities, although encountering a temporary setback, look quite promising, so keep your eyes and ears open.

Tuesday, February 26 (Moon in Leo). The financial theme continues and today could actually be a blockbuster in terms of contacts made, openings investigated, and even a bit of sheer luck coming your way. Also on this upbeat menu could be a career advancement in status and a delightful development in romance.

Wednesday, February 27 (Moon in Leo to Virgo 8:51 P.M.). This could be a routine sort of day, though important in terms of consolidating gains. Interesting communications this evening could include news from a relative, a few important tidbits of local goings-on, and facts about an educational project.

Thursday, February 28 (Moon in Virgo—FULL MOON 1:26 P.M.). Don't look for cooperation, understanding—and certainly not compliments—from those around you today. They are all full of their own problems. Escape into a creative project and bypass a quarrelsome individual in the evening. Rise above the fray.

March 1991

Friday, March 1 (Moon in Virgo). This will be a good day on which to present your important ideas and requests, to see key people, and to try to persuade dissenters to agree with your views. In other words, you are extra articulate and effective in communications now. P.M. may bring a visitor from a distance.

Saturday, March 2 (Moon in Virgo to Libra 1:04 A.M.). Home and family interests are accented this weekend and today is a mixed trend of fortunate dealings with friends and neighbors—not so favorable for contacts with higher-ups or a special romantic someone. By late evening, however, you'll have charmed the latter.

Sunday, March 3 (Moon in Libra). You and your mate, roommate, or other close associate may not agree on the day's agenda, but by late morning you'll have found a middle ground of semiharmony. The P.M. could be notable for a breakthrough in a major problem, a partnership standoff, or a mental block in creativity.

Monday, March 4 (Moon in Libra to Scorpio 8:09 A.M.). Some vestiges of resentment or noncompliance left over from yesterday could dampen a close alliance in early hours. Later, try to avoid confrontational situations at work and at home; opt for diplomacy and the theory that "a soft answer turneth away wrath!"

Tuesday, March 5 (Moon in Scorpio). You'll relax and enjoy this generally peaceful and constructive day, when your love life blossoms, romance intensifies, and eligible Cancerians could be one step closer to the wedding aisle. Late P.M. could bring a declaration of love or perhaps a glamorous social invitation.

Wednesday, March 6 (Moon in Scorpio to Sagittarius 6:36 P.M.). A so-so day at work as routine duties proceed peacefully but sluggishly. The evening may find you eagerly participating in a sports or exercise program, pursuing a rewarding health-and-beauty program, or improving a special talent or skill via practice.

Thursday, March 7 (Moon in Sagittarius). A misunderstanding in the late morning hours may reflect on your career or job status, though this can be easily ironed out if you take the time to do so. Otherwise, it's a positive day for self-improvement activity, boning up on facts and figures for an important conference.

Friday, March 8 (Moon in Sagittarius). Postmidnight hours look dynamically romantic, but though the delightful ambience of the occasion lingers on, you might also en-

March 1991 ♋ 221

counter a few challenges at home or at work. Deal with these in your own inimitable and charming manner, along with a bothersome P.M. call.

Saturday, March 9 (Moon in Sagittarius to Capricorn 7:15 P.M.). An absence of powerful stellar patterns makes today wide open for your own imprint. You may wish to finish up a few neglected chores, tackle a new diet or exercise program, or visit a sick friend. Evening hours focus on a close relationship. *oral*

Sunday, March 10 (Moon in Capricorn). You'll be in the mood to do something different, innovative, and exciting today. You should find a ready companion in your mate or partner, who could initiate a really dynamic itinerary for you to share. Visiting—or entertaining—a distant friend brightens the P.M. *~~oral~~ Thomas called from London England*

Monday, March 11 (Moon in Capricorn to Aquarius 7:32 P.M.). Two distinct themes today feature, on the one hand, love, romance, and travel urges—on the other hand, career-financial aims are accented. Some conflict may accompany your business objectives but the personal interests seem to be well supported.

Tuesday, March 12 (Moon in Aquarius). You may have mixed feelings about a financial matter today, as your inner instincts say "save" while your more expansive urges whisper "splurge!" Be especially cautious with joint funds or if you are responsible for another person's money. Avoid speculative ventures.

Wednesday, March 13 (Moon in Aquarius). Aside from a continuing caution against speculation or other financial risks, today may provide you with a green light for a monetary project. You might also hear some excellent money news late in the day; in some cases this will concern an increase in income or wages.

Thursday, March 14 (Moon in Aquarius to Pisces 5:12 A.M.). At times during the day you may touch bases with an attorney, a travel agent, an academic type, or your great-aunt Harriet! For the most part, any or all of such encounters should produce positive results, and you may be ready to rewrite your scenario.

Friday, March 15 (Moon in Pisces). Mixed trends today support innovative methods of dealing with sensitive topics, creative expression, and romance. What may be difficult to cope with are behind-the-scenes currents working against you and your best interests. A late P.M. conflict with another almost surely concerns money.

Saturday, March 16 (Moon in Pisces—NEW MOON at 3:11 A.M.—to Aries 11:39 A.M.). Your recently evolving change of viewpoint on an important personal matter could be reflected in your handling of a career-related issue after noonday. You can expect cooperation and thoughtful appraisal from a key figure.

Sunday, March 17 (Moon in Aries). An early-day message could shake you onto your feet, and though you will probably have to deal with an irritable colleague or a chronic complainer, you'll find some way to extract the most fun from this up-and-down day. The advice of an expert can ease a monetary worry.

Monday, March 18 (Moon in Aries to Taurus 3:41 P.M.). Remembering that the early bird catches the worm, you'll get off to an early and energetic start and can finalize a business negotiation by early afternoon. However, after that it's all downhill, especially in connection with personal, social, or romantic affairs.

Tuesday, March 19 (Moon in Taurus). The somewhat negative trend in your personal life, which began yesterday afternoon, can lop over into postmidnight hours via friction between you and your mate or partner. Finding a peaceful solution will not take long, though, and by early evening you are once again en rapport.

Wednesday, March 20 (Moon in Taurus to Gemini 6:38 A.M.). In case you find yourself in the mood or the situation for a bit of postmidnight speculation—don't! Make a

March 1991 ♋ 223

note, too, that a business-financial offer you receive this evening could have hidden disadvantages or a deceptive first impression.

Thursday, March 21 (Moon in Gemini). Don't hesitate to call on a private or confidential source for information, advice, even money, in today's early hours. What not to do is speculate or take other financial risk this evening. Protect your security in matters concerning either money or love at this time. *Feeling very bad today*

Friday, March 22 (Moon in Gemini to Cancer 9:28 P.M.). Information you receive this morning can be helpful in a career venture, but news concerning an investment, a love interest, or a youngster's education or welfare could be rather discouraging later in the A.M. You will decide to deal with such problems aggressively.

Saturday, March 23 (Moon in Cancer). Conflict between business or professional interests and personal commitments may seem insurmountable this morning. Nevertheless, the solution could be near at hand. Avoid confrontation with your spouse or partner in the P.M., when you will be light years apart in your thinking.

Sunday, March 24 (Moon in Cancer). A postmidnight misunderstanding with someone close to you might be triggered by a foolish, even trivial, incident; try to keep your priorities and values steady. An excellent career opportunity seems to be in the works at this time; be alert to the potential in the next few days.

Monday, March 25 (Moon in Cancer to Leo 12:44 A.M.). Mixed trends today center on business and financial prospects, which appear to be more promising for your personal finances than for joint funds or resources. Be wary in the investment area. Take advantage of a chance to restructure a shared moneymaking arrangement.

Tuesday, March 26 (Moon in Leo). The investment (speculation) theme continues to include warning signals, but sound business opportunities should be looked into, and *Showed Ch* an offstage agreement with an influential person could have fiscal benefits. Reflect on past errors in financial judgment and don't repeat them.

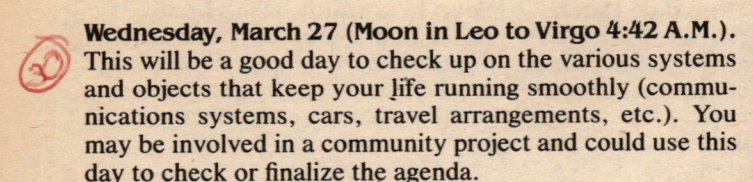

Wednesday, March 27 (Moon in Leo to Virgo 4:42 A.M.). This will be a good day to check up on the various systems and objects that keep your life running smoothly (communications systems, cars, travel arrangements, etc.). You may be involved in a community project and could use this day to check or finalize the agenda.

Thursday, March 28 (Moon in Virgo). This will be an excellent day to follow through on such items as contracts, advertisements, publicity campaigns, academic itineraries, and family-related engagements. You are especially alert and logical and can spot an error a mile away and deal with it adroitly.

Friday, March 29 (Moon in Virgo to Libra 9:50 A.M.). If you are out in the early morning hours, drive carefully and defensively. If you have planned a social evening, especially a get-together in your own home, everything should proceed without a hitch. A partner brings good financial news in the P.M.

Saturday, March 30 (Moon in Libra—FULL MOON at 2:18 A.M.). Postmidnight hours could feature a totally surprising development in a romance, which can have positive effects in your life—although your negative reactions simmer through the day. You may need to be more flexible in adjusting.

Sunday, March 31 (Moon in Libra to Scorpio 5:02 P.M.). Another early-A.M. warning to guard yourself and your loved ones against travel or transportation hazards. Interesting social encounters in the afternoon may help to confirm one of your recent judgments. Late P.M. is still another day when speculation is a no-no.

April 1991

Monday, April 1 (Moon in Scorpio). Be sure to check with your spouse or partner before spending any joint funds. A romantic and glamorous development today could lead to marital opportunity for some unattached Cancerians, enhancement of an existing alliance for others. Your creativity intensifies now, as well.

Tuesday, April 2 (Moon in Scorpio). Concern about a youngster, an investment, or an important social agenda, can be alleviated by using common sense and a little research. Your vitality, energies, and charisma are increased this evening as stellar trends show a new flow of self-confidence and assertiveness.

Wednesday, April 3 (Moon in Scorpio to Sagittarius 3:00 A.M.). This will be a generally fortunate and smooth-running day, at work, home, or en route to a different locale. However, be diplomatic with higher-ups and other authority figures and by all means avoid sudden decisions, anger, and transportation hazards.

Thursday, April 4 (Moon in Sagittarius). A disappointment or mixup in social-romantic plans is a possibility—and there is also a stellar indication of delays, slowdowns, and temporary obstacles blocking plans in general. Be prepared to be patient, thorough, and ready to make alternate arrangements when needed.

Friday, April 5 (Moon in Sagittarius to Capricorn 3:20 P.M.). This may be a touchy day in a personal relationship, as you tend to be more than usually aggressive, while the other person will probably be supersensitive to your dynamic approach. Allowing for all this, you can manage to maintain harmony.

Saturday, April 6 (Moon in Capricorn). Your mate, partner, or other close associate could be in the mood to make the decisions and run the show—which, at this particular time, could strike you as totally unfair. As a result, fireworks may erupt, or some humongous misunderstanding cloud all the issues.

Sunday, April 7 (Moon in Capricorn). Patching up hurt feelings or straightening out misinterpreted statements can take most of the day, but with good results as you and a close associate wind up on good terms once more. You may also be working on plans for a community or family get-together for the near future.

Monday, April 8 (Moon in Capricorn to Aquarius 4:01 A.M.). Sometime today you'll be sorely tempted to overspend on some luxury or overextend a joint credit arrangement. But as you contemplate this rash move, an incident, reminder, or advice from an authority figure will probably yank you back to reality!

Tuesday, April 9 (Moon in Aquarius). A social gathering may be the source of an interesting business-career opportunity today, though there could be a definite element of risk involved in the matter. Much will depend on whether you are a solo performer or part of a team, in considering the pros and cons.

Wednesday, April 10 (Moon in Aquarius to Pisces 2:19 P.M.). A misunderstanding with a friend could concern you today; your very best move is to call this person and get the matter all out in the open and straightened out. Contact with someone at a distance—or perusing travel brochures—gives you a big lift.

Thursday, April 11 (Moon in Pisces). Whether it's a future vacation trip or a spur-of-the-moment trek to some exotic destination, you'll enjoy checking out the possibilities. (After April 28th will be the best timing for this.) Also on today's agenda may be a creative collaboration or shared cultural pleasures.

Friday, April 12 (Moon in Pisces to Aries 8:50 P.M.). A legal matter could take an upturn today, or you may be checking out the advantages of an academic program. A secret romance may tempt you in the P.M., but there could be a question of how to fit this in with an already crowded social-romantic schedule!

Saturday, April 13 (Moon in Aries). You may have to walk a tightrope today, as a career- or status-related situation may depend on your tact and diplomacy, just when you're most apt to speak your mind and let the chips fall where they may! Someone close to you might help out here via advice or guiding the conversation.

Sunday, April 14 (Moon in Aries—NEW MOON at 2:39 P.M.). An early A.M. argument with a cohort might be based on misinterpreted (or inaccurate) remarks by either. Later, a brand new direction could open up to you in career, business, or academic goals; be on the alert for a new trend, new possibilities.

Monday, April 15 (Moon in Aries to Taurus 12:06 A.M.). You may be making plans for social extravaganzas or wild shopping sprees or maybe a glamour trip, but before you put a penny down for any of this, consider how your spouse, partner, or a relative will view your extravagance! (If you are totally solo, go ahead!)

Tuesday, April 16 (Moon in Taurus). A confidential agreement or conference with someone of influence may be just what's needed to give you added clout in your bid for career advancement. In a group situation (social or cultural) try to avoid arousing the jealousy or resentment of a competitive individual.

Wednesday, April 17 (Moon in Taurus to Gemini 1:42 A.M.). Don't be too quick to confide your views, plans, or anxieties to another person, unless you know for sure he or she is a firm friend. On the other hand, working behind the scenes to promote a special goal can be the best way to gain advantages today.

Thursday, April 18 (Moon in Gemini). An interesting financial opportunity may come your way via the good will of an executive type, but best results can be obtained by keeping this strictly confidential. This will be a good day for quiet thinking about current projects and the best way to get them moving.

Friday, April 19 (Moon in Gemini to Cancer 3:18 A.M.). Despite a number of reasons why you cannot push ahead on a major project right now (all of which are beyond your control) you are in the mood to get things done—now! if not sooner. This will apply to P.M. social-romantic meanderings, as well as workaday routines.

Saturday, April 20 (Moon in Cancer). You and your favorite companion will surely not view important issues from the same angle today. In fact, you may both have to work hard to avert an estrangement. Settle on a compromise project, upon which both can agree, and then take it (gently) from there.

Sunday, April 21 (Moon in Cancer to Leo 6:05 A.M.). You might win an honor, award, or some other tangible evidence of esteem, but despite the status boost, you know (and so does everyone else) that hard work was an intrinsic part of your contribution. You could learn a valuable financial lesson in the P.M.

Monday, April 22 (Moon in Leo). Today's early promise for monetary gains might dwindle as the day wears on. Nevertheless, the potential is there and you might learn enough from today's experience to qualify you for a second try for the brass ring. Avoid late-day commitment to a speculative venture.

Tuesday, April 23 (Moon in Leo to Virgo 10:30 A.M.). A contract or other document may require attention today, even though your intuition says "Wait!" If action must be taken, check everything out with extra thoroughness. Meetings, errands, or phone calls may be more distracting than informative in the P.M.

Wednesday, April 24 (Moon in Virgo). A travel plan may be deferred this morning, as a business associate brings information that changes the picture. You could feel on top of the world this evening, perhaps due to the unexpected reappearance of a former romance—or a good friend who has been away.

Thursday, April 25 (Moon in Virgo to Libra 4:37 P.M.). Don't take unnecessary risks during postmidnight hours, or neglect proper protection for money and possessions. An emphasis on domestic issues later in the day can mean guests for dinner, a new appliance, a minor repair project, or a family minicrisis.

Friday, April 26 (Moon in Libra). Mixed trends show an extraactive domestic program, with lots of enthusiasm on your part but little or no cooperation from your spouse or family members. However, you'll proceed full speed ahead and the evening could prove to be an interesting mix of triumph and challenge.

Saturday, April 27 (Moon in Libra). Unfortunately, today could be one of those days when, if anything can possibly go wrong, it probably will. Whether you are concentrating on a domestic project, a family dilemma, a community program, or your own personal whims and hopes, you'll need both patience and ingenuity.

Sunday, April 28 (Moon in Libra to Scorpio 12:35 A.M.—FULL MOON at 3:59 P.M.). Yet another warning about postmidnight hours and possible hazards—in transportation or in personal activities. Today does bring an accelerated pace of action in many areas, as previously delayed projects get moving. Avoid confrontations.

Monday, April 29 (Moon in Scorpio). You'll be pleased to learn that the last two days of April are upbeat and promising, especially for your love life, creative projects, social plans, and matters pertaining to children. Today could also bring the solution to a long-term problem involving an investment or a relative.

Tuesday, April 30 (Moon in Scorpio to Sagittarius 10:43 A.M.). Another positive day, with job and health issues improving (if, in fact, they need improvement) and

230 ⊕ Daily Predictions

the promise of a nice advancement in the near future, with travel benefits for some. A call or meeting with a key figure could confirm upscale potentials.

May 1991

Wednesday, May 1 (Moon in Sagittarius). Your job or career endeavors are becoming increasingly focused and today could find you on your way toward a long-desired goal. A late-evening communication could be just what you've been waiting to hear—perhaps on the subject of romance, travel, or a legal transaction.

Thursday, May 2 (Moon in Sagittarius to Capricorn 10:55 P.M.). With the best of intentions, your efforts to gain the approval and/or the cooperation of those around you do not seem to succeed. Possibly it's a question of people with problems projecting them on to the nearest person (you?). Don't worry about it.

Friday, May 3 (Moon in Capricorn). The morning hours may bring a confrontation of sorts between you and your spouse, partner, or other close associate. You are the one with the dynamic ideas—the other person is the wishy-washy indecisive type. This will have to be handled diplomatically and firmly.

Saturday, May 4 (Moon in Capricorn). This can be a great day to promote new ideas, ride on new trends, unleash your creativity, and encourage a new romance. However, on the debit side, tone down any urge to come on too strong (especially with a higher-up or partner) and make sure communications are accurate.

Sunday, May 5 (Moon in Capricorn to Aquarius 11:52 A.M.). The question of joint funds, or shared income and expenses arrangements, could need to be spelled out a bit more explicitly today. You may be in a spendthrifty mood, while your mate or partner could envision a poor-as-a-churchmouse ending because of it.

Monday, May 6 (Moon in Aquarius). This is not the greatest day for any activity involving another person's money combined with your own. Check out all expenses, bills, split charges, or split fees. You'll never hear the end of it if a financial accounting is not in shipshape form. Usually you want this, too.

Tuesday, May 7 (Moon in Aquarius to Pisces 11:05 P.M.). If you move quickly enough, you can set right an early morning financial concern. Later, a delightful trend toward romance and marriage, or renewed romance in marriage, begins to flavor the day. A friendly P.M. communication could include a travel invitation.

Wednesday, May 8 (Moon in Pisces). This will be a so-so day at work or in your daily routine. The P.M. is another story. A stimulating new trend in your personal life finds your magnetism intensified and your social-romantic calendar filling up rapidly. This same trend supports your seeking favors and special attentions.

Thursday, May 9 (Moon in Pisces). Both business and personal interests proceed rewardingly today, but in the late P.M. resist the urge to speculate or to risk a treasured relationship by a foolish action or attitude. Don't be too trusting of those who promise big profits for small outlay—or instant romance, either.

Friday, May 10 (Moon in Pisces to Aries 6:36 A.M.). You might miscalculate the mood or requirements of a higher-up this morning, if you attempt to promote your ideas or skills. Study the situation first. Evening hours favor social pleasures, sports, or exercise programs, and impromptu gatherings of friends.

Saturday, May 11 (Moon in Aries). Don't expect too much from today, as adverse aspects may help to spread some doom and gloom around your environment. Your

232 ☽ Daily Predictions

ambition or tactics are sure to be misunderstood, while on a personal level your confident approach may cause some individuals to react adversely.

Sunday, May 12 (Moon in Aries to Taurus 10:08 A.M.). Communications improve somewhat in the morning hours, but later in the day a delightful social gathering may have its dark side as well. Finances may somehow become a problem, so make a point to calculate things carefully and concisely for the penny-pinchers.

Monday, May 13 (Moon in Taurus—NEW MOON at 11:37 P.M.). This will be a much more upbeat and encouraging day, with social-romantic interests emphasized, and an attractive itinerary taking shape as you hear from various friends and admirers. A slight problem may arise through someone's jealousy, but rise above it. *Start to feel better*

Tuesday, May 14 (Moon in Taurus to Gemini 11:03 A.M.). Any restraints placed upon you today are most likely to be self-imposed; the way seems to be clear and unobstructed for you to proceed with important matters, but you might develop a few inner qualms, for some unknown reason. P.M. could bring good financial news.

Wednesday, May 15 (Moon in Gemini). Private plans may need a few more finishing touches before they'll be ready for action. Possibly a little more research or study will do the trick. The health of someone close to you might be a cause of some concern, but your fears may be exaggerated at this point.

Thursday, May 16 (Moon in Gemini to Cancer 11:15 A.M.). A confidential memo or call in the A.M. can steer you in the right direction for business-career achievement today. Your self-confidence soars around noon—perhaps lunch with a key person will be productive. Financial indecisiveness due in the P.M.

Friday, May 17 (Moon in Cancer). Your super-romantic mood in the postmidnight hours can make a relationship splendid. Unfortunately, this mood does not continue through the morning hours, when you and a partner could be very much at odds. The good news is that the P.M. brings a chance for reconciliation.

Saturday, May 18 (Moon in Cancer to Leo 12:31 P.M.). Make a note of the hot financial ideas you dream up in the wee small hours of the morning; these could come in handy later on. Later in the day, you might find yourself overspending on a social event, or listening to a friend's well-meant but flawed money advice.

Sunday, May 19 (Moon in Leo). You and your mate or partner may have a brief quarrel shortly after midnight—followed within minutes by a happy resolution of the problem. This may pertain to a matter of material security. After a ho-hum day, your intuition in romance may be off target in the P.M.

Monday, May 20 (Moon in Leo to Virgo 4:01 P.M.). It may take longer than you anticipate to get a business transaction off in the right direction today but keep at it. Don't choose this evening for a showdown with your loved one; stellar patterns show distinct potential for separation or sudden breakup.

Tuesday, May 21 (Moon in Virgo). Today's positive trends include upbeat social-romantic developments, a reconciliation or deeper understanding with your spouse or partner, and a new slant on a private matter that could provide a wider range of options for you. Happy communications brighten the evening hours.

Wednesday, May 22 (Moon in Virgo to Libra 10:09 P.M.). Don't pay too much attention to advice or information concerning financial interests today; facts may be inaccurate and could tend toward exaggeration or the omission of major points. Someone from out of town could have good news for you—perhaps a houseguest.

Thursday, May 23 (Moon in Libra). This can be a fortunate day for household or property interests, and you may be able to purchase just the items you are seeking for a

234 ☋ Daily Predictions

dinner, party, impromptu gathering, or celebration of some kind. However, evening hours become fraught with conflict and/or misunderstandings.

Friday, May 24 (Moon in Libra). Your mate or a family member could be making himself or herself heard in a very definite manner today. You may have to call upon your reserves of diplomacy, ingenuity, and your special ability to soothe prickly feelings, in order to keep peace in your environment on this day.

Saturday, May 25 (Moon in Libra to Scorpio 6:42 A.M.). Your main problem today may be misplaced, misdirected, or marked by insufficient energy—and you may encounter criticism or opposition from people you would most expect to support you. One big bright spot, however, is a midevening tête-à-tête with your *amour*.

Sunday, May 26 (Moon in Scorpio). If you are bound for an early-morning trip or gathering, make sure instructions and information are accurate. On the plus side, you will be especially creative today and could call upon a current or past emotional attachment as inspiration for your creativity in the P.M.

Monday, May 27 (Moon in Scorpio to Sagittarius 5:22 P.M.). Today supports health interests, so if you're scheduled for a medical or dental exam you will probably pass with flying colors. You might be in a hardworking mood in the P.M. and can get things done with the speed of a Triple Crown winner.

Tuesday, May 28 (Moon in Sagittarius—FULL MOON at 6:38 A.M.). Turmoil in your environment will roll off your back like water off a duck; you are in a positive, confident frame of mind and other people's overemotionalism will leave you unmoved. Finances seem to be moving along nicely (personal or shared) as well.

Wednesday, May 29 (Moon in Sagittarius). Don't be surprised if you get a few additional chores or responsibilities today—and you may find that a scheduled social event or romantic date must be rescheduled or altered in some way. Take it all in stride—tomorrow is another (and better) day in your personal life.

Thursday, May 30 (Moon in Sagittarius to Capricorn 5:41 A.M.). You can count on a loyal partner to back you up in business dealings today, or a special someone in your personal life to be there for you. An early-day inspiration could lead to financial advantage, perhaps through contact with a VIP.

Friday, May 31 (Moon in Capricorn). You should get good results from pursuing a goal that includes another person, and you're sure to have that person's full support, even though you might have to make a few concessions or compromises somewhere along the line. The weekend gets off to a happy start with P.M. romance.

June 1991

Saturday, June 1 (Moon in Capricorn to Aquarius 6:43 P.M.). Someone close to you may be opposed to one of your pet plans for the day. Speak and step carefully, for this is one of those occasions when feelings can be easily damaged. P.M. could find you talking with a financial expert, to your good advantage.

Sunday, June 2 (Moon in Aquarius). Some friction may arise between you and your spouse or partner concerning the handling of joint funds; you're inclined toward expansion and taking a calculated risk, your partner seems (to you) to be a worrywart or a doom-and-gloom chaser. Objective discussion could help.

Monday, June 3 (Moon in Aquarius). An early-day theme provides a caution against any kind of risk-taking, whether financial or in the realm of human relationships. The eve-

236 ☊ Daily Predictions

ning brings satisfying communication with a friend or lover, which may establish a party date—or even the date for a wedding.

Tuesday, June 4 (Moon in Aquarius to Pisces 6:37 A.M.). Legal activities or dealings in contractual matters could be time-absorbing today. Although early A.M. might bring inaccurate or confusing information, later day developments clear up this murkiness. You may learn interesting news from a distant contact tonight.

Wednesday, June 5 (Moon in Pisces). Steer away from any behind-the-scenes activities; any possibility of illegality could snowball into an undesirable rumor. Evening may find you in a position to gain through another's confidences; perhaps an investment tip or other monetary advice will prove to be profitable.

Thursday, June 6 (Moon in Pisces to Aries 3:26 A.M.). Your money judgment isn't too hot in the A.M., so delay making any spontaneous decision about your own or another's assets. Later, someone with your best interest at heart could urge you toward a really solvent moneymaking project. A community interest attracts in the P.M.

Friday, June 7 (Moon in Aries). Mixed trends on the career-business scene will require careful assessment of new developments. Someone may be encouraging you to make dynamic changes in your portfolio or reserve funds, but refrain from doing anything on impulse. If you encounter hostility from a partner in the P.M., ignore it.

Saturday, June 8 (Moon in Aries to Taurus 8:14 P.M.). Be prompt in responding to an early-morning opportunity to advance a special career aim. Exchanging ideas with a colleague could be helpful as well. Your social calendar may be subject to various trends and changes at this time, but tonight's agenda looks promising.

Sunday, June 9 (Moon in Taurus). Don't rely on others to be cooperative, on time, or in the mood to enjoy social or cultural pleasures today. You could also find that costs will be higher than anticipated. By late afternoon and early P.M. the situation improves, perhaps nobly assisted by your partner.

Monday, June 10 (Moon in Taurus). The old adage "It isn't what you know but who you know" may fit today's unfolding developments, as you could see a well-connected colleague receiving the extra dividends for which you have been working so hard. On the other hand, you might find delayed benefits will compensate.

Tuesday, June 11 (Moon in Taurus to Gemini 9:37 P.M.). This can be a super day for financial progress, which can be considerably boosted by a private agreement you make with an associate. Meetings and conferences are due to produce solid gains, and a P.M. business-pleasure gathering could be profitable.

Wednesday, June 12 (Moon in Gemini—NEW MOON at 7:07—to Cancer 9:17 P.M.). A lack of agreement or even appreciation of each other's financial views and needs may dim a close alliance this morning. Nevertheless, there is the potential for a new and mutually beneficial course of action for you both.

Thursday, June 13 (Moon in Cancer). A so-so day for routine duties might, however, produce some sort of irritation that reflects adversely in a close relationship this evening. Try to stay off sensitive topics and refrain from bringing up old grievances.

Friday, June 14 (Moon in Cancer to Leo 9:11 P.M.). Dollar signs, horseshoes, or other good-luck symbols seem to surround you today, so be on the alert for a moneymaking opportunity throughout the day. Your dealings with cohorts should be rewarding, especially a special someone who is more than financially attractive.

Saturday, June 15 (Moon in Leo). An early A.M. fiscal disappointment is shortly offset by one or more really promising business opportunities. Your own initiative provides you with sparkling new ideas and methods, which find ready acceptance with an eager-to-advance colleague. Evening could be pleasantly social.

Sunday, June 16 (Moon in Leo to Virgo 11:04 P.M.). Insomnia, anxiety dreams, or simply an emotional upset may cloud postmidnight hours, but all this dissipates as the day progresses. Actually, you can accomplish a lot in business or personal matters today, although much of your activity may be offstage.

Monday, June 17 (Moon in Virgo). Communications will be important today. Explaining details and advantages of an upcoming trip to a friend or lover will challenge your ingenuity; to avoid misunderstanding (or rejection of your plans) opt for charm and diplomacy. Appealing to this person's own self-interest also helps.

Tuesday, June 18 (Moon in Virgo). Early hours bring a delightful trend toward romantic or financial success (either or both!). Don't let any opportunity slip by to promote your cherished dreams in these areas. Fast-forward to late P.M., however, and beware of carelessly losing your advantages.

Wednesday, June 19 (Moon in Virgo to Libra 4:02 A.M.). This could be a day when your noted flair for domesticity and family interests may be challenged, as you really want to pursue some extracurricular goal which requires single-minded attention. By P.M. hours, you will have worked out the routine—and the compromise.

Thursday, June 20 (Moon in Libra). An unusual and innovative solution to a household problem can free you for other interesting plans and demands. Even so, you'll probably have to make extra effort to see that no one feels neglected and no one (including you) is overworked on the domestic scene this evening.

Friday, June 21 (Moon in Libra to Scorpio 12:19 P.M.). A last-minute benefit can be yours around noon, as a VIP influences a business decision in your favor. Later, your vitality, charisma (and romantic appeal) glows and even though late P.M. may bring the stern disapproval of an authority figure, you'll triumph.

Saturday, June 22 (Moon in Scorpio). If you can avoid various excesses today, you can accomplish a lot and have a great time doing so. First on the list of no-no's is financial extravagance, closely followed by overindulgence and overemotionalism. On the other hand, partnership and romance can be guided toward bliss.

Sunday, June 23 (Moon in Scorpio to Sagittarius 11:17 P.M.). Stellar patterns strongly support both love and money today (who could ask for more?). Also on the positive list are social and recreational pleasures, matters pertaining to children, creative expression, and health conditions for you and yours.

Monday, June 24 (Moon in Sagittarius). The workweek begins on a positive note, but throughout the day there is an element of uncertainty and the expectation of an accident about to happen! (To be on the safe side, drive carefully, anyway!) Finances and personal relationships could be targeted for problems.

Tuesday, June 25 (Moon in Sagittarius). Postmidnight hours could bring you a brilliant idea for improving your job conditions. But later in the A.M. your timing might be off in implementing this concept. Business-financial prospects look good, but avoid all forms of speculation. Don't antagonize a loved one, either.

Wednesday, June 26 (Moon in Sagittarius to Capricorn 11:50 A.M.—FULL MOON at 9:59 P.M.). Walk as though you were tiptoeing on eggs today, in your effort to keep from rocking the love boat and/or sinking another person's ego in the deep waters of criticism or recrimination. Everyone is supersensitive today.

Thursday, June 27 (Moon in Capricorn). Today is a refreshing change of pace from yesterday, and you should be able to mend any fences smoothly and permanently.

240 ☺ Daily Predictions

You will be especially articulate, so this is a good time to see business prospects, those from whom you wish to seek favors, or a special loved one for whatever reason.

Friday, June 28 (Moon in Capricorn). Wide open channels of communication can be the answer to any relationship challenge today. You should also note that a financial matter you've been working on seems to be succeeding, while a social, romantic, or investment plan also looks promising, especially in early hours.

Saturday, June 29 (Moon in Capricorn to Aquarius 12:48 A.M.). You and your spouse or partner will be in complete accord on a financial security matter today. This may also be the day on which a special monetary favor you've been seeking is finally available to you. Give some extra thought to securing valuables.

Sunday, June 30 (Moon in Aquarius). With the best of intentions, you and your closest companion may simply not agree on joint interests today—whether it concerns what to do with a business dilemma, where to eat dinner, or who to invite to a birthday party! Give important issues a rest until tomorrow.

July 1991

Monday, July 1 (Moon in Aquarius to Pisces 12:52 P.M.). A legal matter or important communication to a distant contact may require attention today. Travel may also be a focus for your special interest, especially if it includes vacation or other pleasurable aspects. Get your questions and priorities in order now.

Tuesday, July 2 (Moon in Pisces). Stellar trends support your activities, particularly if they pertain to a joint venture, a social bash, or an exciting romance. Don't hesitate to bring up your ideas for improved conditions at work or at home—so long as you phrase them diplomatically and with flair.

Wednesday, July 3 (Moon in Pisces to Aries 10:34 P.M.). Hearing from a family member in another locale might mean a slight—but welcome—revision in one of your travel plans. Involvement in a community project could be especially rewarding to you at this time, and could be the setting for a new friendship.

Thursday, July 4 (Moon in Aries). Be especially careful today not to challenge your spouse, lover, or partner, as stellar trends tend to support separateness rather than close harmony and union. Career-business affairs may also be on a tightrope at this time, so try to refrain from precipitating a break.

Friday, July 5 (Moon in Aries). Today is not much better than yesterday; caution and diplomacy should be your watchwords. Things do ease off in the P.M., when a fortunate financial development could set the stage for cooperation and a happier ambience. Hearing from a special friend will also help.

Saturday, July 6 (Moon in Aries to Taurus 4:53 A.M.). The weekend's social plans get off to a rocky start today. Or, if you are on vacation or traveling, you may be experiencing regrets for your choice. Extra expense and a lack of romantic opportunity may be among the problems. But there's always tomorrow.

Sunday, July 7 (Moon in Taurus). Early A.M. prospects look rosy today, so make the most of getting an early start on your favorite diversion. After midday, however, storm signals are again hoisted, so watch your expenses, avoid friction with a loved one, and make sure your mate or partner understands your signals.

Monday, July 8 (Moon in Taurus to Gemini 7:43 A.M.). Postmidnight hours can be scrappy, so try to keep off touchy subjects with a cohort. (The subject of money is

242 ♋ Daily Predictions

one of the touchy ones.) In the afternoon, there's a simmering down of conflict and a joint decision may be reached which will restore harmony.

Tuesday, July 9 (Moon in Gemini). This can be a low-profile but quite rewarding day in a quiet sort of way. Get caught up on neglected tasks, correspondence, and obligations—and plan on how to handle any upcoming sensitive topics. Health and dental checkups may now be in order for you and dependents.

Wednesday, July 10 (Moon in Gemini to Cancer 8:04 A.M.). This ought to be a thoroughly satisfying day, as stellar trends strongly support financial gains, social popularity, and a romantic coup. Your own confidence increases as the day wears on and you should be well able to steer a romantic evening as you desire.

Thursday, July 11 (Moon in Cancer—NEW MOON Solar Eclipse at 2:07 P.M.). If you can bypass the temptation to challenge your mate or partner over minor and perhaps unfixable problems, this can be your day of days, when your new personal year begins and your confidence, enthusiasm, and know-how make you unbeatable.

Friday, July 12 (Moon in Cancer to Leo 7:36 A.M.). Today's emphasis is on your material resources, personal finances, and steps you intend to take in order to safeguard your security. You may not agree with a partner or ally on monetary matters, but if you wait long enough this person will see things your way.

Saturday, July 13 (Moon in Leo). You may have brought some work home with you this weekend, although your choice is usually to separate your home-family-leisure interests from those of the marketplace. In any event, you may find that early morning is the best time for work and that distractions begin around noon.

Sunday, July 14 (Moon in Leo to Virgo 8:12 A.M.). It looks like another early-to-rise day for you, with a special achievement in view as you find the solution to a monetary problem. Later, it's all social, community-oriented, or romantic, as you hear from—and see—favorite friends or a special love.

Monday, July 15 (Moon in Virgo). Aside from a caution concerning not taking any financial or speculative risks today, the outlook is upbeat, with an early-A.M. communication setting the good-luck theme. This will be a good day to contact people who are important in your life and to see as many as possible.

Tuesday, July 16 (Moon in Virgo to Libra 11:35 A.M.). Be sure to check with family members before proceeding with a home-improvement program or an entertainment plan. It looks as though a few crossed wires might result if you simply plunge into the project. This is another "no speculation" day, incidentally.

Wednesday, July 17 (Moon in Libra). You and your spouse or roommate may disagree on the domestic schedule, which might be undergoing a change or revision. Take into consideration all factors in question, so that later there can be no reproaches! P.M. favors social and cultural interests, contacting special friends.

Thursday, July 18 (Moon in Libra to Scorpio 6:42 P.M.). This is an appropriate day for you to "put your house in order" whether mentally or physically. Perhaps you could throw away some long-saved records, or cut down on the clutter, or rearrange the books. Though you may dread doing it, you'll feel better later.

Friday, July 19 (Moon in Scorpio). Be wary of postmidnight expenditures of joint funds. Later, the day eases into a delightfully romantic haze, as you outline weekend plans with your special someone—or finesse a gathering of favorite friends into following your agenda for pleasure and relaxation.

Saturday, July 20 (Moon in Scorpio). This starts out and could continue as a happy leisure-pleasure day, except for the fact that money once again enters the picture on a stormy note. Things may all cost more than you anticipate, or perhaps a cohort will be reluctant to part with a dime. Try to have fun anyway.

Sunday, July 21 (Moon in Scorpio to Sagittarius 5:17 A.M.). Postmidnight hours can be wonderfully romantic, but later in the day you may receive adverse news concerning someone's health—or your own tummy may be suffering pangs of some excess or other. Opt for diplomacy if talking with a loved one.

Monday, July 22 (Moon in Sagittarius). Today's agenda includes a lot of work, a good sense of accomplishment, and a happy bit of financial news in the early P.M. Finally wrapping up a long-drawn-out job assignment will give you a sense of achievement. An improved health matter could also be a cause for rejoicing.

Tuesday, July 23 (Moon in Sagittarius to Capricorn 5:56 P.M.). This could be an interesting day on which to begin a financial or business partnership. In fact, ironing out details of such a merger could be the subject of a "power lunch." Other possibilities include resolving a personal financial crisis.

Wednesday, July 24 (Moon in Capricorn). You and your mate or partner can really hammer out a joint agreement on a family, property, financial, or strictly personal issue, to the delight of all concerned. Joining forces in a social program is also on the agenda, and the realization of a travel dream may be in the works.

Thursday, July 25 (Moon in Capricorn). This is another harmonious day for you and someone close to you—which can also include a creative collaboration or wedding plans. Agreements in general can be obtained early today, though later some of the interest may taper off. P.M. favors social and cultural entertainment.

Friday, July 26 (Moon in Capricorn to Aquarius 6:50 A.M.—FULL MOON Lunar Eclipse 1:25 P.M.). Postmidnight hours could find many a Cancerian getting engaged or planning the wedding day. (There are also benefits for the already married.) Brace yourself for the P.M. hours, however, when financial friction is rife.

Saturday, July 27 (Moon in Aquarius). Whatever your plans for the day, try to keep a lid on expenses because yesterday's trend toward financial clashes between you and someone close to you continues unabated in the P.M. hours. This is not the time to announce plans for wardrobe enhancement or new interior decor!

Sunday, July 28 (Moon in Aquarius to Pisces 6:36 P.M.). A quietly productive day, even if you merely loll about and review a few of your current game plans. Evening may bring communications from a distance, perhaps with talk of an upcoming trip. In a different context, refrain from overstating your views to a friend.

Monday, July 29 (Moon in Pisces). There may be a gap or a derailment in communications between you and a coworker this morning. Opt for tact rather than verbal brilliance. Comparing notes on current business matters with a colleague in the afternoon can prove helpful to both. Late P.M. brings creative inspiration.

Tuesday, July 30 (Moon in Pisces). An educational project or a fascinating reading program could claim your interest today. You may also be able to interest others in one of your favorite subjects by using the powers of persuasion and suggestion when talking to them. An out-of-town relative may phone in the P.M.

Wednesday, July 31 (Moon in Pisces to Aries 4:21 A.M.). You may feel as though you've found the magic formula to succeed today, as a higher-up supports your theories and your work. The (ever-present) financial picture is glowing with quite-bright hues as well. P.M. may feature a status-y sort of social affair.

August 1991

Thursday, August 1 (Moon in Aries). Be sure you emphasize your corporate loyalty before making an impulsive career suggestion that might otherwise antagonize a higher-up. Too, check facts and figures carefully, as errors are likely. An innovative partnership venture is among today's possibilities, too.

Friday, August 2 (Moon in Aries to Taurus 11:33 A.M.). If someone criticizes you, or your job performance, take it graciously and see if there is a worthwhile message or lesson from it. Evening hours can be enjoyably social, with stimulating communications flowing between you and favorite cohorts.

Saturday, August 3 (Moon in Taurus). Mixed trends today support lighthearted romance, collaborative ventures, creative thinking. Prospects are not so favorable for shopping, saving money (on the contrary!) and indulging in any form of speculation. Mixed signals in the P.M. may have romantic fallout.

Sunday, August 4 (Moon in Taurus to Gemini 3:55 P.M.). Another caution against overspending on social pleasures, or perhaps allowing yourself to get more deeply into an expensive way of life than you intend to. Rely on your inner strengths and inspirations in dealing with a nagging problem that resurfaces now and then.

Monday, August 5 (Moon in Gemini). A confidential tip or piece of advice can result in monetary gains today, but otherwise you could find this a rather "blue Monday." The main cause may be the general attitude of those around you, who seem to be glum, noncooperative, and slow to respond to your winning ways.

Tuesday, August 6 (Moon in Gemini to Cancer 5:48 P.M.). A hidden opportunity may not be easy to focus on today, but if you rely on your intuition you'll spot it. In the evening, your own special brand of charisma (and know-how) will enable you to gain points with an important person and promote a special aim.

Wednesday, August 7 (Moon in Cancer). If your assertiveness is clothed in subtlety and finesse, you'll have an excellent chance of putting across one of your major goals today—or, at least, getting it started on its way. However, don't be surprised if a general slowdown develops and delays rapid progress.

Thursday, August 8 (Moon in Cancer to Leo 6:10 P.M.). Free-wheeling initiative could open a door or two for you today, though don't expect immediate results. You may have a serious financial discussion with your spouse or close associate in the P.M., which could leave you a bit discouraged, unless you resist.

Friday, August 9 (Moon in Leo—NEW MOON at 9:29 P.M.). It may not be a clear-cut signal, but hints and clues today can point to the general direction a business-financial project is due to take in the weeks ahead. Late evening carelessness with cash, or speculation of any kind, is not advised, for obvious reasons.

Saturday, August 10 (Moon in Leo to Virgo 6:36 P.M.). You wake up in a cheerful, optimistic frame of mind that sees you through an unpredictable kind of day and into a safely routine evening's relaxation. In the meantime, early afternoon may bring a shocker in the form of business-related rumor or announcement.

Sunday, August 11 (Moon in Virgo). This should be a thoroughly enjoyable day, and you deserve it. Household and social plans should proceed as desired, your loved ones are there for you, a friend or neighbor brings a welcome bit of news, and the evening ends on a happily upbeat note of love and romance.

Monday, August 12 (Moon in Virgo to Libra 8:53 P.M.). Your involvement in a community program, academic project, or a travel-related group event can be most rewarding.

Good news about a child's health, welfare, or education is encouraging, and evening may bring the family enthusiasm you've hoped for, for a domestic plan.

Tuesday, August 13 (Moon in Libra). Postmidnight hours could produce a message or bit of news concerning a joint project, especially from the financial angle. Later in the day and evening be extra tactful and sensitive to the reactions of your partner if unexpected problems arise in one of your shared interests.

Wednesday, August 14 (Moon in Libra). Happy news is due today, whether you hear it direct or via the grapevine; more than a hint of romance could be part of it. Also on the day's calendar may be a rewarding session with a decorator, painter, or builder, regarding some home improvement you've been planning.

Thursday, August 15 (Moon in Libra to Scorpio 2:34 A.M.). Although the day begins with a nagging worry or perhaps unfounded anxiety on your part, the balance of the day and evening is a delightful setting for love, romance, creative expression, and possibly a musical or artistic performance as well, in the P.M.

Friday, August 16 (Moon in Scorpio). This can be another rewarding day in your love life and/or aesthetic interests. Also on the calendar could be a pleasant involvement in a neighborhood event or plans for a local trip in the near future with congenial companions. A heart-to-heart talk with a friend resolves a problem.

Saturday, August 17 (Moon in Scorpio to Sagittarius 12:12 P.M.). A rash action or comment this morning might reopen an old wound in a friend's heart; guard your reactions and try to avoid unfortunate references. Afternoon tension at work is more than compensated for by great financial news at day's end.

Sunday, August 18 (Moon in Sagittarius). A chore you perform today may be simply a labor of love but your payment is more valuable than money. You could be in the mood for physical challenges via a sports or exercise program, or perhaps you'll be part of a group working for a favorite humane project.

Monday, August 19 (Moon in Sagittarius). The day gets off to a lively but disturbing start with an early-morning communication bringing mixed reports on a special project. Later, time spent with a coworker could be unexpectedly rewarding and informative. Evening hours seem to be active and stimulating.

Tuesday, August 20 (Moon in Sagittarius to Capricorn 12:35 A.M.). A solid spirit of cooperation enables you and your partner to clinch a practical agreement, or jointly promote a rewarding business venture. In the evening, competition could heat up in connection with a career plum, a romance, or a money objective.

Wednesday, August 21 (Moon in Capricorn). A loyal and reliable partner offers just the right words and ideas to help you get your motivation in order. Afternoon could bring an important communication, perhaps of a financial nature. Solidarity on the home front makes P.M. hours relaxing.

Thursday, August 22 (Moon in Capricorn to Aquarius 1:28 P.M.). You may be awaiting word about the progress of a certain business deal, upon which depends a few other plans-in-work. The news could arrive in the early afternoon, to be followed by a firm commitment of some sort. Evening could be celebration time.

Friday, August 23 (Moon in Aquarius). Travel or other forms of escape from the routine may be on your mind today. If you can't get away physically, travels of the mind via an academic course, a museum tour, or immersion in a good book may do the trick. A community party, benefit, or gala may attract you.

Saturday, August 24 (Moon in Aquarius). Romance may have a rocky road to travel in postmidnight hours, but late morning could bring welcome news concerning a relation-

250 ♋ Daily Predictions

ship or a financial matter. After that, the day produces one challenge after another, mostly in connection with joint funds, expenses, etc.

Sunday, August 25 (Moon in Aquarius to Pisces 12:52 A.M.—FULL MOON at 4:08 A.M.). You may find yourself indulging in an impromptu trip, perhaps to visit a relative or in connection with an academic inquiry. In any case, don't expect firm answers to your questions just yet. Unexpected romantic joy due in P.M.

Monday, August 26 (Moon in Pisces to Aries 10:02 P.M.). A long-drawn-out legal matter could wind down today, or a contract finally get ironed out satisfactorily. Lunch with a loved one could be an unanticipated delight. Later, P.M. hours find your mind teeming with new ideas and plans for career-business progress.

Tuesday, August 27 (Moon in Aries). Postmidnight hours could be dynamically romantic, though it's possible it will be a financial coup, rather than your love life, that will be featured. Checking with a VIP regarding your next step in a special assignment will be encouraging. Keep up the good work!

Wednesday, August 28 (Moon in Aries). Since this is not an especially good day for joint efforts, try to work on your segments of any shared venture and leave the collaborative part of it for another time, if possible. Also, check out all the details of a special assignment, before turning it in, as errors may creep in.

Thursday, August 29 (Moon in Aries to Taurus 5:01 P.M.). Progress at work can be as smooth as silk this morning and you might even fritter away the afternoon with frivolous activities. Your social evening begins on a jarring note, however, as someone's problem or a delay or lack of cooperation gets things off to a slow start.

Friday, August 30 (Moon in Taurus). What was missing in yesterday's social agenda is now present—namely, a lighthearted and festive attitude on the part of the participants. A newcomer, or the return of an absent friend, adds further pleasure to the P.M.—which could wind up on a romantic note for some.

Saturday, August 31 (Moon in Taurus to Gemini 10:03 P.M.). A few items on your agenda that have been delayed in recent weeks now become more active. But unfortunately, until late P.M. you'll probably be busy clearing up errors or misunderstandings in your environment. Later, personal interests are rewarding.

September 1991

Sunday, September 1 (Moon in Gemini). You may have to try your best to counteract friction in your surroundings today and it might not be easy. Old grievances will have a way of surfacing when you least expect and relations with neighbors or family members could be somewhat strained. Don't allow pressures to disturb you.

Monday, September 2 (Moon in Gemini). A welcome turnabout today brings a whole series of fortunate trends beginning with an early-A.M. bulletin of some sort relating to a financial upswing. As the day unfolds, encouraging developments are due in your love life, academic interests, social status, and domestic circle.

Tuesday, September 3 (Moon in Gemini to Cancer 1:20 A.M.). You're pretty sure of yourself today and can work wonders in promoting your special schemes and persuading others to follow your lead. True, you may need to tone down your assertiveness for best results, particularly with a close associate.

Wednesday, September 4 (Moon in Cancer). Postmidnight hours may find you wearing either blinders or rose-colored glasses; in either case, you're not seeing things too

252 ♋ Daily Predictions

clear, particularly in a partnership deal or a personal relationship. The picture improves later in the day. Be responsive to creative urges.

Thursday, September 5 (Moon in Cancer to Leo 3:14 A.M.). Poor judgment in a business negotiation, or a stand-off situation between you and your mate or partner may cloud early-morning hours. However, there's an improvement in domestic interests, and you should have a freer hand in resolving any other problems.

Friday, September 6 (Moon in Leo). Though you might want to take a calculated risk in a business-career transaction early this morning, try to resist that inclination. Familiar territory will be better turf for your business-financial interests now. P.M. supports romance and marital progress or potential.

Saturday, September 7 (Moon in Leo to Virgo 4:36 A.M.). You could wake up feeling lucky today, and subsequent events do not make you change your optimistic attitude. Trends favor communications, contractual matters, travel, and legal interests. Evening could bring a pleasant bolt from the blue, as an old flame reignites.

Sunday, September 8 (Moon in Virgo—NEW MOON at 6:02 A.M.). This will be the day on which to get yourself and your agenda well organized, outline your near-future itinerary and your long-range priorities. Creative thinking can work wonders in mundane matters, while a glamorous trend in romance is an intriguing switch.

Monday, September 9 (Moon in Virgo to Libra 6:52 A.M.). You may finally get around to digging in on a long-planned domestic or property project. Lining up things to be done and people to do them is a must, though it may be quite a job to properly harness assorted energies. Guard against sudden friction in the late P.M.

Tuesday, September 10 (Moon in Libra). The domestic trend continues and you could get early-A.M. good news concerning costs and prices. If any of your current projects could benefit from an advertising campaign, now is the time to begin one. A love message in midevening sounds a pleasant note in your activities.

Wednesday, September 11 (Moon in Libra to Scorpio 11:43 A.M.). Except for an early-afternoon disagreement with an authority figure concerning money, the day seems to indicate you'll be in single-minded pursuit of love and romance. Your communications skills are enhanced and you can talk your way into (or out of) anything.

Thursday, September 12 (Moon in Scorpio). The romance theme continues with the added advantage of some practical support from a family member for your career or marital intentions. Late-evening hours may prove that a loved one really can read your mind and heart! In the meantime, creative ideas proliferate.

Friday, September 13 (Moon in Scorpio to Sagittarius 8:15 P.M.). You may be making arrangements for a trip this weekend, whether in connection with seeing a loved one, straightening out a business or personal misunderstanding, or simply because you have a touch of wanderlust. In any case, expenses may be high.

Saturday, September 14 (Moon in Sagittarius). Try to avoid pressuring yourself this morning, since various upsets are due to be straightened out effortlessly by early afternoon. If you are entertaining friends in your home this evening, or out on the town with a favorite companion, you're sure to enjoy yourself.

Sunday, September 15 (Moon in Sagittarius). Don't expend your energies in counterproductive activities—or overdo in such areas as exercise, sports, or working too hard for a group project. There's a chance you might make an unwise health decision today, so before you make a commitment restudy the plan.

Monday, September 16 (Moon in Sagittarius to Capricorn 8:05 A.M.). Get an early start on a business-financial matter and you'll stay a step ahead of the competition throughout the day. Talking over a proposed project, trip, or domestic decision with your mate or partner in the P.M. is the best way to ensure mutual satisfaction.

Tuesday, September 17 (Moon in Capricorn). Listen to the "words of wisdom" offered you by a close associate—no matter how farfetched they may seem—as this could trigger creative solutions in your own mind. Teamwork may not be easy to achieve in all of today's joint endeavors, but weigh the benefits against the irritations!

Wednesday, September 18 (Moon in Capricorn to Aquarius 8:59 P.M.). The success of a joint venture is almost certain this morning, though you may be faced with a knotty monetary problem—or decision—later in the day. Remember the security factors so often uppermost in your game plans, and work toward them.

Thursday, September 19 (Moon in Aquarius). Someone close to you may zero in on your intuitive reactions to a proposed business arrangement—and may even add another unique twist to the possibilities. Be receptive to such an outside influence. Evening hours favor property negotiations and/or family conferences.

Friday, September 20 (Moon in Aquarius). This can be a tricky day for material interests and practical considerations. You may face conflicting responsibilities or the kind of either-or situation where neither alternative is really acceptable. Be on guard against a romantic tiff, as well, especially in the P.M.

Saturday, September 21 (Moon in Aquarius to Pisces 8:21 A.M.). An issue concerning travel, education, or a legal transaction may take precedence over lesser considerations today. Midday overspending or some other form of extravagance or excess is a possibility. Later, word from a favorite person touches your heart.

Sunday, September 22 (Moon in Pisces). An out-of-town trip may be on your calendar for today, and if so, be sure that you and a companion share the same (accurate!)

information or instructions. A light touch of romance in the air in the P.M. can be diverting but not necessarily of big-league dimensions.

Monday, September 23 (Moon in Pisces to Aries 4:57 P.M.—FULL MOON at 5:41 P.M.). Today's trends might place you in the middle of a giant tug-of-war situation between career dreams on one side and home-family obligations on the other. Beginning with a postmidnight choice, the day offers you dynamic potentials.

Tuesday, September 24 (Moon in Aries). When dealing with a higher-up, accentuate points of agreement rather than of difference. And, if you call on a cohort to back you up, make sure the cohort knows what you expect of him/her. Evening hours may not be harmonious, but they could certainly produce action.

Wednesday, September 25 (Moon in Aries to Taurus 11:00 P.M.). A welcome financial development in the A.M. might provide you with the means to take a certain trip in the near future. Your social life is due for an upswing, but brace yourself for a lecture on personal obligations from a helpful type.

Thursday, September 26 (Moon in Taurus). You may head up a group of interested parties in a community project, where your ideas and views could receive a good reception. On a more personal level, a reunion with a long-absent friend, or meeting a newcomer who shares your enthusiasms, makes P.M. hours enjoyable.

Friday, September 27 (Moon in Taurus). An early-A.M. decision is almost sure to concern a pleasure plan and may mean changing a date, time, place (or partner!). You could also learn (later) that costs have escalated. This may be something you'll want to talk over with friend or family member in the P.M.

Saturday, September 28 (Moon in Taurus to Gemini 3:26 A.M.). It's possible that the time has come to launch one of your favorite projects, and in this connection you may be lining up supporters and well-wishers. Don't hesitate to call on a wide variety of contacts for this; avoid relying on a special few.

Sunday, September 29 (Moon in Gemini). Today's plans may be centered in your home environment or on family members, whose efforts can guarantee the success of an afternoon gathering. Late P.M. could be rewardingly romantic and, in a different context, could bring about a potentially lucrative business contact.

Monday, September 30 (Moon in Gemini to Cancer 6:59 A.M.). Despite the way in which you set out at the start of this workweek with your banners flying and your hopes high, don't be surprised if you encounter opposition from associates (perhaps even from family members). Don't be discouraged; trends are changing.

October 1991

Tuesday, October 1 (Moon in Cancer). An early-A.M. misunderstanding with your mate or partner phases out nicely in the afternoon, when you'll both decide that mutual interests are more important than small annoyances. Don't overdo in your domestic labors this evening, as you could strain a muscle; pace yourself.

Wednesday, October 2 (Moon in Cancer to Leo 9:59 A.M.). Aside from an important financial decision in the A.M. (or, it might be a difference of opinion, concerning money, with your spouse or partner) this can be a good day for getting practical affairs in order. There may be a joint funds matter to be resolved.

Thursday, October 3 (Moon in Leo). Postmidnight hours favor communications with family members and/or your mate or partner concerning plans of mutual interest. Early-morning hours, however, could find you and a close associate on opposite sides of a touchy question. By late P.M. the financial angle is worked out.

Friday, October 4 (Moon in Leo to Virgo 12:46 P.M.). Weekend social plans get firmed up nicely by midmorning, leaving you free to concentrate on your work! You might be asked to head a committee or project in a community or other group activity; this could bring pleasure and opportunity, as well as a certain prestige.

Saturday, October 5 (Moon in Virgo). This will be an enjoyable day for meeting and greeting people, as well as for participating in an educational or cultural program. An impasse may be reached in discussing a domestic matter in the midevening, but you'll soon be back on track with this special person.

Sunday, October 6 (Moon in Virgo to Libra 4:01 P.M.). This is an appropriate day for you to put your house in order—literally or figuratively, as you and an associate work out a mutually satisfactory routine. Evening may find you out on the town, visiting friends, or enjoying entertainment with congenial companions.

Monday, October 7 (Moon in Libra—NEW MOON at 4:40 P.M.). Anything that can go wrong with a special project will probably do so today. Make a note, too, not to rely on the support of usually friendly colleagues. Stellar trends are formulating new directions for one of your important aims, so be flexible and observant.

Tuesday, October 8 (Moon in Libra to Scorpio 9:01 P.M.). You could take the initiative in resolving a domestic problem today, and with good results. Refrain from taking financial risks in the P.M. You could find a new romance just around the corner (literally, as your community environment features love potential).

Wednesday, October 9 (Moon in Scorpio). Goals will be more easily attained today, as obstacles melt and opportunities open up. Specifically in love and monetary matters, the way looks clear for you to forge ahead with your inimitable subtlety and finesse. Personal and family issues are also supported now.

Thursday, October 10 (Moon in Scorpio). Your creative flair tends to influence all that you do today, including your routine work chores, dealings with business associates and neighbors, and of course in connection with your love life and favorite companions. The way out of a domestic dilemma is now clear.

Friday, October 11 (Moon in Scorpio to Sagittarius 4:59 A.M.). High energy could make you feel as though you can move mountains with your hands tied behind your back! However, you should take a breather between a hard day at the office and the intense pursuit of pleasure in the P.M. Overdoing has its penalties.

Saturday, October 12 (Moon in Sagittarius). This would be the day to work on your financial agenda, your social calendar, and that list of "must-do's" which could include a workout session and patching up a quarrel with a friend. Top off the day with a P.M. athletic event with a congenial companion.

Sunday, October 13 (Moon in Sagittarius to Capricorn 4:11 P.M.). Household and family interests dominate daytime hours, with perhaps time out to visit someone in need. Evening hours seem just right for shared interests and pleasures with your spouse, partner, or other close associate. Restore peace, where needed.

Monday, October 14 (Moon in Capricorn). Stellar trends are on your side today, especially in matters involving a partnership or alliance. This is when you will be diplomatic, persuasive, and sure to make the right impression on others. A lively but possibly inconclusive discussion can lead to further contacts.

Tuesday, October 15 (Moon in Capricorn). Although there may be forces working against your companionship with another person, you should be able to run rings around the opposition today. There is also a trend toward open discussion and compromise in any areas where total harmony seems to be lacking.

Wednesday, October 16 (Moon in Capricorn to Aquarius 5:05 A.M.). You may be pressed to fulfill monetary obligations today, but the earlier you get on with it the better. The course of true love might not run as smoothly as you'd like this evening, but if you're patient and persevering all will be well.

Thursday, October 17 (Moon in Aquarius). Although an investment may seem to be a spectacular opportunity, you'd be smart to investigate all the angles before laying out your hard-earned money. In fact, this is definitely not the day to engage in any sort of risky behavior, whether in money, love, or health.

Friday, October 18 (Moon in Aquarius to Pisces 4:54 P.M.). A more placid ambience today will be noticeable in your home environment as well as at work or at play. Others are more cooperative and your well-intended suggestions are taken with respect. Evening hours support travel, dealing with distant friends.

Saturday, October 19 (Moon in Pisces). Local travel or visiting relatives could brighten the scene today, but could also drain your energy. However, a romantic bonus awaits some unattached Cancerians in the P.M., when someone you meet in another locale could make a dynamic impression on your susceptible heart.

Sunday, October 20 (Moon in Pisces). The news you hear today could be good in more ways than one, as both financial and romantic possibilities emerge from the communication you receive in the early A.M. Also on tap now could be a special party or entertainment, perhaps a celebration of someone's birthday?

Monday, October 21 (Moon in Pisces to Aries 1:34 A.M.). You're in a gung-ho mood for business-financial advancement today, and provided you've done your homework in terms of boning up on all important details, you can make a great impression on just the right person. Mixed trends in the P.M. favor fiscal restraint.

Tuesday, October 22 (Moon in Aries). Use your foresight and vision to gain a VIP's approval of a business scheme, but be sure to include all the practical details as well. This will be a good time to map your professional objectives and outline ways and means of attaining them. Dispense with nonessentials.

Wednesday, October 23 (Moon in Aries—FULL MOON at 6:09 A.M.—to Taurus 6:56 A.M.). Don't be surprised if this day starts out in a somewhat hectic manner, with colleagues tense, higher-ups demanding, and you in the midst of it, trying to hold it all together! Things simmer down by the P.M., which is gently romantic.

Thursday, October 24 (Moon in Taurus). A few leftover tensions from yesterday may need careful handling, but you'll enjoy asserting yourself with friends and associates as the day wears on. In fact, you may turn out to be the peacemaker in some dispute involving two companions— or a friend vs. a lover.

Friday, October 25 (Moon in Taurus to Gemini 10:10 A.M.). A postmidnight communication is ultraromantic and could set your mood for the entire day! Allot some time to a private matter this afternoon, since it appears that advice from an expert would be a welcome factor. P.M. could be quietly social.

Saturday, October 26 (Moon in Gemini). A nagging problem needs attention and some careful study to pinpoint just what the main issue is. Keep a lucrative idea under wraps for the time being, inasmuch as the whole picture hasn't emerged clearly as yet. Be patient with a relative's complaints you've heard before.

Sunday, October 27 (Moon in Gemini to Cancer 12:38 P.M.). This should be a fine day for personal interests, making helpful contacts for one of your superspecial projects, and directing a romance toward your desired goal. On the debit side, don't overdo your ambition and drive; above all, don't push too hard.

Monday, October 28 (Moon in Cancer). Free-wheeling initiative could be just what's needed in order to open previously closed doors. However, today you may win some (acceptance of a creative idea, a love triumph) and lose some (the apparent failure of a personal or professional partnership).

Tuesday, October 29 (Moon in Cancer to Leo 3:21 P.M.). Your ears listen eagerly to a postmidnight love message that sends your heart soaring. This episode has a second chapter in the P.M.—but in the intervening hours there may be a real Donnybrook when financial friction arises between you and an associate.

Wednesday, October 30 (Moon in Leo). This is not the day to push or shove, either socially or in connection with an investment or a creative project. You'll gain more by watching and waiting. On the other hand, a postmidnight discussion you have with an influential person can help to advance your aims.

Thursday, October 31 (Moon in Leo to Virgo 6:48 P.M.). A friend's financial advice may be well meant, but he or she might not be the expert you've been led to believe. In any case, this is not the day for taking risks—financial or otherwise. Mental pursuits will be rewarding—and inspiring—in the P.M.

November 1991

Friday, November 1 (Moon in Virgo). Togetherness and harmony between you and certain friends are especially strong today. Seek out those people who are closest to your heart. This could also be a rewarding time to participate in a group endeavor, through which both you and the group can benefit.

Saturday, November 2 (Moon in Virgo to Libra 11:13 P.M.). This is when you can see a domestic project right through to the desired conclusion. Harmony should prevail on your home turf and the morning may bring an especially exciting (and prestigious) invitation to attend a social or community event.

Sunday, November 3 (Moon in Libra). Another pleasant and relaxing day, with domestic, family, and community interests featured. However, a small cloud appears on the horizon in the P.M., perhaps in the form of an unexpected challenge from your spouse or partner. This could require tactful handling.

Monday, November 4 (Moon in Libra). Your mind-set is right in tune with the start of a new workweek—and probably in tune with your current assignments and the thinking of the higher-up who designed them. In any case, you could prove how invaluable you are to your employer today. P.M. supports long-range planning.

Tuesday, November 5 (Moon in Libra to Scorpio 5:10 A.M.). You may intend to enhance an ongoing romance today, but if the conversation touches on money or other security factors, guard against an emotional explosion. Keep away from financially risky ventures, as well, even though someone promises you the moon.

Wednesday, November 6 (Moon in Scorpio—NEW MOON at 6:12 A.M.). Postmidnight hours accentuate the intensity of your feelings for a loved one. In fact, this entire day is trimmed with Cupid's arrows and an important relationship could be headed in a new direction in which commitment is one of love's proofs.

Thursday, November 7 (Moon in Scorpio to Sagittarius 1:22 P.M.). Creative tasks should be easy for you today, as your inspiration—and flair—seem boundless. Evening brings high energies and perhaps the desire to expend some of them on a workout program, a dance session, or perfecting an athletic skill.

Friday, November 8 (Moon in Sagittarius). Avoid recklessness in the early morning, especially if it's prompted by someone's comments (which might not be accurate). Throughout the day, your confidence and courage are enhanced, as you pursue your really important interests; one of which is certainly love.

Saturday, November 9 (Moon in Sagittarius). Domestic topics and home beautification are just right for today's stellar trends. You'll probably find that friends or family members will be helpful if you devise an evening's entertainment. A variety of guests can make the occasion both different and special.

Sunday, November 10 (Moon in Sagittarius to Capricorn 12:17 A.M.). An uneasy truce between you and your spouse or partner may start the day off on the wrong foot. However, love, understanding, and common sense prevail, and the evening's plans reflect the sharing and caring between you; communication is open and free.

Monday, November 11 (Moon in Capricorn). This is another excellent day to advance or build on a close relationship, as rapport between you and someone close to you grows and glows. There is also more than a hint of creativity and innovative thinking between you; perhaps a new joint venture is being formed.

Tuesday, November 12 (Moon in Capricorn to Aquarius 1:07 P.M.). Guard your comments to coworkers today as it's quite possible for your remarks to be misunderstood, misinterpreted—and perhaps misquoted, as well. Later, a joint financial venture appears to have a new lease on life; later still, romance reigns supreme.

Wednesday, November 13 (Moon in Aquarius). If you have an idea or presentation to offer to a key figure, midafternoon would be a favorable time to do it. You may gain personally through a colleague's VIP contacts today, and advantages can be made available to you via one of your long-time friends or admirers.

Thursday, November 14 (Moon in Aquarius). Keep a low profile in business today, because even with the best of motives and the most carefully prepared presentation, you just might not make the impression you'll need in order to develop business gains. Review your methods and procedures and doublecheck facts and figures.

Friday, November 15 (Moon in Aquarius to Pisces 1:34 A.M.). Your intuition will be reliable today and help you to make sound judgments and informed decisions. The distance between you and a loved one may seem to be much greater than it is; even so, you'll be in the mood to pay him/her a surprise visit.

Saturday, November 16 (Moon in Pisces). The lure of distant places remains strong, even aside from any romantic motivation. But be realistic about chances for travel at this time; and don't allow yourself to be distracted from a nearby opportunity. P.M. hours can be devoted to lighthearted entertainment.

Sunday, November 17 (Moon in Pisces to Aries 11:09 A.M.). Your presence may be charming onlookers in one location, but your thoughts are far afield—almost in another galaxy! Nevertheless, practical tips may be yours for the asking from a local VIP—someday you'll be glad you extracted this knowledge.

Monday, November 18 (Moon in Aries). Did you ever have one of those days when you have to try harder yet observed fewer results? Challenging stellar patterns may keep you anchored to an old piece of property, an outworn relationship, or a dependent's life-style. Talking things over with a long-time pal can help.

Tuesday, November 19 (Moon in Aries to Taurus 4:50 P.M.). Be alert to a business opportunity in a setting where you'd least expect to find it. Consider, too, the advantages of taking an old project off the shelf and updating it. Do be wary about getting into a severe disagreement with your partner in the P.M.

Wednesday, November 20 (Moon in Taurus). Good news from a friend may set you dreaming about similar occasions for yourself in the not-too-distant past. You can learn more today by watching events develop rather than by directing them in no uncertain terms. Evening hours are rife with inspiration, creativity.

Thursday, November 21 (Moon in Taurus—FULL MOON at 5:57 P.M.—to Gemini 7:23 P.M.). Mixed trends today may influence those around you to be more extreme, or more easily distracted from positive courses of action. All of a sudden, you could find that a rediscovered friend has contacts that can benefit both of you.

Friday, November 22 (Moon in Gemini). Be prepared to cope with behind-the-scenes moves by a close associate. Information you latch onto unexpectedly can have interesting implications. A social or domestic plan may have disappointing side effects in the P.M. but the day ends on an upbeat note of romance.

Saturday, November 23 (Moon in Gemini to Cancer 8:26 P.M.). Early hours may find you under par, perhaps overworked or overindulged. But you gather momentum as the day progresses and evening can bring nice evidences of your popularity. You may have a chance to do something nice for someone who needs a helping hand.

Sunday, November 24 (Moon in Cancer). Take advantage of an opportunity to visit an out-of-town friend or relative and try to ignore the rising tide of criticism and/or opposition to your plans by someone close to you. This is one case when talking things over can only make things worse; in fact, avoid communication!

Monday, November 25 (Moon in Cancer to Leo 9:38 P.M.). Postmidnight hours could be socially disappointing as a party may wind down with a dull thud, or romance lack that certain sparkle and zip. Things pick up later, and you could make surprising strides in a business-financial deal toward the late afternoon.

Tuesday, November 26 (Moon in Leo). Heed the voice of wisdom that comes to you in the wee small hours (perhaps by phone) and advises against hasty financial action. Later, prospects look good for an increase in your income, though it may take a while for this to go through officially.

Wednesday, November 27 (Moon in Leo). Mixed celestial messages today support family-related activities and entertainment plans; also property negotiations. Trends do not support speculation, romance that's too, too serious, and matters concerning children and creative expression. Bypass late-night transportation.

Thursday, November 28 (Moon in Leo to Virgo 12:13 A.M.). Rumors and not quite accurate gossip may be rife in your working environment. You'll be smart to discount most of what you hear. A general slowdown, lasting for the next three weeks, begins today, so don't waste time seeking immediate responses.

Friday, November 29 (Moon in Virgo). A higher-up may have agreed to some revision in your workload, but it's too soon to know how this will affect you. There's a good chance the status quo will be preserved and recognized, which is more than many have experienced. Take a sharp look at a P.M. business offer.

Saturday, November 30 (Moon in Virgo to Libra 4:48 A.M.). You can allow your strongly domestic urges to have full play as today could be just what the doctor ordered for planning a dinner, party, or special celebration. A social or romantic communication opens new vistas of possibility, including a delightful trip.

December 1991

Sunday, December 1 (Moon in Libra). Avoid squabbling with your mate or roommate over the subject of entertaining at dinner or an informal gathering tonight. By the time this affair is over, you'll feel elated at how quickly your guests made themselves at home and participated in the general festivities.

Monday, December 2 (Moon in Libra to Scorpio 11:34 A.M.). An investment opportunity may enable you to put your money to work for you. If you think in long-range terms, you'll realize where your security can be found. A dreary person may try to rain on your parade, but you won't permit this kind of thinking.

Tuesday, December 3 (Moon in Scorpio). This can be a generally fortunate date, with a special emphasis on romance, partnership, creative expression, and matters concerning youngsters. Your relations with a loved one may require a bit of tact in the P.M., when supersensitivity could create a tense environment.

Wednesday, December 4 (Moon in Scorpio to Sagittarius 8:33 P.M.). Your creativity will speak for itself today, and may peak in the early A.M. Evening sets a receptive stage for work, sports, and any form of service to others. Give some thought to how you can restore a damaged collectible item—or an injured friendship.

Thursday, December 5 (Moon in Sagittarius—NEW MOON at 10:57 P.M.). With your dedication and skill you can make a routine job assignment into an outstanding achievement—which will not go unnoticed by a higher-up. In fact, a new trend in your working environment is due at this time, so be prepared to adapt.

Friday, December 6 (Moon in Sagittarius). You may be building up elaborate plans for the weekend, during which the main act could be a glamorous romance. On the other

268 ☺ Daily Predictions

hand, this is a day when great expectations may develop, but the reality is another story altogether. Be flexible and ready to change courses.

Saturday, December 7 (Moon in Sagittarius to Capricorn 7:42 A.M.). The theme for the day is set in the morning hours, when a loved one cooperates with your agenda and gives a great example of teamwork. A friendship that's been rather strained of late now begins to mellow out and the old rapport resurfaces.

Sunday, December 8 (Moon in Capricorn). You'll appreciate the great feeling of knowing your spouse or favorite companion is with you 100% in an important meeting or conference today. Shared pleasure in an out-of-town trip or sports program can be another bond between you, and frosts the cake tonight.

Monday, December 9 (Moon in Capricorn to Aquarius 8:28 P.M.). If you can manage to keep off the subject of money (especially joint monetary interests) you may be able to avoid a rather heavy early-morning session with your mate or other close associate. Tensions remain throughout the day, however.

Tuesday, December 10 (Moon in Aquarius). There's no room in today's itinerary for feeling down because of a minor romantic snafu—but you'll squeeze it in anyway! Nevertheless, compensating stellar patterns ease the pain and by late evening you will have had every opportunity to relegate this to history.

Wednesday, December 11 (Moon in Aquarius). Another person's input can make the decisive difference in a money scheme today. But you should look very carefully into a new health or insurance offer made to you in the late afternoon; there could be hidden conditions. A brief workout in the P.M. is relaxing.

Thursday, December 12 (Moon in Aquarius to Pisces 9:20 A.M.). Travel, adventure, and dramatic changes are probably the stuff of which your fantasies are made today.

Actually, a rather boring regime gives rise to a yearning for escape, but since it's unlikely that you are free to do so, be patient; things will change.

Friday, December 13 (Moon in Pisces). During some portions of today you will really come to believe the "Friday the 13th" superstition! Coworkers and colleagues in general may be scrappy, inconsistent, and uncooperative. However, your keen mind and creative flair will enable you to transform a dreary day.

Saturday, December 14 (Moon in Pisces to Aries 8:07 P.M.). An out-of-town guest or a favorite relative may come to visit—or perhaps you'll be anchored to the phone in happy communication with far-off friends. P.M. hours could find you actively participating in a community project or social bash.

Sunday, December 15 (Moon in Aries). What with holiday plans, family demands, and a special personal project you are working on, little time remains for rest, relaxation, or simple idling. A surprise guest or communication in the evening may lead to a change in holiday travel plans or an educational commitment.

Monday, December 16 (Moon in Aries). The brilliant idea you dream up in postmidnight hours needs an extra dose of realism and a bit more practicality. On the other hand, you'll be right on target in your pursuit of a business-career plum later in the day. This could be the right timing for an innovative approach.

Tuesday, December 17 (Moon in Aries to Taurus 3:11 A.M.). Unexpected romantic delights brighten up the postmidnight hours. Back in the workaday world, however, you may find that an obstacle has developed in a business negotiation; it may be that the influence of a well-meaning friend is not as effective as expected.

Wednesday, December 18 (Moon in Taurus). Mixed trends today support creative work and partnership efforts, as previously delayed projects get moving again. But

270 ⊗ Daily Predictions

speculation and other financial risks are no-no's and romance seems to be rather iffy. Be extra cautious in travel and transportation during late P.M. hours.

Thursday, December 19 (Moon in Taurus to Gemini 6:22 A.M.). In the midst of the frantic pace of holiday shopping, travel, and communications, you can find a refreshing oasis of creativity and contemplation—if you really try! This sort of thing can recharge Cancerian batteries, so try to get some solitude.

Friday, December 20 (Moon in Gemini). The problem you are mulling over is not so much a weighty one as a consistently nagging one. Whether it concerns a relative, a limping romance, or apparently stymied attempts to advance your career, if you think about it objectively, you can come up with options and solutions.

Saturday, December 21 (Moon in Gemini—FULL MOON Lunar Eclipse at 5:24 A.M.—Moon to Cancer 6:55 A.M.). This could be one of those unsatisfactory days when you are either too late or too early for your scheduled agenda, or find that others are totally self-involved, with no time for you to cry on their shoulders!

Sunday, December 22 (Moon in Cancer). You and your mate or partner start off the day on opposite sides of an ongoing discussion; try to keep this from becoming a Big Problem. Later in the day, things mellow nicely and your social-romantic or family agenda ought to be pleasantly active, mentally stimulating.

Monday, December 23 (Moon in Cancer to Leo 6:39 A.M.). You could be busy with personal finances today, or perhaps making updated arrangements in a joint fund venture. Opposition from a close associate in the midafternoon can be amicably worked out if you remember this person's basically helpful nature.

Tuesday, December 24 (Moon in Leo). Last-minute tasks linked with holiday plans can take their usual toll on your time and nerves. However, things do proceed at a fairly healthy pace—especially plans concerning your loved one, as well as matters involving children. But early evening brings romantic hazards.

Wednesday, December 25 (Moon in Leo to Virgo 7:24 A.M.). If you are spending the day with relatives, close friends, or involved with a community or church-related project, you'll be right in tune with stellar patterns. It's a day to mix and mingle and give good wishes as well as gifts to those you love.

Thursday, December 26 (Moon in Virgo). In case you overtaxed your sensitive Cancerian tummy with too many goodies or whatever, early A.M. could bring repercussions! Otherwise, this can be a fun day for a short trip or contact with distant friends and relatives. Early P.M. caution in transportation advisable.

Friday, December 27 (Moon in Virgo to Libra 10:38 A.M.). Postmidnight hours look happily romantic, while household and family-related issues are due to proceed smoothly later in the day (with the possible exception of P.M. friction with your spouse or partner—or a planned entertainment snafu).

Saturday, December 28 (Moon in Libra). You should be warned that today is a day of potential scrappiness and conflict, as those around you tend to overreact and overemote (you, too, may be guilty of these!) The secret is to be objective and to keep your sense of humor handy at all times (even with your true love).

Sunday, December 29 (Moon in Libra to Scorpio 5:04 P.M.). Today is good for those odds and ends of entertaining that come due between the holidays. Impromptu, casual, and relaxed ambience is most successful. Evening hours are likely to bring the start of a delectable romantic minitrend.

Monday, December 30 (Moon in Scorpio). Except for some ever-present anxiety or worry that haunts you in the early A.M., this can be a banner day for treasured relationships, job achievement, and perhaps a go-ahead for a promising new business project. Your creative juices are flowing joyfully.

Tuesday, December 31 (Moon in Scorpio). Always philosophical as an old year draws to a close, you are undoubtedly making arrangements to be with good friends or a special loved one this evening, for the purpose of sharing reflections on the recent past and hopes for the near future. Stellar trends support your plans.

How well do you know yourself?

You are unique. Since the world began, there has never been anyone exactly like you. Sun-sign astrology, the kind you see in newspapers and magazines, is all right as far as it goes. But it treats you as if you were just the same as millions of others whose birthdays are close to yours. A true astrological reading of your character and personality has to be one of a kind, unlike any other, based on exact date, time and place of birth. Only a big IBM computer like the one that **Astral Research** uses can handle the trillions of possibilities.

Your **Astral Portrait** is a unique document and includes your complete chart with planetary positions, house cusps and planetary aspects calculated with precision plus text explaining the meaning of:

- your particular combination of Sun and Moon signs;
- your Ascendent sign and the house position of its ruling planet;
- the planets influencing all twelve houses in your chart;
- your planetary aspects.

Your **Astral Portrait** is a thirty-five-page, fifteen-thousand-word, permanently-bound book that you can read over and over. And, if unsatisfied, you can return the chart within 30 days for a full refund of the purchase price. Your **Astral Portrait** is waiting for you.

©1987 Astral Research, Inc.

For Faster Service — 1-800-533-4676
FAX 508-546-2151 — ASTRAL RESEARCH

Dept. 1G, P.O. Box 879, Gloucester, Massachusetts 01930 ☐ I enclose $23 plus 2.00 for shipping and handling. Please indicate method of payment: ☐ Mastercard ☐ Visa ☐ Check or Money Order. No checks drawn on international banks accepted — Please send money order or bank check equivalent to U.S. dollar exchange. MA state sales tax for residents. ☐ Send a free catalog.

Send **Astral Portrait(s)** to:

Name_____

Address_____

City_____

State_____ Zip_____

Compile **Astral Portrait(s)** for:

Name_____

Birthdate Mo _____ Day _____ Yr _____

Birthtime (within an hour) _____ AM/PM

Birthplace City_____ State____

County_____

Credit Card Number_____ Good Thru Mo _____ Yr _____